Life and Death in
Fifteenth-Century Florence

Duke Monographs in
Medieval and Renaissance Studies 10
Editorial Committee
Arthur B. Ferguson, Edward P. Mahoney, Chairman
Lee W. Patterson, David C. Steinmetz
Bruce W. Wardropper

Life and Death in
Fifteenth-Century Florence

Edited by Marcel Tetel, Ronald G. Witt, and Rona Goffen

Duke University Press   Durham and London 1989

© 1989 Duke University Press
All rights reserved
Printed in the United States of America
on acid-free paper ∞
Library of Congress Cataloging-in-Publication Data
appear on the last printed page of this book.

Contents

▼

Preface

▼

More is known about fifteenth-century Florence than about any other area of Europe before the last half of the eighteenth century. Much of this knowledge has been acquired over the last thirty-five years through the efforts of exceptionally gifted scholars on both sides of the Atlantic. Through use of new methodologies, economic and social historians have successfully asked questions that were considered unanswerable or never even formulated by previous generations of scholars. The application of contemporary approaches of literary criticism to the relevant texts has also yielded precious insights into the mentality of the period. At the same time, painstaking, creative uses of more traditional methodologies of philology, political history, and art history have significantly contributed in this century to our broad and deep understanding of Florentine culture and society. These scholarly achievements have furnished, moreover, questions and models for those working in other geographical areas of Europe in the Middle Ages and Early Modern periods.

The theme of life and death in fifteenth-century Florence as the subject of our October 1986 colloquium at Duke University was designed to celebrate the success of two generations of Florentine studies. We intended that the papers, manifesting a variety of methodologies and interdisciplinary approaches, would demonstrate advances made in the wide range of fields relevant to basic human concerns of life and death. The atmosphere of the conference was collegial, and the discussions following presentations were often intense and surprisingly interconnected. Many of the essays which appear in this volume have incorporated new ideas and information exchanged in those discussions.

Durham, North Carolina, which, with its elaborate complex of hospitals, boasts to be the City of Medicine, seemed to be a particularly fitting place in 1986 to hold a conference on life and death. Whereas until a decade ago the medical community tended to consider death as something of an embarrassment and preferred not to recognize it, death and its implications for life have become very much a focus of medical literature. Liaison psychiatry, a new division of psychiatry, has evolved in part to help the hospital staff in dealing with terminal patients and their families. Modern medicine has finally consented to assist the clergy in treating aspects of the human being which the latter usually associate with the soul.

The death spoken of at the conference was in its own time unhesitatingly acknowledged to be intertwined with life. Domestic and familiar, it was rehearsed and elaborately commemorated by fifteenth-century Florentine society. Proper celebration of the death of their members constituted a central concern for guild and confraternal organizations as it did for individual families. Art, literature, and sermons and tracts on the art of dying constantly reminded citizens of death's presence in their midst. "Did he make a good end" was not simply an attempt to solicit information about the deceased's final hours but about the character of the total life.

In its preoccupation with death in life, Renaissance Florence reflected in its own way a concern common to most societies down to the twentieth century, but the theme seems particularly apt for understanding the city in our chosen century. Death unquestionably moulded the fifteenth century throughout Western Europe. Beginning in 1348 the Black Death struck repeatedly over the next fifty years reducing the population of the subcontinent by perhaps 40 percent of what it had been a century earlier. The demographic tragedy brought with it a severe economic contraction, and then after 1400, as the population stabilized, the economy tended to level off as well. Social mobility slowed and distinctions among classes were accentuated. This general situation had clearly reversed by the opening decades of the sixteenth century as population began to rise dramatically and economic opportunities in Europe and elsewhere multiplied.

Florence largely followed the general European pattern. After fifty years of intense plague, its economy remained somewhat more buoyant than that of most cities. Yet Florence was demographically much smaller, and an obvious diminution in social mobility occurred. Despite shifts in power within the group of leading families, the patriciate dominated political affairs into the early decades of the sixteenth century. The relative political stability of the century encouraged the bureaucratization of communal life and the attendant record keeping which has proved a treasure trove for modern scholarship.

Death as intrusive as the Black Plague could not help but evoke a statistical response: the Florentine government from the 1380s instituted the *Libri dei morti*, registers recording mortality in the city, daily gauges of the ebb and flow of disease. By the early decades of the fifteenth century, life had its turn to be counted as well, when births were being regularly recorded at the baptistry. Clearly a reflection of the wider bureaucratic attempt to define and control society, these particular statistics and others, like those found in the *Libro delle età* of 1429, served to create a more precise personal awareness of the duration of life. We would like to know how widespread the idea of the birthday party, an ancient ritual revived by the humanists in the fourteenth century, became in this period. The Florentine oligarchy realized the fiscal possibilities offered by playing with the mortality rate among young women when it created in 1424–25 the *Monte delle doti* providing dowry insurance.

The routines connected with death, like those pertaining to life, became counters in the struggle for prestige and power among the newly evolved patriciate. Like the upper class culture of Florence as a whole, the celebration of death and burial became informed with a new classicizing aesthetic. Classical models dictated the rules for constructing a funeral oration as well as a tomb. Long-standing traditions and forms were compromised by insistent contemporary standards of "good taste" or *buon gusto*.

A deeper understanding of ancient thoughts on mortality initially gave new dimensions to Christian teachings on the subject. The active life, grounded in service to one's family and fellow citizens, appeared as worthy of heavenly reward as did a life spent in contemplation. Then by mid-century this drive to activity was countered by a revival of Platonism reinforcing the traditional medieval deprecation of the practical intellect. Beneath the confident assertions about the dignity of man made by proponents of both positions, however, ran a deep vein of pessimism as to the value of all human endeavor.

Both Alberto Tenenti and Salvatore Camporeale deal with a long fifteenth century which for the latter begins in the decades after the Black Death and for the former ends by the mid-sixteenth century with the establishment of the Medici principate. Tenenti's article takes as its subject the role of death as a historical force in the writings of Florentines in the period roughly from 1350 to 1550. Although, in contrast with their northern counterparts, Florentine historians treated history as a succession of events defined according to logical and psychological criteria to the exclusion of miracles, they did not altogether exclude supernatural forces. God, fortune, fate, and the heavens could intervene in the temporal order by means of the death of men. That natural and human actions could be causes of death did not necessarily exclude a higher level of causation. Citing a wide range of texts, Tenenti shows how descriptions of the working of the supernatural represented projections of human imagination and needs. Death served as a focus for finding higher meaning in events, especially the assurance of the operation of an underlying moral order. However, by the mid-sixteenth century and the rule of Cosimo, Florentine historians tended to de-emphasize death as divine justice and accentuated its role as punishment for enemies of the regime. In time, death became a tool of *ragione di stato*.

Salvatore Camporeale's Giovanni Caroli clearly identifies the Black Death with its staggering mortality as creating a loss of identity in the medieval communal culture of the city. Caroli saw his Dominican order, a central spiritual force in Trecento Florentine society, increasingly marginalized in the Renaissance city with its new civic and religious concerns. Embracing the organic image dear to contemporary historians, Caroli, in two works, the *Liber dierum* and the *Vitae fratrum*, traces the activity of the Dominicans in the Trecento in almost mythic terms while pointing to their spiritual sterility in his own day. Whatever hope of revival existed lay for him in a return to the order's original emphasis on *caritas* adapted to the new society. In both these works Caroli seems to seek in a study of decay the key to the regeneration of the order and a transformation of his own life.

The focus of the remaining papers lies within the broad chronology set by Tenenti and Camporeale. Ann G. Carmichael's "The Health Status of Florentines in the Fifteenth Century and the Early Sixteenth Century" provides a medical biography of Lorenzo de' Medici and his immediate descendants which reinforces the common impression that even the highest classes of society enjoyed only precarious health. In an effort to place the causes of morbidity in the Medici family into the larger framework of their society, Carmichael, unable to derive adequate data from Florentine death records, turns for this purpose to Milan where statistical evidence is attainable. Among her many findings on chronic diseases, she suggests that tuberculosis, considered a prime killer in later centuries, was probably a major cause of death in the Medici family as well as in the population at large in the fifteenth and early sixteenth century.

In William J. Kennedy's "Petrarchan Figurations of Death in Lorenzo de' Medici's Sonnets and *Comento*," and John McManamon's "Continuity and Change in the Ideals of Humanism: The Evidence from Florentine Funeral Oratory," death is seen as interpreted, respectively, by the poetry of Lorenzo de' Medici and by a new tradition of classicizing oration. Kennedy emphasizes Lorenzo's usage of the Petrarchan mode with its ambiguity of language as a vehicle for conveying his own radically introspective experience and the vision of his role in Florentine politics. Manipulating imagery associated with a complex intertwining of lover with beloved, ruler with ruled, and patron with artist, Lorenzo endeavored to establish his relationship to the Florentine body politic as one of poet-ruler prepared to serve his beloved and, if need be, to sacrifice his life that she might live.

In his study of funeral oratory in the fifteenth century McManamon interprets humanists as utilizing the funeral oration as a means of articulating the program of humanist values and goals. By the 1440s he notes a definite shift in funeral oratory from the overtly republican, imperialistic position based on Attic models so predominant earlier in the century: the accent now falls on the peace-loving qualities of the dead men. McManamon suggests that at least in part this change constitutes a response to the need for Italian unity in the face of the Turkish threat. A further thematic development, signaling the appearance of an ancient Roman influence, occurs early in the sixteenth century when orators, delivering panegyrics for Medici family members, initiate the practice of praising the deceased for their illustrious ancestry.

With Donald Weinstein's "*The Art of Dying Well* and Popular Piety in the Preaching and Thought of Girolamo Savonarola" we move from the Latin funeral oration designed for an elite audience to the popular preaching of Savonarola on death. Beginning with an analysis of Savonarola's *Predica dell'arte del ben morire*, which illustrates the vivid character of the friar's *volgare* style, Weinstein contrasts the simplicity of the religious doctrines found in the sermon with more complex positions on the same subjects developed in Savonarola's Latin works. The rather sharp line drawn by Savonarola and others between the capacities of clerics and of laymen for comprehending spiritual messages leads Weinstein to question whether preachers were meeting the expectations of their lay audiences.

While Donald Weinstein witnesses one aspect of the popular response to death as seen through a sermon of Savonarola, Cyrilla Barr provides another with her study of a lay religious company whose major function was to honor its members' deaths with religious songs called *laude*. Through an analysis of the fifteenth-century records of the Company of St. Agnes, Barr's "A Renaissance Artist in the Service of a Singing Confraternity" produces a detailed sketch of the inner life of one such company among many in the city. Exempt as they were from sumptuary statutes governing burials, the confraternity was permitted to celebrate burials with a lavish display for which private families had to purchase exemptions.

Sharon T. Strocchia's investigation of rituals connected with death in "Death Rites and Ritual Family in Renaissance Florence" results in a rich description of the complexities of the family relations they manifest. Just as was the case with marriage, the celebration of death reflected family status; fifteenth-century Florentines therefore orchestrated the event with a view to representing the honor of the family and in so doing they exhibited the amazing flexibility of family relationships. However, while rituals connected with male death tended to emphasize the patrilineal family line, and those of females reflected their cognate as well as agnatic origins, the character of family attendance for both male and female deceased depended greatly on whether the ritual was the public funeral or the more private requiem, which usually followed it. In the case of females the extent of family participation in both was also a function of their marital status at the time of death. Revealing the shifting nature of the family, Strocchia's work goes a long way toward explaining why recent scholars are producing such contradictory results in their effort to define this central institution of Florentine society.

The monumental tomb of Pope John XXIII in the Florentine baptistry completed in the 1420s forms the subject of Sarah Blake Mc-Ham's "Donatello's Tomb of Pope John XXIII." Having initially received permission for the construction of a tomb of very modest proportions in the baptistry, where no tomb had ever been constructed, the commissioners of the project, who included Bicci de' Medici, managed to evade the restrictions and erect one of the largest in the city. Integrated into the architecture and mosaic decoration of Florence's most hallowed building, the work gave every assurance that the deceased's salvation was assured. Its design was to have a significant influence on tomb construction both in Florence and elsewhere. McHam suggests that the attention devoted to the project by both Bicci and his son Cosimo derived to an extent from the honor they hoped to achieve from being associated with the construction of Florence's most elaborate monument to death.

A fresco cycle of Castagno from a villa in the neighborhood of Florence forms the subject of the final essay in the volume. In his "On Castagno's Nine Famous Men and Women: Sword and Book as the Basis for Public Service," Creighton Gilbert endeavors to explicate the puzzling iconography of a Castagno fresco, which forms part of what was the earliest fresco cycle in a Florentine villa by a major artist. The fresco program containing nine figures—with three soldiers on the left (Pippo Spano, Farinata degli Alberti, and Niccolo Acciaiuoli), three scholars on the right (Dante, Petrarch, and Boccaccio), and three women in the middle (the pagan heroine Tomyris, Esther, and the Cumaean Sibyl)—appears to be a variation on the theme of the Nine Worthies. A detailed comparison with two other Florentine villa frescoes and a third found in a Sienese villa indicates that at least at one level the figures symbolize a curriculum of education for young people, presumably a bride and a bridegroom. In any case, it seems aimed at individuals on the threshold of producing new life to initiate the process closed by death.

These ten scholars whose papers follow have worked within a broad context to give greater definition to this century particularly shaped by death. We wish to thank them for their contributions to this volume, and Professor Valeria Finucci of Duke University who translated Professor Tenenti's article into English. We also wish to express our deep appreciation to Provost Philip Griffiths for his strong commitment to the Center for Medieval and Renaissance Studies and our sincere gratitude to the Duke Endowment whose generous funding and support made possible the colloquium and these proceedings. Finally, we want to recognize our colleagues in the center who attended the sessions and contributed to broadening and enriching the discussions.

Death in History: The Function and Meaning of Death in Florentine Historiography of the Fifteenth and Sixteenth Centuries

▼

Alberto Tenenti

E ven in our times, it could be argued, we do not find ourselves in a more comfortable or more favorable situation than that in which Florentines found themselves during the Renaissance. To be sure, some problems may appear less real today; maybe they are simply further away from our everyday consciousness. Still, were we to ask ourselves similar questions again, we would hardly find different answers from the ones already expressed or offered by those who lived in Florence in the fifteenth and in the first half of the sixteenth century. This is not an indirect way of affirming categorically that in the last few centuries our collective sensibility has not taken steps forward in this area. However, having been unable to say more or to say it better, it appears as if our consciousness has simply repressed and evaded certain questions. Similar anxieties reopen like parentheses in particular moments of uneasiness or anguish.

In order to frame our analysis better and to provide a greater background and perspective, we naturally had to take into account at least the main works written since the beginning of the fifteenth century. On the other hand, it is almost superfluous to note that already in the fourteenth century, within and outside Florence, the prevailing tendency was not to take events far away in space and time as subjects of an historical account, but to look at those close at hand and contemporary, whether they were chronicles in the vernacular or more aulic Latin writings. Moreover, it is not possible to ignore that the most forceful proofs of our argument have emerged in a phase that appeared unusually dramatic, tense, and uncertain to those who lived it, the one precisely in which the political balance of the peninsula was upset—in particular that of Florence—in the more or less fifty years elapsing between 1490 and 1540. It could not have been entirely by chance that so many reflections and so many historical works, all of them having as subject the events of that period, appeared and centered on those decades.

In his *Istorie della città di Firenze*, Jacopo Nardi, faithful follower of Savonarola, wrote about one of those crucial years in the life of his city, 1495: "I soprastanti pericoli e le condizioni de' travagliosi tempi avevano grandemente disposto alla credulità delle profezie gli animi degli uomini, i quali nè tempi avversi spesse fiate ferventemente ritornano a Dio, e rarissime volte nè tempi felici" (Impending dangers and the conditions of those troublesome times had greatly disposed men's souls toward believing in prophesies. In adverse times men often and fervently return to God although they rarely do it in happy ones).[1] These critical observations were no less the fruit of a personal experience than of a precise contact with classical culture. Nardi himself immediately afterward was to recall that a similar emphasis could be found in Silius Italius, a Latin poet of the first century after Christ. The relationship between mental processes and emotional reactions on one side and real situations on the other has always been a complex one. It would help to underline that the history we are talking about is not only general history—that is, the complex flow of any type of events—but chiefly the history of a civic community within a particular conjuncture. The thoughts and the views we will encounter come from far away, from centuries and millennia of reflections. The answers or the attitudes we will be able to survey will not appear in general very original. This is not surprising; rather, it appears natural since the issue at hand is an existential confrontation with permanently relevant questions on how to see and how to grasp the specific world of a particular civilization.

Death is not something easily set apart in such a context since by death we do not mean the daily and more or less anonymous physical dying of each individual. The death we will talk about is a privileged meeting point of supernatural forces and human vicissitudes, more precisely the meeting point between them and the behavior of man as actor in history. This death is not a personality with prerogatives and an autonomous range of action. Therefore, it is not a goddess or an entity operating according to its own criteria. More than once, for example, we will meet Fortune, a representative of, or even synonym for, such superior forces, in fact, one of their many incarnations. For this reason Fortune is perceived as active and is credited with specific interventions. The death our historians speak about—and we could say the same for the majority of their contemporary Florentines—is a significant circumstance, but not a prima donna; it is a dramatic moment with various meanings and consequences, but never a power or a separate form of power.

Such a rationalization could sound perplexing. Personification of death was by then an ever recurring phenomenon in Tuscany, at least from the first half of the fourteenth century. It is even quite probable that the Triumph of Death as an iconographic and literary theme was born precisely in that region. Certainly it had important and decisive manifestations there, not only in art and in literature, but also in theatrical life, as the *sacre rappresentazione* clearly testify. Yet this personified death did not enter historical works either as a law that can be applied or as an agent capable of its own initiatives. The reasons for this disparity and for this missed correspondence between cultural and contemporary domains—such as art, literature, and history—have not been investigated. This is not, however, a strange and abnormal phenomenon. There are not necessarily correspondences and parallelisms among the various sectors of human activity; indeed, frequently there are differences and imbalances. Thus we have to admit that the field and the level of reflection and even of imagination peculiar to historians—in Florence and elsewhere—did not allow death to act as a character—although death appears to them as a central and disturbing fact resonating, often in touching tones, in their story.

It is already sufficiently clear that the impact, the collision point which death offers, takes on the significance of a blow of the supernatural to the order of events. Men are fragile because they unexpectedly can pass on and disappear from the scene. It does not seem admissible that this destiny peculiar to men as actors in history is the effect of chance or of an anonymous, senseless law. For this very reason personified death has no right of citizenship for historians. They cannot admit that death is senseless, a neutral extinguishing of biological life. And yet poets and artists had conceived the new goddess as an unrelenting reaper, deaf, insensible, even deriding. Since the fourteenth and fifteenth centuries they had clearly anticipated the modern and lay sensibility that would have made of death a simple emptiness, something already so foreknown as to be of no importance when it would come. The historians, however—and especially those of Florence in the period examined here—cannot and in any case do not want to imagine this outcome. For them human vicissitudes are at least a drama, sometimes a tragedy; the literary genre that describes them cannot renounce therefore the disruptive, ethically severe, and at the same time metaphysical, meaning of death.

The exception confirms the rule. There has been only one case in which a Florentine has purposely and irreverently wanted to dedrama- tize the collective tension produced by a death warrant. Filippo Nerli relates it in his *Commentarj dei fatti civili occorsi dentro la città di Firenze dall'anno 1215 al 1537*. It was one of those turbulent, Savo- narolian years, 1497, and the time in which two friars, each a cham- pion, respectively, of the Franciscans and of the Dominicans, were to publicly stand trial by fire, the first in order to prove to the Florentines the falsity of Savonarola's theses and the second to prove the truth. Giovanni Canacci, Nerli relates, seems to have offered a "pleasing council" at this point. Indeed, why have them die? If a supernatural event was absolutely needed to convince his fellow citizens, why not find one which did not require the loss of life of at least one man? A much simpler and more persuasive trial by water could be substituted for the trial by fire. Rather than expose the two friars to flames, one could immerse them in two barrels filled with water: the one coming out completely dry would demonstrate the goodness of his cause.[2]

Even if the proposal could be taken as a sign of an open-minded rationality vis-à-vis the mentality of the times, it would be very dar- ing to maintain that a significant number of Florentines, even if not the majority, shared it. All leads us to believe that Canacci was a bi- zarre Florentine spirit and an original, if not an isolated, one. In fact, not only was everything readied for the unrolling of the trial by fire, but the same historian informing us of the fact did not perceive any revolutionary element in such "pleasing advice." Death had to be tra- versed dramatically because the cosmic purport of this, which was an important episode, was conceived in dramatic fashion. Despite the dis- cussed and declared theological and philosophical positions, even the official ones, it does not seem that the educated or average Florentine had clear and precise ideas in this context. In the historical works which reflect current and widespread modes of feeling, the clerical point of view does not occupy a prominent position. Even when divine punishment is mentioned, it is not sins, and thus offenses to Church teachings, that are evoked, but crimes or vices perceived as acts against morality or humanity.

Even though these are lay attitudes, rarely welded to dogmatic positions, they still appear to be marked with religiousness, if we take religiousness as anxiety toward the supernatural. Historians' renderings inject death variously into a context of a philosophical and religious nature. For Bartolomeo Scala death is the limit of a parabolic and natural process;[3] for Giambullari the parabola is still there, but it is a cosmic one. On the one hand, Giambullari re-echoes Scala's emphasis.[4] On the other, as Machiavelli had already done indirectly, he develops in a more explicit fashion the meaning of death at the level of history. For him, that is, there is not only the movement that from birth and growth leads to the extinguishing of the individual, but also an "ordine invariabile delle cose, che i costumi e le età degli uomini di giorni in giorno traendo a 'l peggio ogni cosa creata conduce a morte" (invariable order of things that leads to death, since customs and the ages of men turn every created thing for the worse day after day).[5] Giambullari draws his inspiration out of a clear determinism: "invano certamente si fugge," he writes, "quello che al tutto debbe avvenire; anzi accade il più delle volte che si incorre nel male con la fuga e patiscesi maggior danno dove più si spera salvarsi" (certainly one runs away in vain from what eventually has to befall; indeed it happens that the majority of times man incurs evil by escaping it and suffers more damage where he had more hope of saving himself).[6] A century earlier Giovanni Cavalcanti had tried to establish a voluntaristic thesis by explicitly refusing the doctrine of predestination. To this he opposed Ptolemy's saying "che l'uomo savio signoreggia le stelle" (that the wise man rules the stars).[7] Narrating in detail the end of Count Oddo da Montone, who had clearly dreamt of dying a short while earlier,[8] the fifteenth-century historian insisted that the young man had deliberately neglected that omen and shown himself heedless of Nicolo' Piccinino's warnings. Indeed, the dream had been fulfilled thanks to its victim's will.[9] Machiavelli, however, had thought accurately that the two theses did not greatly contradict each other since the individual had arrived exactly where it seemed it was his destiny to be as a result of his own behavior. In fact, a propos of the conspiracy against Galeazzo Maria Sforza in 1476, he wrote that the duke of Milan had "molti segni della sua futura morte" (many signs of his future death), yet, as if driven by a sort of superior necessity, he managed to go into the very church in which they would have stabbed him the more easily.[10]

The difficulty of our writers in assuming a clear-cut position stemmed from the convictions theology imposed on them regarding God. If on one side God predisposed all things, on the other he gave creatures responsibility for their acts so that he had the right to punish them. Such a God incarnated and reflected the contradictory needs of a dogma that recognized divine prescience (and thus practically made of divinity the supreme cause of everything) as well as the individual capacity to desire and to act freely. Writers such as Cavalcanti or Nerli, for example, who were trying to detach themselves the least from Christian doctrine, were in a more embarrassing position[11] than those—like Machiavelli or Giambullari—who envisioned a true and fitting synchrony between the law of destiny and human conduct. For the latter the two parallel forces would cross and meet; for the former they were not to touch because Hell and Heaven could never blend. But the two tendencies were not actually well separated in the minds of these historians, who would often clearly swing between the one and the other.[12] Their references to fate, necessity, the heavens, and God seem almost interchangeable and recur as current concepts whose meanings overlay and do not appear to oppose one another. After having related the murky circumstances surrounding the killing of Duke Alessandro de' Medici in 1536 and having recalled the premonitions that had preceded it, Benedetto Varchi concludes: "per tutte queste cose fu tenuto in Firenze ed altrove la sua morte esser stata fatale" (for all these reasons in Florence and elsewhere it was understood that his death was fated).[13] A further proof of this approximate process of conceptual osmosis comes from Adriani. He recalls the destiny of those who plotted against the young Cosimo I de' Medici in 1537, the day after the clash of Montemurlo, which was unfavorable to them: "Ciascuno di loro o da necessità sospinto o da poca prudenza o—quello che è più da credere—da divina giustizia fatale tratti in grandissima miseria, sentendosi rimproverare i loro falli, erano menati in parte donde dovevano alla vita loro temere dolorosa fine" (Each of them because of need or of little caution or—which is what should be believed the most—because divine justice led them to great misery, in hearing their faults reproached, were brought to the place where they had to fear a sorrowful end for their life).[14]

Precisely because our historians are not thinkers and make no attempts to limit themselves to rigorous conceptual distinctions, they better reflect a large cultural stratum of Florentine society and remain in direct contact with the most popular tendencies of collective lay sensibility. Moreover, because for the most part they narrate situations and events in which they have participated, been acquainted with, or with which they were at least contemporaneous, their accounts constitute a direct and definitely valuable documentary witness to what the presence of death in human vicissitudes means for a Florentine. As it has been mentioned, in a measure ill defined and not specifiable in their eyes, death is the effect of the work of God or of fortune, of fate or of the heavens. We have previously underlined the variation and the uncertainty with which historians attribute these interventions variously to fate or God. We could say the same of the ambivalence with which they trace it back sometimes to God and sometimes to Fortune.[15] But since each time death occurs it is considered the effect of this or that form of superior power, death constitutes on the one hand the rightful instrument through which the supernatural acts upon history and on the other the means to chasten man whom the supernatural commonly chooses. In other words, death is not for our historians—as has been noticed—a conclusion without importance. Rather, it is the prominent and most visible sign of the activity of destiny or God.

In a sense then, the importance of death in the scheme of human events is not something to demonstrate since it is self-evident and indisputable. Florentine writers of history underline this function in a good number of ways. Death strikes their own professional imagination so that if a king dies the first day of the year—1515 in the case of Louis XII—even Guicciardini does not hesitate to write that his disappearance rendered that date unforgettable.[16] In any case, that imagination loves comparisons, coincidences, symmetries, and does not fail to stress them is not peculiar to the men of those times. Varchi gives us a good example. Although he shows contempt toward such a manner of feeling, he describes in its details the mood in Florence after the death of Duke Allessandro de' Medici. "Nè mancarono uomini ghiribizzosi," he writes, "i quali con vanissima ed anco non del tutto vera o curiosità o superstizione osservarono nella sua morte esser concorso sei 6, cioè lui essere stato ucciso l'anno 1536, avendo 26 anni, a' 6 del mese, alle 6 di notte, con 6 ferite, avendo regnato sei anni" (There were also whimsical men who with a vain curiosity or superstition far from true observed that six 6's had concurred in his death, that is, he had been killed in the year 1536, when he was 26, the 6th of the month, at 6 in the evening, with 6 wounds, after having reigned for 6 years).[17] This mental tendency derives from a desire for attributing to supernatural forces a rhythm of its own and from the assumption that it is possible to grasp its limit in space and time. Giovanni Cambi thus discovers that the dead body of Giuliano de' Medici, son of the Magnifico, followed on March 17, 1516, the same itinerary through the city that his own brother, Leo X, had covered in triumph three months and a half earlier.[18] Not much differently the same Cambi frames Selim's end in 1520: "per divina giustizia in quel medesimo luogho dove avelenò il padre, in quel luogho morì di morbo quando si voleva fare signore della cristianità" (thanks to divine justice, in the same place where he poisoned his father, he died of a disease at the time he wanted to make himself the master of Christianity).[19] Even Machiavelli reacts in an analogous fashion when he registers the almost simultaneous deaths of Castruccio Castracani and of Carlo, duke of Calabria, in these terms: "gli e' rade volte che la fortuna un bene o un male con un altro bene o con un altro male non accompagni" (it is rare that fortune does not follow something good or bad with something else good or bad).[20] The symmetrical games of destiny, beyond those of space and time, also enter family life. Thus Guicciardini notices that because of changes in fortune Filippo Coppola was cut to pieces precisely when he was at the service of Ferdinando, duke of Calabria, whose paternal grandfather had had Coppola's father decapitated.[21]

There is no need to underline that this discovery of the geometry of the supernatural in history was the direct result of a precise way of feeling and also a projection onto the otherworldly of manners of thinking and of reacting which were purely worldly. In any case, with or without symmetry, death appears as an event of determining importance, especially when it strikes individuals having an eminent role in the life of a city or of a people. From Bruni to Poggio, from Cavalcanti to Machiavelli and Guicciardini up to Nerli, Varchi, Nardi, and Giambullari, all Florentine historians assume similar and like-minded positions. Death overturns human interests; it radically upsets situations, both in a positive and negative sense and in the short and long run. Just to give an example, while today we would say that the disappearance of millions of men from the Black Death and the successive epidemics produced catastrophic and lasting consequences on a large scale, Cavalcanti attributed to the murder of a single man, who in contemporary historiography has a much more modest place, an almost equal sum of consequences.[22] Writers such as Machiavelli and Guicciardini assigned a symbolical significance to the death of Lorenzo the Magnificent beyond the real one and saw it as the first link of a fatal chain. The system of distribution of a prince's power, at the time much more linked to physical beings than institutions, makes this extreme sensibility toward the disappearance of first-rate historical actors much more understandable. Guicciardini confirms it in an indirect but eloquent way when he notes the significant exception of Venice in which "per la forma eccellente del governo loro, le cose pubbliche" do not suffer "nè per la morte del principe nè per la elezione del nuovo, variazione alcuna" (because of the excellent form of their government, the public good does not suffer any change either because of the death of the prince nor of the election of the new one).[23]

Obviously death assumed a meaning much more evident in an age dominated by the specter and the fear of unremitting changes and in a period whose vicissitudes offered the most evident proof that these reversals were the leitmotiv of human ups and downs. Thus death takes on an importance of the first order also in the historiographic ritual, that is, in the very fashion in which writers feel they have a duty to present and display events. Dividing line of history and of its developments, death represents on the one hand the meeting point laden with consequences for the future and on the other either the forewarning of a whole process or a central episode foreshadowed in turn. In a sense, therefore, Florentine historians make of death the most relevant time for a judgment of life, of virtues and vices, and of positive and negative functions related to the deceased character. In another sense they focus on death a whole play of lights and shadows, of suspense and uneasiness, of predictions and omens. Because they are historians, and thus expounders of a series of facts of which they know the before and the after, they animate and orchestrate the narration with techniques of suspense which largely utilize death itself. Is Buondelmonte of the Buondelmonti killed in 1215 at the Ponte Vecchio? Here is how the usually sober Leonardo Bruni comments on it: "fu notato questo d'alcuni per mal segno della città" (this fact was regarded as a bad sign for the city).[24] One April night in 1492 Giovanni Cambi sees a shining thunderbolt discharging on the dome of Santa Maria del Fiore. He jots it down: "La brighata giudicò che detto segnio venissi nella chupola per segnificare detta morte di Lorenzo de' Medici, perchè morí . . . tre giorni dipoi" (the company judged this sign alighted on the dome to signify the said death of Lorenzo de' Medici, because he died . . . three days later).[25] A savage duel opposes four young men during the siege of Florence by the Imperial troops and so Segni reports: "Da' sottili interpreti ed acuti ingegni fu preso questo duello per augurio e per segno do pronosticarsi il fine ed il principio di tutta la guerra; conciossiacosachè essendo stato fatto fra i cittadini nobili di quella patria, siccome ancora era la guerra universale, pareva che essendo dall'una e dall'altra parte seguita la vittoria e la perdita, che il fine di quella guerra dovesse essere per l'una e per l'altra parte infelice e che le cagioni che l'avevano mossa fussero similmente ingiuste da ogni banda" (Subtle interpreters and sharp minds took this duel as an augury and a sign prognosticating the end and the beginning of the whole war. This was also done by the noble citizens of that country who, considering that there was still universal war and that victory and loss had followed both sides, thought that the end of that war had to be unhappy for both factions and that the reasons which had started it were similarly unjust on each side).[26] Finally, the weather being absolutely splendid immediately after the murder of Duke Alessandro in January 1536, Florentine exiles wrote: "ciò avveniva per la molta festa che faceva il cielo e la terra" (this happened thanks to the great joy that heaven and earth displayed) for that death. For others, such were "felicissimi segni ed augurii che ne la terra e 'l cielo per la creazione del signor Cosimo" (the most happy signs and auguries that earth and heaven were showing for the creation of Signor Cosimo).[27]

Beyond the differences in interpretations Florentines gave of these deaths, it should be underlined that death appeared to them as the justifiable point of departure and of reference for offering their opinions and expressing attitudes, in a word, for their taking sides. Obviously this could not have happened were death considered an event of the same nature with others. Since its character was different, its purport and sense had to be different. Death excites collective sensibility and stirs minds both to attribute an allusive or symbolical meaning to certain phenomena and to forge others with the imagination. It may very well have been true that after the death of Duke Alessandro a thunderbolt hit Santa Maria del Fiore again and another one the Palazzo Vecchio or that an earthquake shock was felt. But, as Segni relates, did the wooden Baby Jesus placed in the Augustinian church of Sant'Jacopo really sweat for a month?[28] We should not feel surprised that imaginations are moved beyond measure, since Segni himself believes in the relationship between certain incidents and the death of Pope Cervini, Marcello II.[29] Nor should we feel amazed that death is used for the most unexpected combinations, as the one Nardi achieves when he relates a news event which took place in Prato in 1492. In that year two young men from Prato had died following an accident that happened during a pageant given in honor of Cardinal Giovanni de' Medici and in which they were participating. According to the historian, this could have been an omen of the terrible sack of Prato which was to take place in 1512.[30]

Death becomes then the culminating moment of a sort of illogical but comprehensible discourse made of signs and premonitions which surround men in their daily existence. Death is the crucial point of the low-pitched but unceasing, even if nonrational, dialogue woven between supernatural forces and the history of this world. Florentine writers lend their ears to this language because it weaves in both their personal existence and that of their fellow citizens. Within such a discourse death works as a cry no one can avoid hearing. It is possible in fact not to believe astrologers; indeed, some historians deride them palpably. It is also possible to perceive that some speculate on popular sensibility and on its excessive inclination to lend faith to uncontrollable voices and interpretations. But death is an undeniable event of the great dialogue that destiny or God maintains with the community of men. If this is true for the individual dimension, it is also true in a way for the collective and historical one. Nerli surrenders to this evidence when he comments upon the murder of Duke Alessandro: "Vi serrò dentro il duca," he says of Lorenzino who shuts the duke in his own room, "ed egli, accecato dalla sua mala fortuna vi si lasciò serrare e quegli che solamente per sicurtà e guardia della sua persona spendeva tante migliaia di scudi, come faceva, si ridusse solo, disarmato ed a discrezione di uno solo, senza speranza di poter essere, occorrendo, soccorso in modo alcuno" (He locked the duke inside and he, blinded by his own bad luck, let himself be locked; he who was used to spend so many thousand scudi solely to guard and protect his person, reduced himself alone, disarmed and at the discretion of a single person, with no hope, if in need, of being able to be helped in any way).[31] This situation of extraordinary improvidence and insecurity could not have been created by anything else but fate in order to make possible the killing of a man who normally would leave nothing to chance. The fact that there is no valid defense against death means therefore not only that everyone is subjected to it, but that death is the loophole, the slit, that allows fortune or God to intervene in history in a decisive fashion.[32]

This rationalization also means that Florence solidly displayed in this period an ample dose of trust both in the normal and the natural. The social and human context constitutes a web enclosing and supporting everyday life in such a way as to assure it a regular and calm course. Let us not forget that Florentine historians of the fifteenth and sixteenth centuries are able to reconstruct a succession of events on the basis of logical or psychological criteria and on a largely rational scale. History is no more for them the domain of the miraculous; rather, it has a quiet articulate structure, one made up of actions and reactions explainable through exclusively worldly criteria. To make at least a comparison, there is a significant difference between them and their contemporary Philippe de Commynes. The difference is not so much in the kind of world vision as in the measure of the intervention still reserved to the supernatural. While for Florentine writers the area of the supernatural has by now neatly narrowed and thinned, for the French nobleman it remains quite large—no matter how much room he also wants to reserve for men's judgment. Moreover, Commynes channels all superior forces back solely to God while, as we have seen, the pages of our Florentines reflect a repeated presence of natural, or differently hued, powers.

Such observations were indispensable before examining the relationship Florentine historians establish between God and death on the level of events. It can be said with no hesitation that such a relationship has a name, justice. We pointed out a moment ago that it is precisely through the death of this or that actor of history that fortune and fate erupt in the world to provoke shocks or to insert more or less durable processes of change. But the most frequent intervention of God through death is the one that allows divinity to punish men in order to reestablish the supremacy of the good over the bad or at least the balance in favor of the first. Vis-à-vis this phenomenon, it is like drowning in a world in which powerful people almost completely escape the law, both because they make it and because law has not enough might to dominate them. It has just been shown that social life appears to Florentine historians regulated by a steady normality of interhuman relationships. However much this can be true, they are obviously convinced that abuse, arbitrary acts, or malice are still blocked by very few or fragile embankments. Death inflicted for revenge on a man from another man is quite rarely celebrated in their pages without interpreting it as a work of the hand of God. One such unusual case can be found in the tale Giambullari gives of the death of the northern King Aroldo. More than once Aroldo had behaved in vexatious style toward one of his courtiers, Tocco. Thus, when he found himself unexpectedly far away from everybody and alone with his sovereign, Tocco gave vent to his resentment by killing Aroldo with an arrow and thus avenged "con un colpo solo tutte le ingiurie ch'egli aveva già ricevute e insegnò con questa vendetta a' grandi e potenti in che maniera è debban trattare i loro servitori" (with a single stroke all the abuses that he had already received and through this revenge taught the great and the powerful in what manner they should treat their servants).[33] In any case Tocco's gesture does not depart substantially from the kind of intervention that is precisely attributed to divinity. God is patient and knows how to wait, then suddenly, through a single stroke—that of death—he can clearly manifest what is not permitted.

This God appears thus as a creation of men who need to see that sooner or later those who act dishonestly and are too pitiless will be punished. God is imagined exactly as one would wish the force able to repress the excess of wickedness to be. His divine justice does not have scruples about pursuing his designs and does not split hairs on the means employed. Does Valentino have Vitellozzo and Oliverotto strangled? For the pious and Christian Giovanni Cambi there is no doubt that God himself has acted through Cesare Borgia.[34] In a more lay, but fundamentally similar fashion, Machiavelli precedes the news of Giorgio Scali's beheading with this comment: "la insolenzia di messer Giorgio qualche volta doveva avere fine" (Messer Giorgio's insolence had sooner or later to come to an end).[35] In a more moralistic manner the Florentine secretary draws the following lesson from the murder of the Duke of Milan, Galeazzo Maria Sforza: "imparino pertanto i principi a vivere in maniera e farsi in modo riverire ed amare, che niuno speri potere, ammazzandogli, salvarsi" (princes should learn, therefore, to live accordingly and to try to make themselves honored and loved since no one should hope to be able to save himself through murders).[36] As God shows no scruples in administering death, so Florentine historians have no reserve when they have a chance to vent their disdain and their hate by recounting the end of an abhorred character. The case of Guicciardini's treatment of Pope Borgia is eloquent indeed. From the very moment he relates his election the writer expresses a clear prediction of an exemplary future punishment falling on the pope[37] and then exults and sneers in describing his corpse: "Concorse al corpo morto d'Alessandro in San Piero con incredibile allegrezza tutta Roma, non potendo saziarsi gli occhi d'alcuno di vedere spento un serpente che con la sua immoderata ambizione e pestifera perfidia, e con tutti gli esempi di orribile crudeltà, di mostruosa libidine e di inaudita avarizia, vendendo senza distinzione le cose sacre e le profane, aveva attossicato tutto il mondo" (With incredible cheerfulness all Rome assembled to see Alessandro's dead body in St. Peter's. Nobody's eyes ever seemed to tire of seeing dead a serpent who with his excessive ambition and pestiferous wickedness, and with all examples of horrible cruelty, monstrous lechery and unheard of avarice, had poisoned the whole world by selling sacred and profane things with no distinction).[38] To comment on this spectacle Guicciardini does not hesitate then to display his philosophy on the subject and to revile those who presume "di scorgere con la debolezza degli occhi umani la profondita' de' giudici divini" (to discern the depth of divine judgments with the weakness of human eyes),[39] as if he were unable to recognize that they corresponded exactly to his expectations and were taking the forms imagined by the collective Christian sensibility of his contemporaries. Besides, by looking closely at the various ways in which God fulfills his revenge we could clearly discover that these ways do not differ from the totally human and sometimes picturesque figurations that this or that historian give of God's interventions.[40]

This evident appropriation of the actions of God by Florentine writers of history eventually leads toward the middle of the sixteenth century to the identification of divine criteria of punishment with more human criteria of the conservation of the state. Giovanni Battista Adriani, Cosimo I's official historian, offers us a quite transparent demonstration of this idea when he exposes the consequences of the defeat of anti-Medicean exiles in 1537. In relating the beheading of five of them in the Bargello courtyard, the writer concisely states that if, on one hand, the event was worthy of commiseration "pensando all'instabilità dell'umana fortuna" (thinking of the instability of human fortune), on the other it was absolutely necessary for reasons of state, so that not only the law allowed such a death but demanded it.[41] In a similar fashion he frames the suicide of Filippo Strozzi, the main opponent, which followed soon after. The historian surmises that his death is the fated result both of a destiny peculiar to that family and of the intervention of a divine justice bent on punishing Strozzi for having made an attempt against the Medicean power which assured the well-being of Florence.[42] Was not this a means of finally appropriating even God and submitting him to the imperatives of a new supreme lordship over men, that of reason of state? Death was becoming no more a sign and manifestation of the supernatural; rather, it was being annexed as a terrible, but legitimate, corollary of the demands of the Leviathan lurking on the horizon. This was, at least in part, what has brought us to the political tragedies of our century.

Giovanni Caroli, 1460–1480:
Death, Memory, and Transformation

▼

Salvatore I. Camporeale

When we ask why . . . analysis comes upon the death experience so often and in such variety, we find primarily, *death appears in order to make way for transformation.*—J. Hillman, *Suicide and the Soul*

Giovanni Caroli, or to be exact, Giovanni di Carlo dei Berlinghieri, lived from 1429 to 1503. Florentine, and a Dominican friar at Santa Maria Novella, he played a leading role in the conventual and religious life of his order while, at the same time, he was deeply engaged in the cultural and political activity of his humanist contemporaries. He wrote both in Latin and in the vernacular about history and theology, politics and philosophy, as well as upon more specific topics. His complex literary production, which is still largely unpublished, frequently dealt with controversial political and civic problems, as well as philosophical and religious ones. Almost always, he wrote in response to political and/or cultural events, inspired by contemporary trends whether civic, monastic, or religious.[1]

The fact that he began to write at all followed from his realization that he was experiencing a profound crisis in his own religious life. Out of this crisis, which he suffered in mature adulthood, came the first of his most important literary works: the *Liber dierum lucensium* and the *Vitae nonnullorum fratrum Beatae Mariae Novellae*, written between 1460 and 1480.[2]

The first, the *Liber dierum lucensium*, or "Book of the days in Lucca," is densely autobiographical; the second, the *Vitae fratrum*, is a reworking of the earlier text which, going further, sums up and brings to resolution Caroli's process of self-examination. But at the same time, both of these address more general topics: the problems besetting the entire religious system of the order to which he, by his own choice, belonged, and—even more fundamentally—the very nature of monastic and mendicant institutions, both in their contemporary reality and historical perspective.

The *Liber dierum* was begun in the autumn of 1461 and completed the following summer in the convent of San Romano in Lucca. Like a dramatic work, the book displays unity of time (taking place on three consecutive days) and unity of place (the convent of San Romano). Its three parts are structured as dialogues in which the actors express opposing views: they are the conflicting voices of Caroli, conducting a dialogue with himself. A lengthy prologue, setting the scene for the ensuing drama, presents the situation and moral difficulties which are the backdrop for the action.

In April 1460 disagreement and conflict surfaced between the community of Santa Maria Novella, of which Caroli was prior, and Marziale Auribelli, general superior of the order, regarding monastic reform and renewal. This was but a particular case of a more widely spread divergence of attitudes on how to implement the reform already begun by Giovanni Dominici in the early Quattrocento, which was to determine the development of the mendicant orders in Italy for the rest of the century. Caroli argued for a reform that would respect the juridical autonomy and specific tradition of the convent. Auribelli, instead, sought to impose a reform using the authority of his own jurisdiction as general superior, that is to say, with criteria quite unrelated to their local tradition. Despite the support of the Signoria of Florence, who agreed entirely with the convent's position, Caroli was removed as prior and exiled to Lucca in September 1460. However, the convent continued to oppose Auribelli with such strength that he was unable to effect his reform and was himself deposed by Pius II. His removal as master general of the Dominican order was "confirmed," under papal pressure, by the General Chapter of the Order, convened in Siena August 15, 1462. Some historians have seen Pius's absolutely unprecedented interference in Dominican affairs, with the removal of the Avignonese Auribelli, as part of his anti-French policy. It is certainly true, in any case, that after the Pope's death, the same general chapter reelected Auribelli as master general, accompanying the appointment with an encyclical letter of protest against papal interfence in the constitutional rights of the Order.[3]

Caroli was to reflect at length on these events as he passed his days in Lucca. He came to see the events themselves, and their implications, as a personal drama—a conflict between his existential being and the life choices he had made. In order to carry out the reform, he had been obliged to oppose the highest authority of the order. Just as would happen some decades later to Savonarola and the convent of San Marco, Caroli had felt it his duty to renounce monastic obedience to the duly constituted authorities of the order. To save the religious institution he was thus obliged—as anyone else in the same situation would have been—to be institutionally disobedient. Auribelli was the "tyrant" against whom it was necessary to rebel in order to preserve the *libertas conventus*. But in conceiving of the conventual life in these terms, previously reserved for civic affairs, the dilemma of obedience versus disobedience attained a new dimension. For the question of necessary disobedience affected the very roots and foundations of monastic life. The monastic institution had traditionally been thought of, and historically experienced, as based on the principle of obedience; now it seemed that it could only be saved by denying that principle. But this would provoke a profound crisis and a radical transformation of the monastic and mendicant institution, since, by denying the principle on which it was founded, it would, in effect, deny its own reality.

The problem is amply explored in the "first day" of the *Liber dierum* by a Franciscan and an Augustinian who, as guests of the community of San Romano, become the dramatis personae of the dialogue. Heroic obedience, defended by the Franciscan as the evangelical foundation of monasticism, is turned inside out, as it were, by the Augustinian who advocates an equally heroic and evangelical disobedience as proof of Christian freedom. Moreover, having presented his evidence for the necessity of demonstrating Christian freedom in certain historical situations, the Augustinian concludes with a discussion of the greater or lesser disjunctions that necessarily underlie every historical process. In his view radical transformation of any civil or ecclesiastical order is only possible when accompanied by an equally radical break with the past. History, like all natural processes, is governed by the inseparable relation of *corruptio* and *generatio*: just as in the case of organic forms, every birth implies a previous death, so the historical process requires the annulment or, better, the overcoming of the past. *Vetustas et mors*, decline and death, are the inevitable preconditions for any rebirth or renewal.

This reflection on the inexorable alternation of life and death in human affairs evokes an inner tension in Caroli. Confronted by a present reality that he perceives ultimately as the presence of death, he seeks refuge in the memory of the past. This is the point of departure for the dialogue, occupying the "second day" of the *Liber dierum*, between Caroli and his fellow friar Giacomo di Pietro, who had also been expelled from Santa Maria Novella and exiled to Lucca. Caroli, reflecting on the long series of obituaries which make up the ancient *Cronica fratrum* of Santa Maria Novella, interprets these as constituting a single continuous historical chain. They represent the history of a community which, from its beginnings in the thirteenth century, developed as a vital and active organism. Having reached the apex of its grandeur in the early fifteenth century and attained full maturity, it declined rapidly. Caroli's attempts to define the historical segments within this process have a retrograde motion: it is almost as if he hoped to stop himself and his community from being hurled over the precipice, as if his backward glance at the past might somehow prevent the present collapse.

At the end of the second day Caroli withdraws into the silence of his cell, where his reflection continues as a monologue in which voices and images emerge from the depths of his soul. He recognizes with auguish that the past has now run its course and that the present is devoid of hope. Now he gives himself up to that *tedium vitae* which he had hinted in the prologue was the real cause of his personal crisis: "tedet itaque hominum, tedet et morum, et, si verum fateri velim, non-nunquam tedet et vite."[4] And the anguish which he had sought to escape in sleep reemerges in his dreams. The third part of the *Liber dierum*, conceived "ad modum Somnii Scipionis," is a dream vision, a premonition of the future: the destruction of the conventual structures of Santa Maria Novella and the dissolution of the Florentine community.[5]

The dream reveals a vast plain lit by a sinister moonlight gleam as the last rays of the sun fade. Along the side of a mountain, rising in the middle of the plain, the conventual buildings of Santa Maria Novella gather around the church; the glimmering moonlight throws into sharp relief the architectural contours of the complex. While the Dominican gazes, fascinated, at the splendid nocturnal scene, an enormous multitude surrounds the monumental edifice and attacks it from all sides. The structures, so harmoniously arranged, collapse one after another, as if torn apart stone by stone. Nothing remains but an immense pile of rubble; a vast expanse of rocks and falling walls stretches out beneath the vault of heaven. Now the friar gazes with profound sadness at the great ruin of what was once a splendid work of art, erected and enlarged over the course of centuries. Aeneas's exclamation over the sight of rising Carthage comes to his mind but in a reverse sense: "O *in*-fortunati quorum iam moenia *ruunt*."[6]

The dream vision of the great destruction summons up figures from the remote and recent past. Giovanni Dominici and Antonino Pierozzi, whom Caroli considered the last of the great men of his order, appear in his dream and interpret its significance.

The history of institutions, says Dominici, their birth and death, growth and decay, needs to be understood in relation to a human will and human freedom. The cyclical process of history is an integral part of the human adventure on earth. If the mendicant religious system and, in particular, the Dominican order and the Florentine community are in decline, this is because the spirit which inspired its founders has died. Just as Priam's kingdom fell because Athena, goddess of wisdom, abandoned it, so—continues Dominici—the Dominican community is in decline because of insufficient love of divine truth. Hence the disintegration of its monastic and religious life, the decline of theological inquiry and of that civic and cultural commitment which was the vital source of its existence through the centuries.

Caroli could hardly have chosen better than to attribute such considerations to Dominici, who had been one of the most active proponents of religious reform in the late fourteenth and early fifteenth centuries, and he seems to have understood his subject well, when he makes Dominici conclude his speech saying: "Quis aliud in rebus humanis umquam vidit, nisi finem et obliquitatem. . . . Sic et regum et urbium et populorum ac familiarum clara atque lata imperia incurvata ac tandem extincta sunt. Nusquam stabilitas esse potest, nusquam firmitas, nusquam rectum sine obliquo vidisti. Ubi lune imperium, ibi mobilia et desinentia omnia."[7]

Pierozzi, the other character of the dream, goes beyond the discussion of the cyclical historical process to which institutions are subject and of cultural change. He interprets Caroli's vision of the disintegration and dismantling of the architecture of Santa Maria Novella as signifying internal discord and breakup. Caroli witnesses this destruction in the fleeting last rays of the sun and during the rise of the moon with its ill-omened signs of Mars and Saturn in opposition: "solis fulgor subrubens et obliquus, ut cum ad occasum flectit exiles radios fundens; lunaris autem globus cum infestis orbium signis, que Saturni ac Martis dicimus, domui incumbebant."[8]

Pierozzi, with images and metaphors that verily match Caroli's vision, speaks of the need for the Florentine community to regain spiritual heat and sunlight by returning to its original state and through the renewal of *caritas*. The architectural contours and the harmony of the "spiritual edifice" can only be restored and rebuilt on the foundations of "living stones," such as once were the best representatives of the institution. Thus Pierozzi calls for institutional reform of the order and the development of a spiritual and cultural scope better suited and more adequate to the contemporary *rinascita* of the *studia humanitatis*.

This is the second mention of the *studia humanitatis*: the first appears early in the prologue of the *Liber dierum*. In the pages that intervene between these two affirmations of the *studia*, Caroli gives his detailed analysis of the decline of the religious and mendicant way of life. It seems clear that for him the crisis in the Dominican community was the simultaneous result of, on the one hand, the progressive erosion of the institution's foundations and, on the other, of a split (equally progressive over time) between the traditional *studia divinitatis* and the *studia humanitatis* of contemporary culture. In fact, Caroli's sense of historical change is powerfully shaped by the new learning and its own sense of rupture with medieval past.

The *Liber dierum*, then, is an exposé, from the inside, of the crisis of monasticism, specifically in its mendicant form. While antimonastic polemic, common among the humanists, was almost always motivated by, and conducted along the lines of, moral and often moralistic thinking (the great hypocrisy of the friars!), Caroli's criticisms are on another plane altogether. His analysis focuses on the mendicant community's loss of its historical role, following on the transformation of Florence from a Trecento communal society into the fast-growing city-state of the Quattrocento. The Dominican's self-criticism of the monastic system has therefore a decidedly historical character: the religious institution, born in the thirteenth century, was now in deep decline because—as might happen to any other institution—it seemed to have lost its civic and religious function, its historical role, and its justification with the coming of the new Renaissance society.

Given this realization, Caroli, having reentered the Florentine community, had only one choice: to relive in the present the story of the past. The memory of the past, which underlies the whole *Liber dierum*, had been sketched out in the second book of the dialogue. This skeleton was now reworked in a new context and for other purposes barely a decade later, in the 1470s, as the *Vitae fratrum*. The direct source for Caroli's revision was the *Cronica fratrum* of the Florentine convent, whose uninterrupted series of *obitus* had already been mentioned by the Dominican in his *Liber dierum*.

The *Vitae fratrum* is a collection of seven biographies, recounting the lives of men famous in the history of the convent from its foundation in the first half of the thirteenth century to the first decades of the fifteenth. The biographical series is arranged in chronological order. The first two lives describe the careers of Giovanni da Salerno and Aldobrandino Cavalcanti, the founders of Santa Maria Novella, who died respectively in 1242 and 1279. These are followed by the lives of Simone Salterelli, bishop of Pisa, and Angelo Acciaiuoli, bishop of Florence, the former dead in 1342 and the latter in 1357. The fifth and sixth biographies concern Alessio Strozzi, the "master in theology," who died in 1383, and Guido da Raggiolo, the "master of grammar," deceased in 1397. The seventh and last is the life of Giovanni Dominici (1355/6-1419). The whole collection is preceded by a letter of dedication to Cristoforo Landino. Each biography is introduced by a preface; some are dedicated to Florentine humanists who were friends or acquaintances of Caroli: Giorgio Antonio Vespucci, Donato Acciaiuoli, Roberto Buoninsegni and his son Giovan Battista, and Francesco dei Berlinghieri. An extensive *laudatio domus* of Santa Maria Novella, whose last pages speak of the Pazzi Conspiracy, is placed as a proem to the biographical series. On the basis of both internal and external evidence, the composition of the entire work can be dated between 1474–75 and 1480–81.

This, in brief, is the compositional structure of Caroli's book. But even from this summary description one might deduce that the *Vitae fratrum* constitutes a history of Santa Maria Novella from the thirteenth to the fifteenth century. The book is linked by the correlations and sequence of the biographical facts of each of the subjects, the interconnections made between the periods in which each of the seven Dominicans participated in the religious, civil, and cultural life of Florence, and the description of Santa Maria Novella, whose architectural development was the fruit of these friars' patronage.

But, going further, I can clarify the significance of Caroli's compendium of biographies by saying—and this, I believe, best expresses the historiographical significance of the work—that the *Vitae fratrum* is a story of communal Florence seen from the viewpoint of the historic memory of the mendicant community at Santa Maria Novella. It is within this perspective of the past, to which is accorded the status of a mythical era of original and authentic beginnings, that Caroli develops his views on the present crisis of the monastic and civil life in late fifteenth century Florence. This particular aspect of the work is most clearly and explicitly seen in the introductory and dedicatory portraits: the *epistola* to Landino, the *laudatio domus,* and above all, the *praefationes* to the individual biographies.[9]

There is, for Caroli, a profound difference between late fifteenth century Florence and the earlier communal city in terms of cultural, civic, and political life. In fact, the civic and religious life of the present is the exact opposite of that communal past, and underlying each individual biography is the comparison between Medicean Florence and the communal past—irrevocably lost and, just for that reason, the stuff of myths. The historical break between past and present is placed, by Caroli, at the end of the Trecento and beginning of the Quattrocento—more exactly, with the advent of the Black Death. The shadow which this great epidemic cast over the medieval city in the second half of the fourteenth century was also the death of a historical period. The plague brought about a *"dissolutio morum et religionum,"* which caused the destruction of a previous era that had sought precisely to *"erigere domus et componere mores."*[10]

What reasons does Caroli give for this decline, which signifies, for us, the end of the Middle Ages? The causes range from the inevitability of death—intrinsic to all natural life and, according to the Augustinian concept of history, also to human events—to the schism in the highest echelons of the church, schism which ripped open all of Western Christianity and disrupted its balance. But it is above all the demographic disaster of the Black Death of 1348 and its returns in 1363, 1374, and 1400 (this last, according to him, as devastating as the first) that Caroli considers to have been the principal agent in bringing the communal era to an end. The high death toll interrupted the normal succession of generations and, as a consequence, the cultural and spiritual continuity of civic and religious life. Just as this violent and unforeseen generational break threatened the physical survival of conventual (and, more generally, urban) life, so the break in transmission of cultural traditions led to a loss of identity for an entire culture.

Thus Caroli projects his own sense of death, which had surfaced with his consciousness of both personal and collective crisis, onto the historical memory of the past. And for this reason he reelaborates in the *Vitae fratrum* the same concept of history as a cyclical process of life and death, which he had asserted in the *Liber dierum*.

The evolution and decline of an institution are discussed by Caroli in terms of the life phases of an organism. The extremes of minimum and maximum on the graph of historical process are described as birth and growth, life and death. Thus his narrative is not so much about the foundation, consolidation, and deterioration of the institution as a juridical and organizational structure, as it is about the birth, growth, and maturation of a community or social group, its breakup at the height of its powers, and its fragmentation in unexpected collapse—just as death, a constant and eroding hidden presence, lies in waiting to disrupt a living organism. Undoubtedly, one of Caroli's presuppositions, in both the *Liber dierum* and the *Vitae fratrum*, is this notion of an "organic" fall and death in historical process, an assumption which is claimed, in the final analysis, as the resolution of the antinomy of greatness/decline:

"Equidem ita se habet rerum ipsa natura, ut quicquid oritur occidat nihilque sub sole perpetuum vel sub lune globo eternum. Proinde equa pene conditio est et ineuntis etatis et in senectutem vergentis ut morbis plurimis sint referte, quasi iam in finem suum metipse asciscant; solum id interest: quod infantiles ad purgationem morbi, seniles autem tendunt ad mortem, nature virtute, que in infantibus augescit, in senibus decrescente."[11]

By virtue of its nature as an association of individuals over a succession of generations, the Dominican community had a unique role in the political and social activity of a communal city like Florence. Because of this relationship, the biographies of some of the prominent members of the community have a special representative status: they allow Caroli to spell out his large historical vision of the antinomy greatness/decline in individual biographies. Thus the essential elements of the passage from origin to decline are considered within the framework of each single individual's life and the events which concerned him. And each of these, in turn, is considered within the framework of the convent's history from its foundation to its contemporary crisis. Thus, the notion of organic decay in historical process not only shaped the subjective motivations that inspired Caroli to write the *Vitae fratrum*, but it also determined his methodical choice of a narrative, structured as a series of biographies. In this way the fundamental problems of history and historiography reciprocally influence and define one another.

The *Vitae fratrum*, then, can be seen as a last effort to recover and reconstruct, in a literary way, that cultural and architectural edifice which was, for Caroli, the convent of Santa Maria Novella. This last attempt to restore the past was prompted by his dream vision of the complex in disintegration and reduced to a mass of ruins. Indeed, Caroli himself makes explicit references to his personal motivations for writing the work: to his tension, to the point of insomnia, during its composition and to his sense of internal compulsion to set down those events worthy of being remembered.

His awareness of a present-day crisis and his vision of historical process as an inexorable movement toward the finality of death led Caroli to consider the Black Death of the Trecento (beginning in the 1340s) as the waning of an epoch: the communal and religious era of the Middle Ages. Caroli had read and understood much about the Black Death in the dense series of *obitus* in the *Cronica fratrum* of Santa Maria Novella and in other Florentine chronicles. Also, between the lines of the *Liber dierum* and the *Vitae fratrum*, I believe that one can detect the writings of Petrarch, which are almost all (from the *Epistolae* to the *Secretum*) pervaded by his personal experience of the Black Death. Within such a contextual frame the *Liber dierum* dis-

plays a "cogitatio mortis," expressed as an internal drama in which conflicts and anxieties reveal themselves or reemerge from the depths of
his being, and the *Vitae fratrum* are a commemoration of the past,
dominated by a strong sense of the transience of all human things.
Death figures as a constant presence within the vitality and grandeur
of human achievement.[12]

I have already noted in several places that Caroli cites passages
from Virgil's *Aeneid*. Actually, these occur far more frequently in
his work than I have so far indicated, beginning with the first lines
of the prologue to the *Liber dierum* and continuing into the last pages
of the *Vitae fratrum*.

As we saw, Caroli begins his reflections on the events which had
occurred and on his personal situation by considering his flight from
"the great destruction" and by expressing his deep sadness at "the
anguishing realization" of total loss. Here occurs his (first) reference
to the *Aeneid* (book 2, verses 274–79) where Hector, appearing to
Aeneas in a dream, informs him of the imminent destruction of Troy
and exhorts him to flee. The relevant passage of Virgil's poem must
have been enlightening to Caroli's mind, bearing deeper significance
to his thought—"recte familie nostre ruinas eisdem versibus, quibus
poeta noster Troiana excidia in hectorea similitudine flebat, deplorare
possimus."[13] In the autograph manuscript, Caroli himself added a
marginal gloss at this point: "metaphorice intelligenda sunt hic."[14]
And in fact, from this point on, all of his Aeneas metaphors—the
flight from his native city, whose grandeur had fallen together with
its walls; the wandering in search of new shores and new cities; the
descent to Hades in order to recall, in conversations with the ancient
heroes, those deeds which had made his native land great—are invested with personal meanings by Caroli. The Dominican implements
a mythical metaphor to understand his own existential crisis and to
express it in the most appropriate language. Rising up from, or delv-
ing deep into, the depths of his being, Caroli gives form and meaning
to his own life experience by acting out a symbol of transformation.[15]

His awareness of the decline of the monastic and religious system,
of its loss of historic purpose, and perhaps even of the end of an
era, led Caroli to pass in review the century-long duration of that
cultural, political, religious, and artistic complex which was the Florentine community of his order. His historiographical research appears

to him as a journey into the shadow and darkness where famous men of the past are held imprisoned by the oblivion of the living. These seem to be awaiting liberation, to be brought back into the light. This is a descent into Hades in order to make deeds and ancient figures live again by telling the stories of their lives. The *Vitae fratrum* opens with the words: "in has vitas describendas descendi"—just as Aeneas descended to the kingdom of the dead to talk with the ancestors and ancient heroes and thus acquire from the past the strength and inspiration to reconstitute a city for his Trojan people.[16]

This consciousness of destruction and death, which returns as a dream vision and dramatic dialogue with himself in the *Liber dierum*, becomes historical memory in the *Vitae fratrum*. If it is the decadence of the present which urges Caroli toward the memory of the past, writing about the past is the only means he can find in some way to redeem the present. Thus it will not seem—he writes—that I have spent this time of conflict and decadence in vain, without acting or without caring.[17] In this sense the discussion of a "being for death" and the historical reflection of the *Liber dierum* and the *Vitae fratrum* can be seen as prospects for a rebirth of the past or, better, for a rebirth of origins out of the ruins of the present. His reflection on death is a search for solutions that will make possible personal and collective transformations, and it is, above all, a final attempt to survive and somehow transfigure his own mortal anguish—the *tedium vitae* of the prologue to the *Liber dierum*—into existential choice.

After the Pazzi Conspiracy of 1478, Caroli seems to have radically changed direction. In the 1480s Caroli would go on to write a kind of *defensio* of the Medici regime, opposing the well-known humanist, Filelfo. Later, in 1489, he was to criticize the famous *Theses* of Pico della Mirandola, using the most traditional Scholastic arguments. After this, he strongly opposed (together with the rest of the community at Santa Maria Novella) Savonarola and the religious experience which the Frate had brought to San Marco and Florence.[18] But all of Caroli's literary works and conventual activity in the last two decades of his life are still the subject of investigation. It is necessary, therefore, to await the results of that research before determining the relations and connections between the Caroli of the *Liber dierum* and the *Vitae fratrum* and the Caroli of his last years, ending with his death in 1503.

The Health Status of Florentines
in the Fifteenth Century

▼

Ann G. Carmichael

F ive hundred years ago urban Florentines had to expect that at least one-third of those born would die in infancy and that no genera-tion of survivors would reach adulthood without experiencing in some way the relentless cycles of recurrent plague.[1] Epidemics, domi-nated by plague, occurred three times every two decades, sweeping into the grave defenseless babies and the chronically ill. High infant mortality and epidemic disease were essentially refractory to the best medical remedies of the day. The wealthy were, for the most part, able to escape plagues by leaving the city for safer countryside re-treats, and thus actual experience with the plague, including the powerful *mentalité* of fear its recurrences created, was bound to the expectation of a differential mortality between rich and poor.[2]

These violent, acute infections capture the imagination in our cen-tury and have drawn the attention of contemporary scholars of medi-cal history. On the other hand, far less attention has been given to the background, nonplague illnesses of the Renaissance. It is difficult for recent generations, burdened with chronic rather than acute dis-eases, to realize that the "ancien régime of disease," as the preindus-trial past has been called recently, was not fully dominated by the savage rapacity of acute pestilences and plagues.[3] The fact is, how-ever, that chronic illness and infection throughout the life course were decidedly a part of life five hundred years ago. With or without sick-ness many lived through the young and middle adult passages escap-ing plague, the sequelae of childbearing, and other acute infections, only to die of debilitating chronic illness. Unlike the various acute infections, exposure to these kinds of diseases among urban Italians in the Renaissance did not depend on wealth and social class.

This paper will explore, in a very preliminary fashion, the kinds of ordinary illness and death experiences that were typical in Renaissance Italian cities, drawing from some reconstructions of family medical history, from clinical narratives of illness and death written in the late fifteenth century, from fiscal records reflecting the average burden of illness carried by households of this period, and from causes of death in ordinary nonplague years. It is not always possible to find Florentine records that show the typical patterns of sickness, so, assuming that urban morbidity and mortality were uniform across northern Italy, I will utilize materials from other areas in my assessment of the Florentine situation.

Retrospective diagnosis is very difficult and uncertain, even with good medical records, but the evidence presented in the following pages strongly points to the role of tuberculosis as the major killer among urban populations in northern and central Italy in the Renaissance. Social and medical historians usually associate this chronic disease with the early phases of the industrial revolution, possibly because during that time physicians everywhere in Europe began to describe its ravages. But two hundred years before John Bunyan labeled this disease "captain of all these men of Death," and two hundred years before John Morton provided the first classic medical description of acute and chronic pulmonary tuberculosis, the disease was endemic in the growing, crowded cities of Italy,[4] and for both rich and poor exposure to this common pathogen seems to have influenced all subsequent experience of illness and death.

Starting from a detailed case study of the last illness of Lorenzo di Piero di Lorenzo de' Medici, duke of Urbino, I will outline the history of his illness and briefly reconstruct a family history of the Medici that illustrates how tuberculosis could have been a common pathogen in the Renaissance.

Lorenzo, the last direct male heir of Cosimo the Elder, died in Florence May 4, 1519, at the age of twenty-seven. He may have had other medical problems underlying his terminal illness—consuming the last half-year of his life—but there is little reason to challenge the diagnosis of pulmonary tuberculosis that was made seventy-five years ago by Andrea Corsini, drawing upon the minutely detailed records of both the secretary and the physician to the duke.[5] In the next few paragraphs I summarize the clinical course that led Corsini to this diagnosis.

As early as 1515–16, when in his early twenties, the duke of Urbino suffered leg ulcers and blisters described as "French boils" by one contemporary, but nonmedical, observer. From this point on he carried the diagnosis of the French disease, or syphilis, justly, some said, because of his *sfrenato libertinaggio*. The death of his wife, Maddalena Tour d'Auvergne, shortly after the birth of their only child, Catherine de' Medici, was blamed on her innocent infection with the "new disease" of the sixteenth century.[6]

In March 1517, two years before his death, Lorenzo sustained a head wound in battle, and many physicians debated whether or not the skull had been "tainted" (*maculato*). After several days a fever appeared, the sign they had all feared, and so Lorenzo's skull was trephined. During his long convalescence his uncle Giuliano died of tuberculosis, and Lorenzo returned to Florence from Urbino against medical advice in order to visit his mother, Alfonsina Orsini, during an acute episode of her chronic bouts with "bloody flux."[7]

In September 1517 Lorenzo had to delay another journey because of a poorly healing abscess on one foot. In March 1518 he was well enough to proceed with wedding plans and left for France in May. In August he and his bride returned; within ten months both died. During the same period, after a year-long remission, Alfonsina's health worsened, and she could no longer disguise her difficulty sleeping and her recurrent vomiting. Throughout the fall of 1518 she battled kidney and stomach pains, debility, fever, fatigue, and the flux. As two generations of Medici women before her, she abandoned hope that the physicians' purges and emetics would help and left for the mineral baths of Volterra.[8] Despite bland foods and mineral water therapy, her bleeding, blood-tinged vomitus, and anorexia continued through the winter. In November the duke himself fell gravely ill, so little attention could be paid to his mother's suffering.

Lorenzo's last illness began with chills, fever, and headache, treated, as was usual, with purges.[9] Fever, profuse sweating, and abdominal pains followed—the exacerbations usually at night—and so the physicians withdrew six ounces of blood, which they thought to be of "a bad quality."[10] Purged again, moderate diarrhea followed, along with understandable difficulty sleeping. Syrup of poppies helped, along with other tonics. In mid-December, after a brief remission, the fever, chills, and vomiting and diarrhea returned, so his doctors tried measures to open his pores, allowing another exit for bad or corrupted humors. After a remission there began abdominal pains, night sweats, and fever. Sometimes the fever was described as putrid, sometimes choleric, sometimes double tertain, melancholic, or hectic. As the winter wore on, joint pains, debility, and anorexia added to Lorenzo's miseries, despite gentler, dietary treatment with chicken broths and syrups.[11] By April 21 a *catarro*, slightly productive of sputum, became the focus of medical efforts. The physicians indeed declared that "catarrhal phlegm" was the efficient cause of his death on May 4: the failure to bring up the phlegm had "suffocated his heart."[12]

Whether or not Lorenzo ever had had the "French boils" of syphilis, Corsini noted that the duke was never treated for this disease during his final illness. Nor is there any hint in this brief sketch that the complications of tertiary syphilis—commonly either neurological deterioration or sudden death from a dissecting aortic aneurysm—ended his life so early. Instead his clinical course was characterized by infection (fever), with intermittent gastrointestinal and pulmonary symptoms over a six-month period, a course suggesting the diagnosis of tuberculosis. A likely explanation is that Lorenzo was first infected as a child, "seeded" the organism at many different sites, and then recovered. The infection then reactivated in his third decade.[13]

Although we could devote considerably more attention to the description of his illness, as Corsini has already done, it seems reasonable to assume that tuberculosis was the cause of Lorenzo's final illness. Certainly the treatment he was given confuses diagnosis of the underlying problems from our medical viewpoint, but there is other evidence for tuberculosis infection in the Medici family, mingled among other case studies of Medici illnesses and in letters between members of this family.

Two deaths in the family were roughly contemporary with Lorenzo's. Maddalena died two weeks after delivery, one week before her husband's death. Although she may have been, or become, infected with either tuberculosis or syphilis (her pregnancy was several times threatened by fevers), her death was nonetheless a classic course of puerperal sepsis or postpartum infection (usually streptococcal), commencing two to three days after delivery. Lorenzo's personal secretary noted that this was an illness common among puerperae in Florence that year.[14] Lorenzo's mother, Alfonsina, died the following winter in February 1520, two years ill with *flusso*. It is not unlikely that tuberculosis complicated her final illness, one Corsini thought consistent with a diagnosis of uterine cancer. While neither of these two cases provides much additional evidence to my primary hypothesis, neither do they exclude coinfection with tuberculosis.

The familial illness usually associated with the Medici is gout. Piero di Cosimo was nicknamed *il Gottoso* for his crippling arthritides, nearly lifelong. Cosimo, his father, suffered "a touch of gout" during the last decade of his life, and both father and son frequented the hot mineral baths together. To a lesser extent both Lorenzo di Piero (*il Magnifico*) and his youngest son, Giuliano, duke of Nemours, suffered arthritic pains described as gout.[15]

Although gout could explain a four-generation family history of joint pains, exclusively among men, once again coinfection with tuberculosis is possible. Looking at the problem more closely is necessary because none of the skeletal remains of Cosimo the Elder, Piero, Lorenzo, and Giuliano, duke of Nemours, provide evidence of gouty arthritic destruction of bone.[16] Piero *il Gottoso* suffered foot pains but never the classic swollen toe, and his first affliction was said to have occurred in childhood, an exceedingly rare onset for true gout. Cosimo's pains were described by his wife as "a slight thing"—few sufferers would so describe gout's crises—and the years of his gout (1450–63) were punctuated by febrile episodes: "gout fever," "an attack of the plague," and, finally, a "cold."[17] Moreover the Medici males were not the only sufferers of arthritic pains in this family. Hot mineral baths do not usually relieve gout, though they are enormously beneficial to sufferers like Lucrezia Tornabuoni, Piero's wife, who sought relief from "rheumatic gout" all her adult life.[18] Furthermore, victims of gout usually survive to a much older age than did *il Gottoso*'s gouty heirs. Lorenzo the Magnificent died in his early forties "tormented by pain all over his body," and four of his seven children died in their late thirties (between 1516 ond 1521), of febrile illnesses, not gout.

Unfortunately, the paleopathologists who exhumed the Medici

bones over thirty years ago failed to consider tuberculosis.[19] A concurrent history supporting a diagnosis of tuberculosis exists, beginning with Giuliano di Piero di Cosimo, who died in his mid-twenties during the Pazzi conspiracy. In 1463, at the age of eleven, Giuliano suffered from a chronic fever, much worse at night, throughout the summer. Pale and weak, exhausted by the evening fevers and the remedies applied, Giuliano nevertheless appeared basically healthy to his physicians and his mother once he was able to get rid of "the phlegm which is in him." His illness then abated.[20] These barebones details and the age of onset suggest the possibility of primary pulmonary tuberculosis.

Four years after these events his mother, much sicker than usual with "rheumatic gout," went to the baths and "brought up much phlegm and nastiness which must have been there a long time."[21] Tuberculous arthritis, a remote possibility in Lucrezia's case, classically involves the hips, knees, elbows, shoulders, and small joints of the hands and feet, with pain on motion and usually some swelling. Of course, other arthritides, especially crippling rheumatoid arthritis, would also have been common. Lucrezia was willing to cope with "bugs as big as capons" in the shabby accommodations at the baths, in order to obtain relief.[22]

Lorenzo the Magnificent, whatever retrospective diagnosis one may favor in his own case, was married to a woman described consistently as a "consumptive" for the last ten years of her life, dying, as did most of their children, in her late thirties.[23] Even with careful new attention to the medical genealogy of the Medici, however, this line of reasoning has rather obvious flaws: I have deliberately selected the tidbits of supporting information to show that many members of this prominent family suffered from some of the common, protean symptoms of tuberculosis infection. Because tuberculosis is such a chronic, multisystem infection, diverse in clinical presentation and often only a contributing cause of death, one could easily subsume the medical histories of many prominent individuals and families of the Renaissance under this diagnostic category, tidying up varied and tortured efforts at deciphering five-hundred-year-old patient records trapped in distinctively unmodern medical accounts.[24] Occam's razor, applied to retrospective diagnosis, would favor the tuberculosis connection through this family medical history because it is the most parsimonious explanation. Only Lorenzo, duke of Urbino, and his uncle Giuliano certainly died with the disease, so the more cautious conclusion at this stage would be that whatever the cause or causes of all these illnesses, suffering mediated the lives of the Medici as much as it did the existence of their poorer, less advantaged contemporaries.

These difficulties with retrospective diagnosis are actually increased when we use a collection of patient records and autopsies of wealthy Florentines done during this period. Florence claims the "father" of pathological anatomy, Antonio Benivieni, who dissected the corpses of his patients with apparently none of the stigmatization of that procedure that led Leonardo da Vinci to conduct anatomies in secret.[25] In a casebook devoted to the "hidden and secret causes of illness" and death, Benivieni casually recorded his postmortem findings for patients who died. Benivieni's brother posthumously gathered these notes to create the *De Abditis Nonnullis ac Mirandis Morborum et Sanationum Causis*, 111 brief studies such as "death resulting from the stimulation of a cancerous ulcer," or "worms ejected," or "death due to intermittent fever." Fifteen of the 111 cases include description of necropsy; permission was apparently easily granted so that Benivieni could search the cause of death, not so that he could learn anything of normal human anatomy.[26] As a result these accounts are hopelessly confusing if used as an index of what diseases were prevalent in Florence, but as a record of common illnesses, they are richly diverse. Fevers, intestinal worms, hernias, fistulas, cholecystitis (gallstones), and the sequelae of trauma make up the bulk of the small volume, revealing perhaps as much about what Benivieni found interesting as about the illnesses common to the upper classes he served.

Of all these only two stand out as possible examples of tuberculous infection. In the first,

> the daughter of Rogerio Corbinelli had almost continual pain in her right flank. . . . At last she died. It was decided to open the body. The femur was found to be eaten away and most of it reduced to powder. Moreover around the *os matricis* were four yellowish lumps, like balls, three filled with watery fluid, and the fourth raised a little above the others, and tuberculated [*den-

tatus], rough, and hard as to the surface, seeing that it was gendered of flesh and black bile.[27]

This is typical of Benivieni, providing little clinical or postmortem detail apart from attention directed to the site of a patient's principal complaint. His concern was to defend the differing "opinions and pronouncements of physicians" showing how internal changes could not be easily diagnosed from outward signs. This case might be attributed to a tumor in the bone, but tuberculosis of the head of the femur was before 1900 the commoner cause of this pathological process.[28] To this girl's case he added an ineresting codicil: "For I also knew the son of Antonio Iaccetio who suffered terrible pain in the hip and fell first into a state of extreme weakness and then died, as neither physicians nor remedies availed. When his body was cut open a noxious humor [*pestifer humor*] was found in the hip. By this most of the bone had been eroded and looked as though reduced to ashes."[29] With two such cases it is less likely that a bony tumor caused both illnesses than that tuberculosis did so.

Nowhere in Benivieni's casebook is there a straightforward case of pulmonary tuberculosis with bloody sputum (hemoptysis), although he describes pleurisy as "coughing and fever and blood coughed up with the phlegm,"[30] but then Benivieni does not seem to be interested in recording what was typical in Florence, even in his own practice, despite his considerable clinical experience in hospitals and private practice.[31] The only other case perhaps suggestive of tuberculosis is the patient with an abscess over the thoracic spine, which had eroded the underlying tissues so that the heart was exposed to view.[32] These three examples of possible tuberculosis infection are rare complications of the disease, more to be expected if the organism were prevalent in the general population.[33]

To put the medical problems of the Medici in the perspective of the population and times in which they lived, we must look to some other data besides those afforded by imperfect, individual case studies. These other sources are especially important in any effort to assess the levels of prevalence of tuberculosis in Renaissance Florence. Even though I believe the prevalence of tuberculosis was high at this period, the lesser, more general assertion I make that chronic illness was as important as acute epidemics in determining patterns of morbidity and mortality clearly finds support from a study of population-level medical data discussed below.

Mortality registers are one of the most accessible sources of historical data reflecting the overall health status of a population because they encompass a broader segment of the general population than do other records of illness and death. Ignoring, for most of this preliminary study, that the circumstances or immediate causes of one's death do not necessarily have any direct relationship to illness and suffering experience in one's life, we need to know, as a first approximation of the health status of Florentines, when during the life course individuals died. Studies of the careers and interests of physicians, particularly the written *consilia* or consultations that formed a very lucrative part of the practice of university-trained physicians, reflect many of the common problems and common successes of wealthier patients treated by elite physicians, but this kind of information has rightly been exploited to tell us about the system of medicine and the priorities of those using or delivering services in the medical system of Florence in the Quattrocento, and I will repeat none of that material here.[34]

The two greatest problems one encounters in trying to determine the causes of morbidity, or ordinary illness, in a population so far removed from our own times are that causes of illness must usually be inferred from causes of death and that the reconstruction of normal health problems of that society must often be done with comparisons to more populous, subtropical, "Third World" populations in our own day. For a study of morbidity at the population level, one cannot use fifteenth-century medical textbooks alone.

In Florence there are few sources for investigating morbidity and all reveal the problems encountered by inferring disease from deaths and thus deriving a speculative reconstruction of likely health environments. Florentines kept registers of mortality, which I have discussed at length elsewhere.[35] From 1424 many entries are accompanied by a cause of death provided in vernacular terms. Because the purpose of recording diagnoses was related to early identification of plague in Florence, "healthy" years did not warrant inclusion of even the ordinary causes of death, much less illness. Nonplague diagnoses provided by the Florentine death registers, moreover, often give very little information. "Old age," "fever," "long illness," and diarrheal diseases are the most frequent causes of death given for nonplague victims. Rough age categories of the victims can only be guessed, for example, because a name showed that the individual was dependent upon another person and thus was likely to have been a child.

During epidemic years scattered diagnoses of nonplague deaths provide some of the few clues to the basic health conditions of fifteenth-century Florentines. Epidemics took a heavy toll among very young children, in part because diarrheal disease rapidly dehydrates and kills infants and toddlers, and the proliferation of gastrointestinal pathogens inevitably accompanied summer disease crises. One of the most basic features of health conditions in the Renaissance city, the fact that one third of all individuals born died before their second birthday, is a consequence of omnipresent gastrointestinal pathogens. Even that commonplace is difficult to see when a baby died in a plague-infected household, and there was apparently no reason to refine the diagnosis of death further: most (over 90 percent) of the diagnoses reported attribute deaths to plague.

The nonplague illnesses were certainly noticed by Florentine diagnosticians. For example, between 1424 and 1458 "dropsy" occurs ninety-six times; *tisico,* or consumption, 169 times. Both of these diagnoses could easily encompass many cases of chronic pulmonary tuberculosis, but we have no idea what level of tuberculosis this might represent in the population, even if every one of these deaths were indeed due to tuberculosis, because the diagnoses are provided only during years of high mortality. There are three deaths attributed to gout in this period, and all were male. The point here is that out of over 60,000 registered deaths during the period of records before 1460, very few entries give us any hint at all that chronic disease was as important to Florentines as the recurrent epidemics in foreshortening the life course.

The catasto of Pisa, smaller and thus easier to survey for morbidity than the catasto (tax records) of Florence, brings a very deceptive picture of morbidity among the local population.[36] Here families sought tax relief when they had members incapable of contributing to household resources. Illness meant for many acute financial crisis from loss of work and income, but in the catasto only the crippling debility of an adult warranted tax relief. Sixteen blind individuals and fifteen *atratto* (cripples) are listed, 74 percent of whom (twenty-three of thirty-one) are older than sixty years.[37] Of the nineteen individuals described as gouty, only five are younger than sixty years, the young-est a forty-eight-year-old man with gout and flank pains possibly re-lated to kidney stones. Three of these nineteen gout sufferers were women, which is an exceptionally high proportion of women. Only the overweight Maori of New Zealand have in the twentieth century approximated this level of gout in a population, with 10 percent of all cases those of females.[38] It is more reasonable to assume that the diagnosis of "gout" in the fifteenth century is quite different from our own more rigorous definitions than that Tuscans were as gouty as this atypical, inbred population consuming high meat and fat diets. In the catasto the only debility consistently assigned to younger per-sons (in their twenties and thirties) was mental illness.

In other words, the catasto reflects an impression, I believe mis-taken, that one sees in prescriptive medical treatises on old age during the Renaissance: adults who do not die from epidemics can live in relative good health until senescence, when the multisystem problems of gout, other arthritides, catarrh, dysuria, and apoplexy reflect the gradual desiccation associated with a loss of "natural heat."[39] From the dietary literature that underlies this picture one would assume that in the fifteenth century one only needed to avoid plagues and eat the right foods appropriate to one's age and humoral complexion in order to escape chronic pain and illness. Few adult members of a family were considered tax-deductible burdens, whatever their actual health status.

Thus, Tuscan records of both mortality and tax-deductible morbid-ity are limited because they give very little information about two critical features of ill health: age at death and cause of death in all years. Both pieces of information, however, are supplied by the sur-viving years of the *Necrologi*, death registers kept in Milan after 1452. Moreover, the Milanese causes of death were certified for every individual over the age of two years at death, in each and every year, and by university-trained physicians, members of Milan's College of Medicine. Thus the diagnoses appear in traditional Latin medical ter-minology, presumedly with reference to texts of the day. My prelimi-nary analysis of Milanese mortality data is drawn from the records of nonepidemic years of the late fifteenth century, including 1453,

1459, 1469, 1471–72, 1474–75, 1478–80, 1482, and 1503. I coded the data for 27,291 deaths, of which approximately 35 percent are infants and young children (less than three years at death) and usually carry no note of cause. Thus the total "population" of deaths in the data presented below is roughly 18,000.[40]

In difficult or disputed cases several members of the college would be involved in a diagnosis, for the Milanese also were interested in early identification of plague deaths. Milanese physicians recognized over fifty types of fever, twenty kinds and colors of urine, and twenty varieties of diarrhea—a reminder that their diagnostic categories were not naive observations of suffering. On August 7, 1479, for example, the death of a fifty-year-old man was judged by one physician as due to "simple tertian fever with a bad regimen," with the additional note that the man had maintained almost no contact with his neighbors. A second physician questioned this diagnosis on the grounds that "simple fevers easily resolve," and thus the poor diet must have permuted the fever.[41] Diagnoses were accompanied by age of the victim and often by the temporal sequence of symptoms leading to death. With data this good one can attempt identification of specific causes of illness leading to death. For example, a nine-year-old boy who died June 11, 1479, of phthisis, dropsy, and an "immoderate" diarrheal "flux" close to death reflects a fairly good descriptive sequence of a child overwhelmed by tuberculosis. The dropsy, or collection of fluid in dependent limbs, in this age group usually indicates difficulty returning venous blood, thus either lung disease or right-sided cardiac disease, such as acute rheumatic fever with destruction of valves in the heart or inflammation of the heart muscle.[42]

Even though the majority of entries do not give quite so much "modern" sounding clinical detail as the foregoing cases would lead us to hope, the frequency and age distribution of a few of the readily identified symptom complexes may help to illuminate the extent of morbidity in fifteenth-century Italian cities, illnesses not quickly resolved by death. From an epidemiological point of view the age distribution of death by cause is the crucial information supplied by Milanese records that is simply unavailable from Florence at this time.

Figure 1 illustrates aggregate numbers of deaths from phthisis, hemoptysis (the production of bloody or blood-tinged sputum), and the hunched-back scoliosis, "gibbosity," characteristic of pulmonary

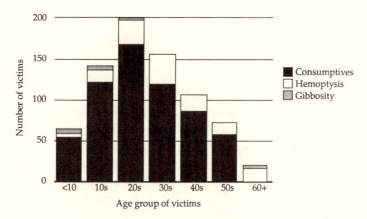

Figure 1. Late Fifteenth-Century Deaths in Milan Caused by Diseases Resembling Pulmonary Tuberculosis

tuberculosis, together used here as a proxy for mortality from pulmonary tuberculosis. The diagnosis of phthisis alone, "consumption" the best translation of the Greek word, need not reflect tuberculosis, but any wasting disease included in other chronic infections and cancers. Nevertheless, in the case of an eighteen-year-old girl who died March 28, 1479, after a year's suffering from phthisis and a subsequent "rupture of a vein in her chest," little else besides tuberculosis is likely. A fifteen-year-old girl who died December 31 that year, of phthisis and ulcerated lungs, is another of these typical cases. Among the eighteen thousand individuals older than two years of age at death, the subset of these records where diagnoses were routinely provided, there are 769 victims from causes that included fulminant pulmonary tuberculosis and its complications. The proxy may include many young people who died of nontubercular "consumption," possibly due to other chronic infections, but by the same token it excludes cases of pneumonia deaths attributed to pleurisy, some of which were associated with hemoptysis and "ulcerated lungs," as well as all of the chronic diarrheal diseases due to gastrointestinal tuberculosis, the most common extrapulmonary form of this infection. Were we to include the 874 victims of catarrh, a chronic hacking cough usually productive of sputum, then at least 1,643 individuals of the 18,000 (9 percent) died with chronic respiratory infections. In many older people a final, respiratory catarrh could have been due to a wide variety of different respiratory pathogens, but nonetheless tuberculosis must be included: the pattern of reactivated tuberculosis with a decline in immunity associated with aging is characteristic epidemiological experience with that disease. Even if only 6 percent of the overall noninfant death rate can be attributed to this "phthisis," the burden of morbidity underlying such a figure is considerable: René Dubos estimated ten to twelve individuals living with tuberculosis for every one who died. It is quite possible that the "epilepsies" which claimed the lives of infants in such numbers included tuberculous meningitis and miliary (widely disseminated) tuberculosis. The pattern of mortality from chronic respiratory disease in Milan around 1500 is, I argue, indistinguishable from that three hundred years later when tuberculosis "threaten[ed] the very survival of the European race."[43]

Figure 2 reflects the age distribution of deaths from three of the five most common respiratory diseases. (I am omitting asthma and empyema altogether in this essay, diagnoses which overlap considerably the range of pneumonias and other lung infections, chronic and acute, that caused death.) Here the age distribution by cause clearly signals the likelihood that pulmonary tuberculosis accounted for much of what was called "phthisis," because the peak of deaths by this cause occurs in early adulthood. By contrast those who survive these critical years, already infected with tuberculosis in childhood, would

Figure 2. Late Fifteenth-Century Deaths in Milan Caused by Acute and Chronic Respiratory Diseases

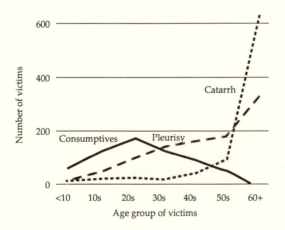

live until old age, then fall easy prey to reactivated disease: "catarrh." Pleurisy, on the other hand, is an acute disease, and over half of the 975 individuals in my sample who died with this disease died within seven to ten days: a typical course for acute bacterial pneumonia. Not surprisingly, deaths from this cause rise steadily with age.

It is important to note that among the 27,291 counted, 22 percent were age sixty or older at death. One-third of all those diagnosed thus were among the elderly. Naturally there is a bit of "age inflation" in the attribution of age in the older categories, typical in all preindustrial populations, but what it shows us is that the chronicity of illness or infection throughout life was a vital part of the disease pattern five hundred years ago.

Looking further at the features of chronic illness in the Renaissance, figure 3 considers another long illness, deaths from "dropsy," and illustrates a couple of interesting features about the spectrum of ordinary illnesses. This is a very ambivalent diagnostic category from a twentieth-century perspective because the peripheral edema characterizing the disease could be caused commonly by two different physiological disturbances. Difficulty in returning venous blood for oxygenation either in cardiovascular dysfunction including incompetence of peripheral veins or in right-sided cardiac disease (usually due to a damaged valve) is a common cause of dropsy. William Withering's discovery of digitalis in the eighteenth century helped these cases. The second general cause of dropsy, more usual in our day, logically relates to difficulty clearing fluid, that is to renal disease. Primary renal disease could probably be dismissed from the probable differential diagnosis if we could be sure that dropsy never referred to generalized edema, but we cannot. The diagnoses of anasarca and ascites do appear, if rarely. Tuberculous infection of the kidneys is not uncommon nor is destruction of renal tissue from streptococcal infections.

The graph of dropsy deaths illustrates why other causes besides lung disease contributed to the burden of illness many carried through life. The double peak of deaths from dropsy misses just the age group hard hit by phthisis. Significant is the peak before age ten, and the dramatic rise in deaths during middle adult years. A probable explanation of this biphasic peak is that streptococcal diseases, such as acute rheumatic fever with destruction of cardiac tissue, struck in

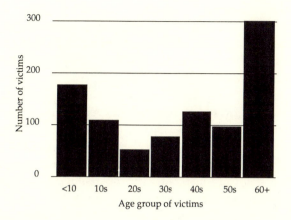

Figure 3. Late Fifteenth-Century Deaths in Milan Caused by "Dropsy"

childhood, peaking among the six to ten year olds, just as it did a century ago in the United States.[44] Many recovered, only to die of "dropsy" or its associated infectious sequelae (pneumonias, septic emboli, and endocarditis) later in life. Dropsy is rarely associated with lung diseases productive of sputum ("asthma" and fevers are the most common associated diagnoses with dropsy). It may be possible to refine the practical diagnosis of dropsy further with more death data, but at present the data seem to indicate that some Milanese passed through their most productive adult years debilitated and fatigued, in early congestive heart failure.

The final graph (figure 4) illustrates an unusual cause of death from our perspective. Aggregated are the cases of fistulae and ulcers, including *ulceribus sordidis* and *ulceribus cancrenosis*, many of which must have been leg ulcers. (Ulcers on the trunk or neck were to Milanese diagnosticians suspicious signs of plague, or were described as "scrofula" or "struma.") Leg ulcers are not unusual in twentieth-century clinical experience, but the age distribution of these fifteenth-century deaths is not at all like that seen today. Draining fistulae and sinus tracts are now more typical in older adults who have forms of peripheral vascular disease or diabetes, and there are a significant number of these among the Milanese sample as well. The problem is, again, the biphasic peak, with deaths among those aged three to twenty making a significant contribution to deaths from this cause. Since fever was an associated diagnosis at death in most cases of youthful ulcers, we have the problem of accounting for chronic, superficial infections in a segment of the population best able, immunologically, to resist many common infections. Superficial infections of the skin generated by insect bites or eczema and encouraged by rare changes of clothing would of course be expected among poorer children. The problem is that in a significant number of children such infections led to death. Cutaneous tuberculosis, rare in the twentieth century, might have been more common in the past, but it is more likely that those already infected with tuberculosis had impaired immune responses to a wide variety of other infections. Children compromised with one infection could have considerable difficulty meeting immune challenges by other infections.[45] Another unpleasant possibility is that the young suffered a high incidence of comminuted fractures, with subsequent osteomyelitis and draining fistulae. A breakdown of figure 4 would show fistulae more common in the younger ages, ulcers more common among the aging. Moreover the diagnosis of fistulae as a cause of death is usually (over 75 percent of the cases) associated with fever. Finally, nutritional deficiencies, especially of vitamins A and C, if severe enough, could render individuals incapable of healing cutaneous injuries quickly. "Land scurvy" was

Figure 4. Late Fifteenth-Century Deaths in Milan Caused by Ulcers and Fistulae

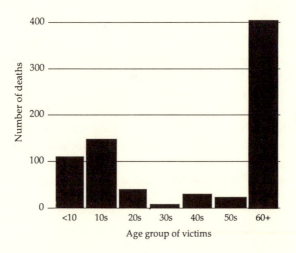

probably responsible for the high incidence of leg ulcers among young adult men in late eighteenth-century British hospitals, accounting for over 25 percent of all admissions to hospitals.[46] The social and economic status of the Milanese victims and a study of recommended diets for older children may shed light on the problem.

Thus among the ordinary health problems likely to affect Florentines as much as Milanese of the fifteenth century, the high incidence, and high social and economic costs, of chronic illness among younger and middle-aged adults can be seen, even if faintly and imperfectly, through the study of deaths. But it is a picture far different from the one usually painted for the periods before 1900. It is probable that acute diseases then dominated mortality patterns, or, more especially, acute infections accounted for the proximate causes of death. Nevertheless, chronic illnesses, which within the late twentieth century are "responsible for over eighty percent of all deaths and for an even higher fraction of cases of total disability," likewise underlay the morbidity patterns of temporally more distant generations.[47] Included in the chronic diseases were also many cancers, arthritides, nephroses, and "fluxes," but, at least before the advent of syphilis, dominating all was tuberculosis. This disease played a far greater role in determining morbidity and mortality than has been realized.

Significantly, with all its methodological problems providing a true reconstruction of fifteenth-century medical evidence in late twentieth-century terms, medical and epidemiological information from this era lends two novel ways of looking at the health status of Renaissance Florentines. Tuberculosis, long thought to be a disease of industrialization, would better be understood in the context of rapid urbanization, which Renaissance Italian cities certainly experienced at this time. Second, however dramatic and disruptive were the epidemics that so characterize this period to us now, the codominant experience then was of chronic and debilitating disease, punctuating and determining many life choices. We often consider medicine of this period ineffective and tradition-bound at best, superstitious and a hindrance to normal healing at worst. In fact, medicine and medical men may have served well the common disease problems of life, gently navigating the sick along fragile boundaries between tolerable and incapacitating illness.

Petrarchan Figurations of Death in Lorenzo de' Medici's Sonnets and *Comento*

▼

William J. Kennedy

L orenzo de' Medici composed his varied and extensive poetry in an unstable cultural and political world. During his lifetime, and partly as a result of his patronage, ideas about literature were changing dramatically. In classical scholarship, moralized allegorical modes of critical commentary on earlier texts were giving way to formalistic, rhetorical, and philological modes. In vernacular poetry modes of composition were shifting from popular carnival songs, *canti a ballo,* proletarian satires, and *sacre rappresentazioni* to exploratory imitations of classical forms, refined adaptations of learned traditions, and bold conflations of ancient authors with the *Stil nuovo,* Dante, and Petrarch.[1] The political climate was changing too, and as a ruler Lorenzo monitored its course. At times he used his literary talents to reflect or at least reinforce his own political agenda.[2] The popular appeal of *La Nencia da Barberino,* the *Uccellagione,* the *Canzoni a ballo,* the *Canti carnascialeschi,* and the religious verse seems crafted to meet Lorenzo's governing needs. Their form and content belie a canny attempt to identify with the culture of the lower bourgeoisie and proletariat, a sly scheme to promote the culture of the Florentine populace in the larger world of Italian power politics.[3]

The rarefied tone of Lorenzo's Petrarchan verse in his *Rime* and *Comento sopra alcuni de' suoi sonetti* is different, and its appeal to the patrician classes and the upper bourgeoisie seems crafted for other ends. This verse earned the highest praise from Poliziano, Ficino, Pico, and other leading humanists, and among Lorenzo's elite aristocratic audience it enjoyed the greatest favor of all Lorenzo's literary efforts.[4] The *Rime* and especially the *Comento* nonetheless play important roles in Lorenzo's managerial agenda. They publicize a conviction that Tuscan can express as many ideas as Latin and both function as virtuoso displays of cultural imperialism in annexing texts for political ends. In them Lorenzo's appropriation of the Petrarchan mode—an appropriation that forecasts sixteenth-century Petrarchism—augments the Medicean design. It does so through its representation of the ruler's sacrificial offerings to Love. These offerings symbolically enact a dialectic between Lorenzo's submission to the state and his domination of it. Like a Petrarchan lover Lorenzo defers to a self-proclaimed ideal that he yet tries to bend to his will. The rhetorical world of Petrarchan poetry circumscribes the intricate world of Medici politics.

Of all the literary modes at his disposal, the Petrarchan mode certainly enabled Lorenzo to win approval from the patrician classes and upper bourgeoisie whom it attracted. It allows him to proclaim his personal misfortunes both as a public figure and as a private individual. It invites the audience's sympathy with his plight, and it gives him powerful rhetorical tools to attract that sympathy. Finally it encourages a prose commentary that expands his possibilities for self-representation. The commentary permits him to fashion an *apologia pro vita sua*, an unabashed autobiographical platform upon which to shape and reshape the events of his life as he wants his Florentine audience to perceive them. This poetry and its accompanying commentary is a work of masterful rhetoric in the disputative, controversialized, highly agonistic sense inscribed by Renaissance humanists. As Salvatore Camporeale has shown in his account of Giovanni Caroli's texts elsewhere in this volume, the essentially contestatory nature of humanist rhetoric discloses a web of social, political, and cultural functions. Not the least of these functions is a regulatory one. The opposition of book and sword in Andrea del Castagno's fresco discussed below by Creighton Gilbert suggests that in humanist practice language displaces combat, and rhetoric becomes a weapon of aggression. In fifteenth-century poetic representations of life and death in Florence, rhetoric encodes a ritual significance no less powerful than the ritual action associated with funerals that Sharon Strocchia and John McManamon demonstrate in their contributions to this volume. Petrarchan figurations of death in Lorenzo's poetry enact this significance.

One rhetorical element that Lorenzo exploits is the homophony between his own name—Laurentius, Laurus, Lauro—and the elusive laurel that Petrarch sought throughout his career. Lorenzo himself adopted the laurel as a personal emblem, and it was as a laurel under whose cover Florence rests in peace that Poliziano addressed Lorenzo in his *Stanze per la giostra:* "E tu, ben nato Laur, sotto il cui velo / Fiorenza lieta in pace si riposa" (1.4.1–2) (And you, well-born Laurel, under whose shelter happy Florence rests in peace).[5] As an evergreen, the laurel enjoys immunity from death; its only mortal threat comes from Jove, whose thunderbolts kill. As a controversial political figure, however, the human Lorenzo faced death practically every moment of his political life, especially after the Pazzi conspiracy perpetrated on April 26, 1478, and the conspiracy of Giovanni Battista Frescobaldi discovered on June 2, 1481.[6] As a poet Lorenzo could benefit from Petrarch's figurations of death. To the elite audience that Lorenzo seeks, Petrarch's representation of death as an act of finality, as a barometer of human instability, offers a special and direct appeal.

In the prologue of his *Comento* Lorenzo turns to Petrarch to draw sympathy from his audience. He indicates this purpose with a direct quotation from the first sonnet of Petrarch's *Rime sparse:* "spero trovar pietà, non che perdono" (I hope to find pity, not only pardon).[7] Lorenzo cites Petrarch's line twice. The first citation implies his own insecurity about being able to imitate Petrarch. Petrarch's speaker designates his modest intention to win sympathy because he distrusts his own rhetorical skill to achieve a higher goal. So too does Lorenzo, with an added gesture of self-abnegation in declaring his intention by humbly comparing himself with a superior poet. He begins his argument by admitting insecurity about the worth of the amatory topic. His love may not have been a perfect human love, because perfection is rare, but it was nonetheless a good love and one worthy of celebration in the manner of Petrarch. If detractors cite flaws in his representation, he may beg sympathy from other readers who know the difficulty of the topic: "e se, pure con tutte queste ragioni, non risponderò alle obtrettazioni e calunnie di chi mi volessi dannare, almanco, come disse il nostro florentino poeta, appresso di quelli che

hanno provato che cosa è amore: 'spero trovar pietà, non che perdono'" (And if even with all these reasons I will not answer the
detractions and calumnies of those who wish me harm, at least as
our Florentine poet said, among those who have experienced love,
'I hope to find pity, not only pardon').[8]

Two pages later Lorenzo cites Petrarch's verse again. Here the context registers a grave uneasiness about winning his audience's political
approval. He begins by referring to his well-known personal and
political misfortunes at the hands of his enemies, other men, and fate.
Later references explicitly link these misfortunes with the Pazzi and
Frescobaldi conspiracies. Compassion ought to move his audience to
pity him: "la compassione almeno mi doverre' giustificare, perché,
essendo nella mia gioventú stato molto perseguitato dagli uomini e
dalla fortuna, qualche poco di refrigerio non mi debbe essere negato"
(17) (Compassion at least should vindicate me because, hounded as
I was in my youth by men and fortune, such small solace should not
be denied me). Still, Lorenzo knows that his audience will be divided
in its political estimation. He therefore refers to Petrarch as his final
court of appeal: "E però torno al sopradetto verso del nostro fiorentino poeta, che dove sia chi per pruova intenda amore cosí questo
amore che io ho tanto laudato, come qualche particolare amore e ca-
ritá verso di me, 'spero trovar pietá non che perdono'" (18) (And
still I return to the already quoted verse of our Florentine poet, that
wherever there may be one who understands love by experiencing
it—both this love that I have so praised and some particular love and
charity directed toward me—'I hope to find pity, not only pardon').
Some readers may not support Lorenzo's political goals and they may
shed no tears for his political adversities, but all might share in his
amatory misfortunes. Lorenzo seeks an audience of lovers who have
experienced Love's torments. He seeks Petrarch's audience.

The forty-one sonnets of Lorenzo's *Comento* advertise their relationship to Petrarch's *Rime sparse*, and they do so in a characteristically Petrarchan way. They restate the powerful rivalry that Petrarch
felt with his own precursor, Dante, by insisting on the rhetorical presence of Dante's *Vita nuova* as a rival subtext throughout the *Comento*.
At the outset Lorenzo's sonnets invert the topos of death canonized
in the *Vita nuova* and reworked by Petrarch in the *Rime sparse*. Instead of depicting the speaker's passionate love for a woman who dies

before the sequence ends, as Dante and Petrarch had done, Lorenzo begins his sequence with the death of a young woman whom the speaker hardly knew. Most biographers identify her as Simonetta Cattaneo, the wife of Marco Vespucci, a cousin of the explorer Amerigo. She captivated Lorenzo's brother Giuliano and became the heroine of Poliziano's *Stanze*, "vergin sovrana / o ninfa o dea" (1.49.1–2) (sovereign virgin, nymph or goddess), but she died in April 1476 at the age of twenty-three.[9] After mourning for her in the first four sonnets, the speaker encounters another woman who kindles his desire. The remaining sonnets depict his relationship with her. Unlike Dante's Beatrice or Petrarch's Laura, however, she returns the speaker's love, reciprocates his passion, and even suffers as he does when distance separates them. Most biographers identify this woman as Lucrezia Donati, Lorenzo's own mistress whom he had courted even before his marriage to Clarice Orsini in 1469.[10]

Lorenzo's dramatized relationships with Simonetta and Lucrezia generate a highly allusive textuality. Though neither woman fulfills the narrative paradigm established by Beatrice or Laura, each nonetheless fulfills a poetic design adumbrated by Dante's and Petrarch's contrasting poetics. Throughout his poetry Lorenzo pays overt homage to Guido Guinizelli, Guido Cavalcanti, Cino da Pistoia, and other *Stilnovisti* as well as to Latin and Neo-Latin poets, but he inscribes the *Comento* with especially pointed citations from and references to Dante and Petrarch. In the rivalry between them, Petrarch overtakes Dante. The reason is stylistic. In a letter of July 15, 1484, Giovanni Pico della Mirandola commended Lorenzo for improving the philosophical defects of Petrarch with the sublimity of Dante and the stylistic defects of Dante with the formal elegance of Petrarch: "Sunt apud vos duo praecipue celebrati poetae florentinae linguae, Franciscus Petrarcha et Dantes Aligerius, de quibus illud in universum sim praefatus, esse ex eruditis qui res in Francisco, verba in Dante desiderent" (There are two celebrated Florentine poets, Petrarch and Dante, about whom in general it is right to assert that among the learned some perceive a defect of content in Petrarch, of form in Dante).[11] In this remedial action, however, Petrarch's style powerfully modifies Dante's content. That style does not always fulfill its promises: "Hoc addiderim, Franciscum quandoque non respondere pollicitis, habentem quod allectet in prima specie, sed ulterius non satis-faciat" (800) (I would add that sometimes Petrarch does not fulfill his promises; what seems seductive at first sight does not satisfy further). The instability of Petrarch's language, its elusive grasp of oxymoronic opposites, its deceptive echoes that fade before recall, all subvert the stable assurances of Dante's content.

Lorenzo's first three sonnets and his commentary on them exploit Dante's and Petrarch's rival figurations of death. In Sonnet 1 the speaker praises a star that has absorbed all the luminescence of the dead young lady: "O chiara stella, che co' raggi tuoi / togli alle tue vicine stelle il lume" (O bright star that with your rays draw light from neighboring stars). In the commentary the loss of the young lady inspires in the speaker and in all who knew her a great desire for her, "uno ardentissimo desiderio" (26). In Sonnet 2, just as the sunflower scans the horizon for the return of the sun, so the speaker awaits a new dawn, but he knows the lady will not return to this life: "O Clizia, indarno speri vederl'ora" (O sunflower, in vain I hope to see her now). At the same time, by limiting access to her, death confers a value upon her: it makes the speaker and others desire her more than ever before: "le cose mortali si debbono amare come cose finite e sottoposte alla necessitá della morte" (29) (mortal things ought to be loved as finite things subjected to the necessity of death.) In Sonnet 3 the speaker develops the paradox that by pursuing her in death he seeks a higher form of life: "Di vita il dolce lume fuggirei / a quella vita, ch'altri 'morte' appella" (I would flee the sweet light of life for that life that others call death). The paradox catches the speaker in a double bind. On the one hand, death induces in him a will to live so that he can express his desire in a language that op-poses death. On the other hand, death removes the very cause of his lament; it marks the cessation and end of the life that he mourns, and hence it implies the futility of mourning itself: "in quanto era fine di questa dolorosa passione, era odiata da me, e tanto piú doveva essere odiata, quanto la morte per essere stata negli occhi di colei si poteva stimare piú dolce e piú gentile" (30) (insofar as it was the end of this dolorous passion, I hated it, and so much the more should it be hated; as for having been in her eyes, it could be esteemed sweeter and more gentle). As one consequence death becomes a productive force that spurs the survivor's creative ability. As another, death emerges as a destructive force that asserts the aleatory nature of all human experience.

Lorenzo's conflicting perspectives on death in the *Comento* have literary ancestry in the rhetorical rivalry between Dante and Petrarch. In Dante's *Vita nuova* death certifies the beloved's transcendence. By experiencing her loss the lover now recognizes just how much she meant to him then. Henceforth her death provides a goal, a transcendent marker for him to reach in the *Divina commedia*. His desire to attain that goal motivates him to exercise his power of speech:

> Li occhi dolenti per pietà del core
> hanno di lagrimar sofferta pena,
> si che per vinti son remasi omai.
> Ora, s'i' voglio sfogar lo dolore,
> che a poco a poco a la morte mi mena,
> convenemi parlar traendo guai.

The eyes grieving through pity for the heart / While weeping have endured great suffering / So that they are defeated, tearless eyes. / And now should I desire to vent that grief, / Which gradually leads me to my death, / I must express myself in anguished words. (*Vita nuova* 31.1–6)[12]

Dante's poetics of desire represents an attempt to substantiate human desire in the accidents of language, and the process of doing so enacts a positive and productive relationship between physical existence and spiritual reality. Human understanding stabilizes the concentric layers of analogic meaning in prodigious acts of semiosis, and poetry helps it to do so by articulating in the chain of being links that elude direct statement.

Petrarch's figurations of death and their consequences for his poetics trace a different pattern.[13] For Petrarch death means separation and it entails finality. It represents an end, not the beginning of a quest. It substantiates loss and asserts the radical instability of human existence. It posits the aleatory nature of all human experience. The liminary sonnet of Petrarch's *Rime sparse* that Lorenzo quotes at the beginning of his *Comento* summarizes this view: "che quanto piace al mondo è breve sogno" (that whatever pleases in the world is a brief dream). This topos recurs as a thematic motif throughout the *Rime sparse*, but even stronger than its verbal articulation is the impact of this view on Petrarch's rhetoric and poetics.

Sensitive to the disjunctions between signifier and signified, Petrarch articulates a poetics of the sign that makes all signs ambiguous. Words are a breath of wind, fleeting, evanescent, insubstantial. The bond that links signifier to signified is equally tenuous. As words drift, so do their meanings, with the result that the sound of a word and even its position within the syntactic unit continually defer from their desired meaning and intention. Homonymy, antinomy, puns, and paronomasia epitomize this condition of Petrarch's language. "Laura" signifies a woman's name, a laurel leaf, a breath of air, a golden hue, but no concentric orders of natural logic or reason bind this polysemy into a stable whole. These meanings acquire poetic resonance through their radical difference from one another, not through layers of profound synonymy as in Dante. This principle of radical difference generates Petrarch's oxymoron, the figure that expresses rhetorical tension, paradoxes, and contrariety. Oxymoron provides the cornerstone of Petrarchan aesthetics, and its operation pervades every level of Petrarch's poetry. It also underlies the rhetoric and poetics that animate Lorenzo's *Comento*.

Lorenzo did not compose his *Comento* all of a piece. Evidence suggests that he chose various poems begun in the late 1460s and early 1470s and framed them with a prose commentary begun in 1474.[14] He returned to this project in the 1480s after the Pazzi and Frescobaldi conspiracies that he broods upon in the commentary. References to diplomatic events of 1483 and financial setbacks in the Medici fortunes imply that Lorenzo expanded his *Comento* in the later 1480s, but he worked toward a design that he never achieved. The commentary nonetheless reflects the most troubled years of Lorenzo's reign, years when the threat of death by assassination loomed all too large for the Medici ruler.

The *Comento* assembles its forty-one selected sonnets in a way that no other commentary before it had done. The author points to Dante's *Vita nuova* as its model, but in too many ways Dante's commentary differs. The *Vita nuova* was not a popular text in the fifteenth century. Though the manuscript edition that Lorenzo used evidently unites its prose with its poetry, other contemporary editions separated the one from the other. The poetry of the *Vita nuova* did not appear in a printed edition until 1526 and its prose not until 1576.[15] Lorenzo's attraction to the *Vita nuova* and especially to its prose commentary is therefore unusual, but despite this attraction, the aims of his own commentary only superficially resemble those of Dante's. Lorenzo's major concerns border on the differences between philosophy and rhetoric as do Dante's, but unlike the latter they advocate the primacy of rhetoric.[16] The *Comento*'s philosophical statements receive both less intensive and less extensive treatment than they require as vehicles of systematic thought. For the most part they constitute *quaestiones*, propositions or theses that the audience may submit to rhetorical debate. Like their counterparts in the rhetorical criticism of Cristoforo Landino and Angelo Poliziano in the 1470s and 1480s, they are designed to stimulate *controversia* through the narration of topics, division of ideas, confirmation of argument, and confutation of opposing arguments.[17]

Lorenzo's rhetorical commentary presages an important stage in the development of critical and analytical commentary in the late fifteenth and early sixteenth centuries. Like Landino's and Poliziano's commentaries, it came to serve political ends that Lorenzo's own early efforts at literary criticism adumbrate. In 1476 the Medici ruler sent to Federigo of Aragon, son of the king of Naples, an anthology of Florentine poetry with a prefatory letter extolling the preeminence of Tuscan over other Italian usage. The letter, possibly ghost written by Poliziano, associates greatness in poetic composition with greatness in the social and political order. Great poets not only celebrate great deeds in the past, but they also encourage great deeds in the present and future. The letter refers to Petrarch for support. In *Rime sparse* 187 Alexander the Great longs for a Homer to celebrate his heroism: "O fortunato che si chiara tromba / trovasti et chi di te sì alto scrisse!" (O fortunate one who found so clear a trumpet, one who wrote such high things of you!)[18] Lorenzo recognizes that effective rulers encourage not only the production but also the reception of poetry. Pisistratus inspired the populace when he resurrected Homer, at once authorizing both heroic poetry and the deeds it might inspire: "Per la qual cosa nessun altro titolo sotto la sua statua fu intagliato, se non quest'uno: che dell' insieme ridurre il glorioso omerico poema fussi stato autore" (4) (For this deed no other title was inscribed upon his statue but this: I have authored the reassembly of the glorious

Homeric text). Lorenzo goes further than Alexander and Pisistratus. Not only does he collect samples of the best Tuscan verse in his *Raccolta*, but he also composes verse himself. By appending to the *Raccolta* a sample of his own verse, including four sonnets later used in the *Comento*, Lorenzo asserts Tuscan's linguistic hegemony, Florence's cultural hegemony, and the Medici's political hegemony.

Just as the *Raccolta* needs the explanatory frame of its letter to Federigo to enforce this political point, so Lorenzo's own poetry requires the frame of his *Comento*. When the *Comento* seems most concerned with Petrarchan style, it often turns out to be promoting Medici ideology. In this respect it has an important precedent in a controversial series of lectures on Petrarch that Cristoforo Landino presented in 1466–67. Landino dedicated the lectures to the young Lorenzo de' Medici, then seventeen years of age, "acciò che con quelle possiate eliminare e crescere la lingua patria" (so that with these examples you can prune and extend the language of the fatherland).[19] Like Landino's prolusion, Lorenzo's *Comento* raises the issue of the vernacular and its capacity to sustain great poetry on a par with the classical languages. For Landino a cultivated vernacular nourishes free republican expression as well as a Medici ruler's power to unite the populace and persuade it to follow his will. Landino's reasoning is overtly political. Eloquence is a vital adjunct to the pursuit of free speech in a republic: "Né cosa alcuna si troverrà che in una libera e ben governata republica più utilità e ornamento seco arrechi che la eloquenzia" (38) (Nothing will be found that in a free and well-governed republic should yield more usefulness and adornment than eloquence). Lest democratic oratory challenge Medici hegemony, however, Landino takes care to suggest that eloquence can enhance the despotic ruler's own prestige: "che dove manca ornato di parole e retto e vero ordine, . . . ivi manca riputazione, mancavi auttorità, mancavi fede" (39) (Where eloquence is lacking, there too is lacking reputation, authority, trust). Above all the ruler can unite the populace through eloquence, thereby shaping its attitudes and bending its will: "La eloquenzia poté da principio gl'uomini . . . in uno ceto e congregazione ragunare, e, ragunati, alle leggi e al giusto vivere sottomettergli" (39) (Eloquence can unite people anew . . . into rank and file, and, reunited, can encourage them to submit to law and order).

Landino directs his remarks about the vernacular to a political purpose, and so does Lorenzo, but in his *Comento* Lorenzo dares not refer to his own administrative use of language as such an instrument of public control. Instead he refers to the literary language of the Tuscan people as a collective achievement, and he refers especially to the master texts of Dante, Petrarch, and Boccaccio as proof of its power. Lorenzo argues that political illusions lead us to attach greater value to some languages rather than others. Linguistic or poetic hegemony, the prestige that one language or set of poetic conventions acquires over another, results from carefully contrived assertions of power by ruling parties that use the language or style. Rulers manufacture this illusion about the superiority of one language over another in order to assert political mastery: "l'essere in prezzo e assai celebrata una lingua nel mondo consiste nella oppinione di quelli tali che assai l'apprezzano e stimano" (19) (The idea that a language is highly valued and exalted throughout the world consists in the opinion of such people who value and esteem it). In his historical view Lorenzo attributes the hegemonic success of Latin to the designs of the Roman imperium. "Questa tale dignitá d'essere prezzata per successo prospero della fortuna è molto appropriata alla lingua latina, perché la propagazione dell'imperio romano non l'ha fatta solamente comune per tutto il mondo, ma quasi necessaria" (20) (The Latin language has acquired such prestige because the spread of the Roman empire made it not only universal but also designated it a necessary vehicle for communication). At the same time, just as imperium spreads the language, so also language spreads the imperium by inscribing reality in a classifying and differentiating system. Latin made the world Roman. There is no reason to suppose modern Tuscan less capable of promoting Medici interests throughout Italy.

As proof that Tuscan has already succeeded as a literary language, Lorenzo cites the great number of commentaries on Dante, "come mostra l'esempio per molti comenti fatti sopra alla sua *Commedia* da uomini dottissimi e famosissimi" (21) (as exemplified in the many commentaries on the *Commedia* composed by extremely learned and highly renowned readers). Their number suggests that deep meaning animates Dante's texts, but their diversity also gives way to hermeneutic controversy. Not all commentators understand the text in the same way. In the *Commento*'s first pages Lorenzo recognizes "la confusione che nasce dalla varietá de' comenti, ne' quali il piú delle volte si segue piú tosto la natura propria che la intenzione vera di chi ha scritto" (12) (the confusion that arises from the variety of commentaries in which the commentator usually follows his own inclination rather than the actual intention of the one who wrote). While some simply fail to understand the text on any level, others represent it as inherently contestable to advance their own interpretive arguments. In both cases competing commentaries furnish a rhetorical paradigm of divergent understanding. They afford less a vehicle to clarify univocal meanings than a baffling mirror that deflects and defers such meanings.

Particularly when his own poetry approaches autobiographical statement, Lorenzo deflects and defers its emotional meaning through his commentary. It sometimes seems as though he were using rhetoric to displace the experience of grief. In Sonnet 10, "Se fra gli altri sospir ch'escon di fore" (If among the other sighs that issue outside), this displacement performs both a narrative and a symbolic function. The poem dramatizes an act of deception that results from the use of a Petrarchan oxymoron. Cruel fate ("mia dura sorte") sends the poet a host of woes, among which are his amatory tribulations. These sweet woes bring relief to his other bitter woes: "Amor qualcun ne mischia, par che porte / dolcezza agli altri e riconforti il core" (3–4) (If Love is mixed among them, it seems that it brings a sweetness to the others and that it comforts my heart). Fortune, however, fails to distinguish amatory sighs that please the speaker from other sighs that pain him, with the result that it believes itself victorious over the speaker:

> Fortuna invidia vede que' sospiri
> che manda Amor dal core e li comporta,
> credendo che s'arroga a' miei martíri.

Invidious fortune sees these sighs that Love sends from the heart, and it bears them away believing that they are added to my suffering. (9–11)

As these oxymoronic signs of love deceive Fortune, rhetoric impinges upon reality. Rhetorical figures effect a cure for woe.

In the commentary that follows, Lorenzo seeks to undo his other sorrows with similar acts of verbal displacement. Lorenzo had implied in the prologue of the *Comento* that these other sorrows refer to setbacks in his personal and political life. In discussing these setbacks he now cites with a resonant pun on his own name the example of those *medici* (doctors) who exaggerate patients' illnesses in order to make their treatment seem more efficacious: "sopravenendo pure la morte, la colpa sia piú tosto della natura che della cura; venendo la salute, la cura ed opera si mostri tanto piú efficace"·(51) (If death does occur, the fault would sooner seem the result of nature rather than of the cure, but if health returns, the doctor's work would seem so much the more efficacious). The enumeration of trials that follows concludes with the statement that death would indeed be welcome in this context: "essendo ad un medesimo tempo nell'anima con escomunicazione, nelle facultá con rapine, nello stato con diversi ingegni, nella famiglia e figuoli con nuovo trattato e macchinazioni nella vita con frequenti insidie perseguitato, mi saria suto non piccola grazia la morte" (51) (being afflicted in my spiritual life with excommunication, in my household with theft, in affairs of state with many exigencies, among my family with betrayal, and with plots against my life, death would have been no small favor). Lorenzo's sonnets now function as a form of therapy for these misfortunes. They are the Medici's *medici*.

The pun on *medici* resonates ironically throughout the text, just as John Shearman has shown that it resonates throughout visual art later in the period.[20] On a conceptual level the pun is an ambiguous one. It represents Lorenzo through language as a potential healer of both corporeal and political bodies that he rules, but it equivocates his power to heal. In the context of his statement about physicians Lorenzo might be one of those *medici* who inflate the value and prestige of their own skills by publishing a false prognosis. He might also be one of those *medici* who cannot cure their own ills. On a political level the pun insinuates a threat to Medici rule. It suggests that Lorenzo might resemble those *medici* whose skills become obsolete as soon as the patient is cured. Ironically this possibility has its basis in the Platonic philosophy that Lorenzo so ardently patronized.

In Plato's dialogues the figure of the *medico* (*medicus* in the Latin translations of Ficino, who advertised himself as a man of medicine, a *medicus*) functions as a trope for the plight of Socrates.[21] In the *Symposium*, for example, Eryximachus, a physician, explains how the body consists of such opposites as hot and cold, moist and dry, at war with each other. When the physician adjusts the balance between them, he substitutes healthy desires for morbid ones. Medicine is a science of love, the art of generating harmony and concord among opposites, a good and healthy temperament. Socrates himself is a physician of love (*Symposium* 185c–188e). In his commentary on the *Symposium* Ficino explains how this physician of love instructs us in "amoris caritatisque modus ad deum, ad patriam, ad parentes, ad alios, tam ad vivos quam ad defunctos" (the practice of love and charity toward God, fatherland, family, and others living and dead).[22] Here the medical and political intersect as they do elsewhere in Plato. In *Gorgias* Socrates elaborates upon this intersection through a powerful analogy between physicians (*medici*) and politicians. Physicians aim to produce order and regulation in the human body; politicians should aim to do the same thing for the public body. Just as physicians restrain sick persons, so should politicians chastise those who corrupt the soul of the state (*Gorgias* 504a). Ficino in his epitome of *Gorgias* comments that the health of the state is not just a metaphor nor a mere matter of opinion, but a real condition that the good politician brings about: "Ex quo fit, ut quemadmodum virtus corporis vitiumque non in opinione, sed in re ipsa vel naturae consentanea vel opposita reperitur, sic virtus vitiumque animi non ad humanam opinionem sed ad naturae legem dijudicetur" (1319) (Just as the excellence or defect of the body is found not in opinion but in the body itself, either agreeing with nature or opposed to it, so the excellence or defect of the soul might be judged not by human opinion but by the law of nature). In *Philebus*, however, Socrates confronts the limit of his own powers. When the physician establishes a healthy ratio between warring opposites within the body, he releases the patient. He does not try to make the patient healthier by passing beyond this ratio. If he did, he would only upset the balance and give the patient a new disease. Having reached this limit, all physicians, including Socrates, become obsolete (*Philebus* 26d).

Socrates's obsolescence assumes a sacrificial character in Plato's dialogues, and this character has special import for a Medici ruler patterned on the Platonic model. The need to block designs of Pope Sixtus IV upon Romagna and of his successor, Pope Innocent VIII, upon Naples; the need to keep peace among Milan, Venice, and Naples so that none could attack Florence and each would aid the others against the popes; the need finally to block the threat of a French invasion encouraged by injured parties in the Italian alliance, all demanded heroism of an unusual sort. At the height of his opposition to Pope Sixtus IV in December 1479, Lorenzo presented himself as a public sacrifice to King Ferrante of Naples as the latter was aiding the pope's advance upon Tuscany. The boldness of Lorenzo's action persuaded King Ferrante to break his alliance with the papacy. Until the exile of the Medici in 1494, Naples remained an ally of Florence.

Lorenzo repeats this sacrificial gesture in the *Comento*. This time it assumes a rhetorical form for which the Petrarchan lyric supplies a model. Lorenzo ruled at an historical moment when he could identify his own private interests with those of all Florence. His rhetorical problem was to explain how his private design to get and hold power might coincide with the greater public need to build strong defenses against outside forces, or to explain how they might seem to coincide. One solution is to identify the private ruler with the public ruled. Here the topos of love offers a dynamic poetic vehicle. In the torments of love as Petrarch represented them, lovers sacrifice themselves to the beloved. To perceive the ruler as a sacrificial victim of love brings him to the level of the ruled while it marks him as someone special. It implies that his very rule, like his love, serves to reconcile opposites and prepare the way for a higher form of order. When this order occurs, however, his rule may be rendered obsolete and done away with, and he may be expelled like a pharmakon. His sufferings and transgressions, real or imagined, therefore play an important part in this sacrificial drama. In them the ruler's subjects see an enactment of their own aberrant desires. Just as the ruled are able to displace their own transgressions on to this sacrificial ruler, so they can project their own longings for release upon him.

In this complex self-dramatization Lorenzo succeeds in attributing, if not to his own political intelligence, at least to his own rhetorical skill, a victory over death. He achieves this victory through a symbolic enactment of the Petrarchan lover's sacrifice. The lover must give himself wholly to the beloved, just as she in turn will encourage him toward a death of the self. In Sonnet 14 the beloved's hand draws the bow that wounds him and at the same time heals him.

La vita e morte mia tenete voi,
eburnee dita, e 'l gran disio ch'io celo,
qual mai occhio mortal vedrá né vide.

You hold my life and death, ivory fingers, and the great desire
that I conceal, which mortal eye will never see, nor ever did see.
(12–14)

The topos refers to Petrarch's Sonnet 159 in whose last stanza Love
simultaneously heals and wounds. There Petrarch appropriates Plato's
topos of love as a medicine that effects a reconciliation of opposites
in the soul: "non sa come Amor sana e come ancide, / chi non sa
come dolce ella sospira / e come dolce parla et dolce ride" (12–14)
(he does not know how Love heals and how he kills, who does not
know how sweetly she sighs and how sweetly she speaks and sweetly
laughs).

In his commentary on this poem Lorenzo traces this topos to the
mythic lance of Achilles that had the power to wound and heal at
the same time. "Ferisce adunque e sana, cioè accende il desiderio, di
poi lo adempie, come si dice faceva il telo, cioè la lancia, d'Achille
figliuolo di Pelleo, la quale avendo due punte, dicono i poeti che con
l'una feriva, con l'altra sanava le ferite" (64) (It wounds and heals,
that is, it kindles desire while allaying it, just like the lance of Achilles,
son of Peleus, which poets say had two points, wounding with one
and curing wounds with the other). As Lorenzo explains the allusion,
the figure of the warrior blurs into that of the physician, the *medicus*
whose work averts death. Both figures find their ultimate locus in the
speaker's own sacrifice. Achilles faced the choice of living a long
but undistinguished life or meeting an early death through which he
would earn fame by offering himself to the public body. Lorenzo
ponders a similar choice, but rather than execute it in the world of
politics where the consequences are real, he represents it in the world
of Petrarchan poetry where the consequence is symbolic.

Sonnet 15 begins with a direct quotation from one of Petrarch's
most celebrated poems *In morte di Laura*, sonnet 300, "Quanta invidia
io ti porto, avara terra" (How I envy you, greedy earth). Petrarch's
speaker envies the greedy earth that entombs Laura. Lorenzo by contrast envies his own heart because the beloved has made it the em-

blem of her conquest: "Quanta invidia ti porto, o cor beato, / che quella man vezzosa or mulce or stringe" (How I envy you, o happy heart, whom this graceful hand now caresses, now clasps). The beloved has mastered his heart as a writer or artist would by inscribing her name upon it as though upon a page and by painting her face upon it as though upon a canvas. In the last tercet the speaker exclaims that the beloved's eyes might transform his heart to solid diamond.

> O mio bel core, oramai piú che speri?
> Sol ch'abbin forza quelle luci dive
> di trasformarti in rigido adamante.

O my dear heart, what more do you now hope for? Only that those divine eyes might transform you to solid diamond. (12–14)

Such a substance will retain the beloved's artistic image for all time. It will achieve a conquest over death.

This poem generates a commentary on the relationship between the artist and patron, but the commentary curiously inverts the relationship between them implied in the poem. Whereas the lover in the poem submits to the beloved as artist, the artist in the commentary submits to the patron as ruler. As he does so, however, the artist himself performs the work of a ruler in constructing monuments that resist death. On his canvas he can, like a ruler, erect buildings, regulate the landscape, fight battles on land and sea, and call people to dances and other merrymaking. The patron judges these canvases the way the populace judges the work of the ruler: what counts is what seems good in his eyes, "secondo la natura di chi debbe vedere" (68) (in harmony with the nature of the person who is to see it). Creighton Gilbert has observed that the examples listed in this commentary represent undistinguished topics common in "industrial art" of the time, "all intellectually humble and old-fashioned preferences, and all to the exclusion of those [symbolically complex] choices in the works of the leading individual masters in Florence."[23] The discrepancy between the artist's highest ambitions to render a symbolically complex design and the patron's restraining wish for a simple representation implies that the artist must sacrifice his complex design to please the patron. The trick in Lorenzo's rhetoric is to sort out the Chinese boxes within which the figures of artist and ruler exchange roles. As Medici and poet he himself is a poet-ruler who commands the ruled, a ruler-poet who submits to the claims of the ruled, a patron of the arts who makes claims upon artists who serve him, and an artist himself who seeks to please his own beloved, all in an effort to husband the body politic and shield it from death.

This equivocal shifting of roles informs Lorenzo's self-dramatization in other sonnets. Poliziano referred pointedly to Lorenzo's ability to exchange roles and to the political consequences of that ability in his position as a statesman. Poliziano's reference occurs in an éloge to Lorenzo as statesman and poet that ends his long poem about poetic art, *Nutricia* (1486). Poliziano represents in Lorenzo an idealized conjunction of ruler and artist, one who composes poetry as a pastime after his day's work managing affairs of state:

> Quodque alii studiumque vocant, durumque laborem,
> Hic tibi ludus erit, fessus civilibus actis
> Huc is emeritas acuens ad carmina vires.
> Felix ingenio, felix cui pectore tantas
> Instaurare vices, cui fas tam magna carpaci
> Alternare animo, et varias ita nectere curas.

What others call study and hard work will be a pastime for you; exhausted with affairs of state, you nonetheless begin honing your veteran powers in song; gifted with wit, you are gifted in being allowed to play so many roles, to move from one great deed to another with an expansive mind, and to bring together such varied concerns. (*Nutricia*, 769–74)[24]

In the *Comento* Lorenzo exploits his ability to shift roles by associating it with acts of public good.

Sonnet 23, for example, construes the desire for death as a sacrificial drive that paradoxically renews life. In it the beloved expresses a wish for her own death as a form of *contemptus mundi*. Her attitude motivates the speaker to adopt a similar stance.

> Sí dolcemente la mia donna chiama
> morte nelli amorosi suoi sospiri,
> ch'accende in mezzo agli aspri miei disiri
> un suave disio, che morte brama.

So sweetly my lady calls for death in her amorous sighs that amid my rude desires she kindles a soft desire that longs for death. (1–4)

When the speaker sacrifices himself, he finds to his surprise that his own longing for death strengthens his grasp on life.

> Questo gentil disio tanto il core ama,
> che scaccia e spegne in lui gli altri martíri;
> quinci prende vigore e par respiri
> l'alma contra sua voglia afflitta e grama.

So much does my heart love this gentle desire that it drives out and extinguishes its own sufferings; hence the soul takes vigor and appears to have respite against its afflicted and miserable will. (5–8)

As the commentary asserts, a desire for death drives out of the heart those worldly afflictions that trouble it, and in so doing it renews a will for life in this anxiety-ridden world: "Per questo si dice che ogni altro desiderio e passione e tutti i martíri ed affanni che si sentono, erono spenti nel cuore sopravenendo questo dolce desiderio della morte; ed essendo tutte queste passioni, e restando solo il dolce pensiero della morte, la vita ne pigliava vigore e respirava alquanto" (93) (For this it is said that every other desire and suffering and all torments and anxieties that are felt are extinguished in the heart when this sweet desire for death occurs; and alone with the sweet thought of death, life takes strength and a bit of respite). In this sonnet, then, sacrificial death functions as a powerful metaphor for creative renewal. Sacrifice becomes a way of entering history so that Lorenzo can transform himself by playing a ritual role. It is not the role of Dante's sublime lover who rises from time to eternity through love, but the role of a Petrarchan lover who validates his existence in this fallen world by sacrificing himself to love.

Ensuing sonnets in the *Comento* show how this problematic renewal draws Lorenzo deeper into the orbit of Petrarchan equivocation. In Sonnet 33 the motif of springtime's bloom celebrates wonders of nature that the speaker can barely comprehend:

> Ove madonna volge gli occhi belli,
> senz' altro sol questa novella Flora

fa germinar la terra and mandar fòra
mille vari color di fior novelli.

Wherever my lady directs her beautiful eyes, without any sun
this new Flora causes the earth to bloom and sends forth a thousand different colors of new flowers. (1–4)

The adequacy of words to things diminishes as Lorenzo falls back on
Petrarchan clichés to enumerate the joys of spring, and it vanishes
altogether when he tries to celebrate his beloved's relationship to
them. Part of the irony is that its colors and flowers, figures of the
beloved's beauty, are also conventional figures for rhetorical ornament, the colors and flowers of speech. The poem multiplies the
production of these rhetorical figures. In the final tercet, however, a
Petrarchan topos of ineffability dramatizes language's failure to cir-
cumscribe the speaker's intentions:

Or qui lingua o pensier non par che basti
a intender ben quanta e qual grazia abbonde,
là dove quella candida man tocca.

Now here language or thought do not appear sufficient to conceive both how much and what kind of grace she abounds in.
(12–14)

The fragility of the speaker's linguistic resources, no matter how rich
the rhetorical tradition that has nourished them, gives way to mute
silence.

As the *Comento* draws toward this silence, its penultimate Sonnet
40 represents the speaker in paralyzing indecision. "Lasso, ormai non
so più che far deggia" (Alas I no longer know what I ought to do).
The oxymoronic contrarieties of elation and dejection divide his judgment. The beauty of the beloved's eyes draws his attention, yet when
he looks at them he sees only his own death: "veggo la morte mia
che in lor lampeggia" (4) (I see my own death shining in them). The
sonnet's final tercet pits the familiar Petrarchan antitheses that proclaim the beloved's eyes and other features as "sweet enemies"
against the now powerful antithesis that the speaker lives just to
think about his own sacrificial death:

> Da tali e tanti dolci miei nimici
> ho mille dolci offese, e ancora aspetto
> sí dolce morte, che a pensarne vivo.

From so many such sweet enemies of mine I suffer a thousand sweet injuries, and yet I await so sweet a death that I live just to think about it. (12–14)

On the one hand in the figurative convention of the Petrarchan mode death absorbs the personified Amore, the Lover's initial adversary and now his final conqueror. On the other hand according to the narrative conventions of the Petrarchan mode, the beloved's eyes, limbs, gestures, words, and other beauties assault the lover as carriers of yet another death, here imagined as an attack upon the senses, "la speranza di molto piú dolce morte dalli inimici gia detti" (139) (the hope of a much sweeter death from these already mentioned enemies.) To these metonymic equivalents the speaker adds a third in the *Comento*, the neo-Platonic surrender of the self in contemplating the beloved: "che non importa altro che lo adempiere il desiderio, che si adempie quando l'amante nello amato si trasforma" (139) (which means nothing more than the fulfillment of a desire that is accomplished when the lover is transformed into the beloved). With this motif of fulfillment through transformation, the Petrarchan mode yields to a higher philosophical strain than any yet announced in the *Comento*.

At this point, however, the text comes to an abrupt end. The lover and the beloved begin to share a mutual enamorment. The focus now shifts to the beloved and her response to her newly awakened love. The sequence's final sonnet initiates a new narrative in which the lover undertakes a journey away from the beloved and wonders how she will respond to his absence. The sonnet's final lines dramatize how the speaker wards off his own death-dealing despair:

> E, se non pur che ad ora ad ora spero
> gli occhi veder, che sempre il mio cor vede,
> per la dolcezza e per pietá morria.

If I do not hope from hour to hour to see her eyes that my heart always sees, I will die of sweetness and pity. (12–14)

The unfinished state of the text allows us only to speculate how the germ of this narrative might have developed.

One possibility is that it might not have developed at all. As a sequence the forty-one sonnets of Lorenzo's *Comento* do not advance a very clear or compelling narrative.[25] After the first four poems about the dead young woman, the speaker celebrates his own beloved by grouping several sonnets on conventionally limited motifs—for example Sonnets 7 to 12 on her eyes and heart, Sonnets 13 to 16 and 30 to 32 on her hands and heart. In Sonnet 29 the beloved's smile implies her innocent surrender to the speaker, but in Sonnets 35 to 37 and again in Sonnet 41 the lovers are temporarily separated. On the whole a coherent narrative plays only a small role in organizing the sequence. For the commentary this impoverishment of the narrative bears some significance. At some point Lorenzo might have envisioned linking the sonnets into a fully developed narrative sequence. Petrarch's example in the *Rime sparse*, however, counseled against any obvious sequence. Lorenzo's gravitation toward the Petrarchan mode pressured him to admit aleatory, undecided, oblique, and problematic open-endedness into his poetry. If Lorenzo had followed Dante's mode, he would have sought a transcendent order, a stable center, a fixed correspondence between words and things. Instead, forecasting the choice of the later Renaissance, he set Dante aside and followed Petrarch.

Through the Petrarchan mode Lorenzo represents service to the beloved as an act of sacrifice that allows him to exploit the political implications of his own service to the state as an act of sacrifice. The price that he pays is to admit the instability of his own best intentions. When the Petrarchan mode emerges as a rival to Dante's poetry, it comes to function as a relativized unstable barometer of a relativized unstable history. In Lorenzo's case, it does so all the more after it has passed through the crucible of his own personal biography fraught with its ambiguities, uncertainties, and indetermination. For this instability the transcendent assurances of Dante's poetry and that of the *Stil nuovo* offer no model. The disjunctions between signifiers and their signifieds in Petrarch's poetry, however, offer a powerful example for the Medici poet. Lorenzo's use of Petrarchan figuration with its turn toward radical introspection and its beckoning of stylistic semaphores that take on different shades and tones with each new performance serves his rhetorical purposes. In its confrontation with Petrarch, Lorenzo's *Comento* inscribes a political vision while it confronts the pressures of life and death in fifteenth-century Florence.

Continuity and Change in the Ideals of Humanism: The Evidence from Florentine Funeral Oratory

▼

John McManamon, S.J.

"Farewell then, my dog, and insofar as I am able to influence matters, may you be immortal as is natural that your virtue desire." With these words Leon Battista Alberti closed a funeral speech for his canine companion. Alberti composed the tribute as a diversion on a hot summer's night in the 1430s. He used the portrait of his dog to satirize the characteristic form and exaggerations of a funeral oration and to present an ideal for the human person with thinly veiled reference to himself.[1] By treating the portrait as the foil it was intended to be, one can measure continuity and change in humanist ideals against the characteristics of Alberti's pet.

That Alberti would write a satire of funeral oratory by 1438 indicates how well-rooted the species had become in Italy. In fact, several of the most popular humanist funeral speeches, which thereafter molded the form, had been delivered by that date. They included the eulogies of Gasparino Barzizza for Iacopo da Forlì at Padua in 1414, Andrea Giuliano for Manuel Chrysoloras at Venice in 1415, and Leonardo Giustiniani for Carlo Zeno at Venice in 1418. Poggio Bracciolini introduced Europe to the classicizing form of the species when he commemorated Francesco Zabarella at the Council of Constance in 1417. Zabarella had served as cardinal-bishop of Florence.

The fact that Alberti's speech was never delivered publicly also makes it an appropriate foil for comparison to Florentine oratory. The most famous eulogies from Renaissance Florence, those by Leonardo Bruni for Nanni Strozzi and by Poggio for Niccolò Niccoli and for

Lorenzo di Giovanni de' Medici, circulated only in written form. Throughout the Quattrocento the various regimes at Florence respected the potentially explosive character of a public funeral. The Medici consciously refused the honor lest funerals become open celebrations of their hegemony. Florentine governments normally sponsored public obsequies for ecclesiastics like Baldassare Cossa and Bartolomeo Zabarella or for humanist employees of the government like Coluccio Salutati, Leonardo Bruni, and Carlo Marsuppini.

Alberti began his speech by giving his reason for composing it: "It was a custom among our ancestors to praise deserving citizens." The humanist defined deserving citizens as those who were outstanding in their knowledge of the "good arts" and in their morals and piety. In rhetorical terms they were persons of ethos, whose studies affected the conduct of their lives. The arts that they pursued were called "good" in the sense of an Aristotelian final cause. Their study fostered excellence of character. Alberti saw the virtue of integrity as the essence of Christian living. A believer lived morally by practicing the ideals that he advocated.

Alberti then characterized panegyric as an act of equity; citizens of integrity earned their public reward. Praise should also spur the youth of a state to practice virtue. Listeners would be enticed to imitate the excellence of the exemplar. Alberti's use of the verb *illicere* reflects a Western tradition of thought that assigned a seductive and almost magical power to the art of rhetoric from the time of the Greek sophists.[2] His exordium stated abiding convictions of Florentine and Italian humanists. Like Ovid (*Pont.* IV.2.35–36), they were convinced that virtue increased with praise. There was an intimate tie between the eloquence of praise and blame, which humanists overwhelmingly pursued, their fundamental commitment as educators, and a peculiar tenet of their anthropology that held that human persons were attracted to virtue.

Alberti's exordium also reflects the humanist cult of imitation. Humanists delivered funeral eulogies to imitate ancient custom and used them to present exemplars worthy of imitation. In Alberti's case one can be even more specific. He stated that he was imitating a custom among "our ancestors." Roman rhetoric emphasized the persuasive power of ethos more strongly than the Greeks had. In the concise formulation of Quintilian (I.Pr.9) the orator must combine virtues with gifts of speech. Alberti appropriated that peculiarly Roman approach to eloquence.

What qualities did Alberti commend in his dog? First of all, the dog descended from a distinguished line, whose origins could be traced to antiquity. His breed had produced numerous *principes,* a word that seemed to delight humanist orators because of its ambiguity. The word was widely used at Florence to mean "leading citizens," but it could not be stripped of its more specific, monarchical connotations.

Alberti drew information on the heroic canine ancestors of his own pet from Pliny's *Historia naturalis* and Plutarch's *Moralia.* Plutarch was especially appropriate, for he wrote history in the manner of an epideictic orator. He tried to show the effects of virtue and vice on human events. Moreover, Plutarch had once stated his belief that the sight of virtuous deeds moved the beholder to imitate them. His approach helped shape funeral oratory in Italy from the beginning of the fifteenth century.[3]

Alberti specifically commended the heroism shown by his dog's ancestors in battle and contrasted their virtue to the normal behavior of soldiers. The dogs who defended the Colophoni and Castabalenses from enslavement accepted no pay for their service. They were the antithesis of the avaricious mercenaries of the Quattrocento. Theirs was an act of pure benevolence. Alberti also used the dogs to censure treachery in warfare. Courage must be combined with loyalty, humanity, and justice.

Alberti criticized the whole enterprise of warfare when he discussed how his dog dealt with this legacy of heroism in combat. The humanist condemned wars that were fought for any other reason than self-defense. Given that his dog was, frankly, puny (*pusillus*), the justice of his cause was virtually guaranteed. Still, Alberti assured his readers that his dog never fought except for justice and honesty and never refused to fight to protect justice and liberty. The dog at first carried on the virtuous traditions of his ancestors in battle.[4]

In a brief digression, Alberti elaborated his criticisms. He chided those contemporaries who would reduce excellence of character to courage in battle. Leonardo Bruni had done just that in his eulogy for Nanni Strozzi. Alberti asked rhetorically whether such courage was really more commendable than the heroism of justice exercised in a society at peace. His question reflected an abiding conviction among rhetoricians, who saw eloquence as a civilizing force in society. Speech set men apart from animals. War bestialized them. Troubled by these matters, Alberti's dog eventually decided to spurn arms for the study of letters. Alberti created that conversion as a symbolic call to his fellow humanists. Their praise for martial virtue in the early Quattrocento had become propaganda for unjust wars.[5]

Alberti applauded his dog for abandoning "the art of inhumanity" in order to pursue disciplines that fostered moral excellence. He went to study under Alberti's guidance, thereby initiating their friendship. Alberti noted that his new student possessed the essential talent for humanist studies, an acute memory for words and concepts. He used that ability to master the three languages of Alberti's curriculum: Latin, Greek, and Tuscan. The little beast's talent and commitment were proven when one considered that he learned the languages in less than three years.

In subsequent moments of the speech, Alberti filled out the picture of his pet's learning. He recounted that his dog liked to visit the university and "sniff around" eclectically among the teachings of the Academics, Stoics, Peripatetics, and Epicureans. He did not waste his free time, often passing whole nights "singing" to the moon. Humanist orators liked to commend their subjects for their musical abilities. The Venetian Leonardo Giustiniani apparently invented the topic in his speech for the admiral Carlo Zeno. Humanists used it to prove the superiority of Italian statesmen to the Athenian Themistocles. Without musical training, Themistocles had to refuse invitations to play the lyre, and for that reason he was considered "less than learned" (*indoctior*) by Cicero and Quintilian.[6]

The pursuit of the best arts had its desired effects. Alberti adduced his dog as a norm of moral living. There were numerous indications of his spirit of detachment, especially from riches. He had only one suit of clothes, went barefoot no matter what the season, only slept out of necessity, and avoided expensive wines and rich sauces. To promote moral living among his contemporaries, the dog exercised the arts of an epideictic rhetorician. He censured impure and obscene behavior and only befriended upright persons. His life attested that one should combine scholarly leisure (*otium*) and public service (*negotium*).

The interweaving of themes of learning and a committed way of life brought Alberti's speech back to its starting point. His dog was one of those deserving persons who excelled in the good arts and in moral living. Among the actions that exemplified that moral life, Alberti particularly emphasized the dog's decision to break with family traditions and contemporary opinions, which reduced public virtue to courage in battle. He felt that the pursuit of justice in a society at peace more beneficially exercised the arts of humanity.

One can now compare the ideals that Alberti advocated through his dog with those presented in Florentine funeral orations. Such a manner of proceeding does not imply that funeral orations are the only source for humanist ideals at Florence or even the best ones. However, since Italian humanism is now accepted as a characteristic phase in Western rhetorical culture, such orations are appropriate sources. Rhetoric primarily means speechmaking. Italian humanist rhetoric was predominantly epideictic and sought to instill a sense of values or reinforce them. Humanist speakers, who commemorated the death of public servants, challenged their Florentine listeners to evaluate their fundamental values.

Florentine ideals did change, and their evolution becomes apparent by noting how humanists manipulated the rhetorical topics of their funeral speeches. In the earliest eulogies of the Quattrocento, orators practically ignored the topic of ancestry, so important in the case of Alberti's dog, and focused upon the topic of birthplace. Leonardi Bruni pioneered that approach when he composed a panegyric of Florence around 1403–4. Consequently, Florentine humanists did not find their original inspiration in Roman rhetorical principles but looked to Athenian models. Roman funeral oratory had celebrated the historical individual and his ancestry. It underlined the nobility and excellence of the governing aristocracy. The first Athenian funeral orations commemorated the anonymous victims of the previous year's wars. Athenian orators focused their praise on the state and its ideology.[7]

Whatever the demerits of his thesis, Hans Baron correctly credited Leonardi Bruni with using Athenian models to trace a republican ideology for Florence. Bruni introduced his ideas in his *Laudatio* of the city and developed them in his funeral oration for Nanni Strozzi (1428). In the *Laudatio*, Bruni argued that government existed to protect citizens, not to tyrannize them. In a society composed of economic classes, the poor majority was more vulnerable and had greater need of government's protection. That protection was assured through the strict enforcement of justice by impartial magistrates rotated in and out of office.

Bruni elaborated his republican stance in his treatment of the topic of birthplace in the oration for Nanni Strozzi. He described Florence as a popular republic, whose offices were open to all. That factor naturally stimulated a competition for virtue among those who aspired to hold public office. It also provided a rationale for an education in the good arts. Much of Bruni's propaganda sought to break the monopoly on moral government that the "mirror-of-princes" literature had granted to monarchs. Republics rewarded the virtuous with office; monarchs inevitably feared them.[8]

Ostensibly the defender of republican liberty, the humanist from Arezzo also functioned as an apologist for Florence's bourgeois oligarchy. At the outset of the *Laudatio*, Bruni guided his readers through the elite's urban palaces. In a later digression he emphasized that he had not written the speech to curry favor with the mob of citizens. His praise for constitutionalism in the panegyric focused on the Ordinances of Justice of 1293, which had defeudalized the commune by excluding the nobility from public office. That constitutional enactment had propelled the merchant oligarchy to a position of dominance. Bruni applauded the majority of Florentine citizens for consistently following the views of the aristocracy. In the funeral speech for Nanni Strozzi, Bruni carefully distinguished Florence's popular regime from monarchy, but he passed over in virtual silence any criticism of oligarchy.

Both speeches sought to solidify oligarchic control by fostering internal consensus among the elite while rallying popular sentiment to defense of the city-state. Was Bruni then merely a fawning servant of that elite? Must we reject as hypocrisy his praise for Florence's system of government, which opened public office to all worthy candidates? Like most historical problems, this one defies a simple answer. Bruni's humanist mentor, Coluccio Salutati, had taught that excessive praise could function as subtle criticism. "What biting criticism it is to praise someone above his merits or when he has none. . . . Who is so empty-headed that if given exaggerated praise he does not feel he has been warned about the perversity of his life with a view to his reform or instruction?"[9] Bruni surely knew in 1428 that Florence's elite maintained severe restrictions upon holding office. His speech for

Nanni might be read as propaganda for the Albizzi oligarchy or as implied criticism for its increasingly restrictive practices. From the perspective of internal politics Bruni's speeches are masterfully difficult to interpret.

From the perspective of foreign policy, the speeches were effective weapons in a battle for public support during the wars of the Quattrocento. Milan and Venice recruited humanists to defend their own positions and rebut Bruni's. Yet Italian humanists came to perceive their involvement in that propaganda war as contradictory and dangerous. Take the case of Nanni Strozzi, whom Bruni cast as the ideal citizen-soldier. Bruni's portrait emphasized that wars fought by mercenaries left little room for virtue or patriotism. Mercenaries frequently broke their contracts. Florence's chief condottiere, Niccolò Piccinino, had abandoned Florence to serve Milan in 1425 just after the outbreak of hostilities between the two states. Consequently, treachery, not courage, often determined the outcome of a campaign. Bruni probably designed Strozzi as a contrast to Piccinino.[10]

The difficulties of Bruni's task become more apparent when one recalls that Nanni Strozzi, the ideal Florentine citizen-soldier, was the son of Florentine exiles living in Ferrara. Contradictions also emerged if one honestly assessed the character of wars fought in Italy in the first half of the fifteenth century. Humanist orators everywhere presented those wars as just; they were said to be legitimate acts of self-defense.[11] Florence's wars against the Visconti or Ladislaus of Hungary were perhaps defensive. Still, the speeches Bruni wrote to defend them were openly imperialistic. His *Laudatio* contained a stirring and controversial passage on Florence as the direct heir of Roman imperialism and was written a few years before the conquest of Pisa. Bruni's speech for Nanni was completed in 1428 on the eve of the fateful decision by Florence's regime to try to annex Lucca. He emphasized in the speech that Florentines descended from Etruscans and Romans, who had dominated Italy and the entire world respectively.[12]

Alberti designed the story of his dog's conversion to challenge fellow humanists to see the danger of their ways. He invited republican ideologues to confront a question that still begs for an answer. In simplest terms, what does liberty have to do with empire? His dog rejected precisely those sorts of combat. Courage was never displayed when a stronger opponent defeated a weaker one. Moreover, the problem of continual warfare posed grave risks for those dedicated to the culture of the rhetor. Florentine humanists were familiar with Cicero's contention that eloquence thrived in a settled society but was overwhelmed by the passions of warfare.[13] His assassination during Rome's civil wars gave poignant ethos to that affirmation. By mid-century Florentine humanists retreated from overtly ideological positions in their funeral oratory.

Leonardo Bruni's state funeral in 1444 supplies evidence for this change. None of his three panegyrists mentioned Bruni's impassioned defense of republican liberty when they eulogized him. In fact, the only subsequent use of those ideas in Florentine funeral oratory occurred in Marcello Adriani's eulogy for Giuliano de' Medici in 1516. Adriani contended that the popular character of Florence's government where offices were open to the virtuous explained why the Medici became leaders (*principes*) in the republic.[14] Bruni himself made no allusion to his propagandistic speeches in the "Journal" he composed in 1440. He mentioned only a private address to Pope Martin V, who lived in Florence from 1419–20. Martin had been enraged by a jingle that the youth of Florence chanted to mock him. Bruni calmed his anger by reminding the pope of the benefits he had received during his Florentine stay. By 1440 Bruni wished to be remembered for his persuasive diplomacy on behalf of Florence.[15] Diplomacy exploited the art of eloquence.

Two events in the middle of the Quattrocento sealed this change in humanist ideals. In 1453 Constantinople fell to the Turks. The following year, protracted negotiations among the peninsula's states yielded a peace settlement at Lodi. Humanists applied two paradigms from antiquity to mark these events as a watershed. The fall of Constantinople dramatized that the civilized world was threatened by the advance of barbarian hordes from the East. An oration written to honor Ioannes Hunyadi in 1456 presented Hungary as the eastern bulwark of Christendom. The oration's author, who may well be Donato Acciaiuoli, recalled that Hunyadi had struggled to defend the common liberty of Christians against the contemporary equivalent of the Goths and Vandals.[16]

Italian humanists interpreted that moment in history as "Isocratean." Isocrates has earned a place among history's fuzziest ideologues. His most consistent political ideal was a Panhellenic alliance against the

barbarian Persians. Humanists at Florence and elsewhere advocated a
similar, pan-Christian crusading alliance against the Turk. The appeal
of Isocrates at Florence, which in itself indicates a relaxation of republican ideology, is further supported by the history of the translations of his works. Lucia Gualdo Rosa has demonstrated that Venetians
and Tuscans participated actively in that endeavor. In fact, the Florentines Carlo Marsuppini and Lapo da Castiglionchio (the younger)
were among the first humanists to translate the *Ad Nicoclem*.[17]

If the paradigm of Isocrates shaped reactions to the fall of Constantinople, that of Augustus influenced humanist celebration of the settlement of Lodi. Now that the peninsula was at peace, political leaders
could realize the highest Roman ideals. Romans like Virgil considered
themselves superior to the Greeks because they demanded a standard
of humanity in rulers. In Virgil's words, political authority should be
merciful to the submissive and crush the arrogant (*Aen.* 6.853). Like
their Roman forebears, Florence's governors would assure true peace
and concord by infusing politics with a moral standard that went beyond expediency.

These themes are prominent in the decrees drafted by Florentine
humanists in 1465 to explain why the Signoria posthumously named
Cosimo de' Medici *pater patriae*. Alamanno Rinuccini opened his text
by asserting that the leading members of a republic ought to reward
deserving citizens and punish harshly those who break the law. In a
public speech to commemorate the award Donato Acciaiuoli asserted
that Cosimo earned the title for piloting Italy to an era of peace and
Florence to civic concord for the first time in her history.[18] Cosimo's
achievements mirrored those of Augustus. The choice of the title "Father of the Country" was appropriate. Ostensibly republican in character, given its primary associations with Cicero and Camillus, it had
likewise been awarded to Julius Caesar and Augustus. Its abiding Roman character indicated the paternalistic nature of good government.[19]

Humanists at Florence also used their orations for fellow humanists
to prove that they adeptly practiced the Roman art of governing. The
eulogy of Cristoforo Landino for Donato Acciaiuoli in 1478 illustrates
this usage. Landino and Acciaiuoli had formerly been bitter enemies.
Acciaiuoli once described Landino as an intellect unworthy even of
the town of Prato. Moreover, Acciaiuoli had vacillated in his support
for the Medici regime until the peace of Lodi. He then accepted a vari-

ety of governmental responsibilities and was even chosen to deliver the official oration in honor of Cosimo de' Medici, "father of his country."

At the funeral Landino presented Acciaiuoli as the ideal public servant. His dedication to peace and concord proved the sincerity of his religious belief. Acciaiuoli could never be bribed from the impartial administration of justice, the essential virtue of good government. He even managed to conciliate the Pistoians, seemingly the essence of factionalism for Florentine orators. Faithful public servant in all his magistracies and embassies, Donato gave his life for Florence when he died en route to France on an important diplomatic mission. Landino used Acciaiuoli to call for loyalty to the Medici regime in a delicate moment.[20] The speech was delivered in the summer of 1478, only a few months after the attempt on Lorenzo de' Medici's life. Landino offered a vivid description of that attempt in his eulogy, tying the death of Giuliano de' Medici to the liturgical sacrifice in which it occurred.

The history of Medici funerals in Florence supplies final evidence for the evolution of humanist ideals. Cosimo and Lorenzo forbade any ceremonies in their honor. The posthumous award to Cosimo was arranged by a commission appointed by the Signoria at the urging of his son Piero. After the exile of the Medici in 1494 and their restoration in 1512, state funerals were organized for Giuliano, the duke of Nemours (1516), and Lorenzo, the duke of Urbino (1519). The ceremonies were consciously designed to assert Medici hegemony. The funeral procession for Giuliano followed the same route traveled by Pope Leo X during his triumphal entry less than a year before. Public rituals, which previously were forbidden because they might stir resentment for Medici control, were used in the Cinquecento as a means to assure it.[21]

Sixteenth-century eulogists for the Medici also changed the emphasis of their speeches. They broke with Quattrocento patterns and focused their praise upon the ancestry of the deceased. Francesco Cattani made the nobility of the Medici family the leitmotiv of his speech for Lorenzo. The orators singled out specific deeds of Medici ancestors like Cosimo and Lorenzo to delineate a program of government in keeping with humanist ideals. In general, the Medici of the fifteenth century had crushed revolts, curbed factionalism, and supplied vital funding and counsel to the state. Cinquecento orators recalled that Cosimo had helped to negotiate peace for Italy and that Lorenzo did not use arms but the prudence and eloquence of an orator to prevent Neapolitan intervention in favor of the Pazzi conspirators.[22]

Eulogists also used their speeches to foster Medici patronage by praising that practiced in the past. They underlined that patrons should support projects for the common good, not for private enjoyment. The Medici rebuilt churches and supported the revival of the liberal arts, seeking thereby to enhance the sacral character of the state and spur its moral improvement through education. In Lorenzo de' Medici humanists commended one who practiced what he patronized.

Humanist panegyric therefore changed at Florence during the Renaissance. Thanks to Leonardo Bruni, it initially pressed a republican ideology and supplied propaganda for Florence's wars in the early Quattrocento. By 1440 humanists abandoned their emphasis on the form of government in favor of praise for ethical governors and bureaucrats. They urged that peace and harmony reign in society, conditions essential to the practice of eloquence. The topics and models for their speeches reveal this basic change in emphasis. Bruni was inspired by Athenian oratory and imitated its use of the topic of birthplace to celebrate the state's ideology. Subsequent orators shifted their inspiration to Roman precepts, which stressed that ethos persuaded. They worked from within the aristocracy. By the sixteenth century the Medici abandoned their reserve for state funerals and their panegyrists followed suit. They used their oratory to celebrate Medici ancestors, who had first acquired leading roles in the state. Florentine humanists were moral reformers who looked backward to Roman antiquity for their models. Their search led them away from the "new matters" of revolutionaries.[23]

The funeral orations of Florentine humanists also supply ample evidence for the ideals that they consistently supported. A commitment to rhetoric shaped humanist culture in significant ways. Rhetoric is not simply a question of style. In fact, the character of humanism as a rhetorical culture is probably most apparent in a common conceptual framework underlying the humanist act of communication. The shared mental assumptions, in turn, helped to shape the ideals that humanists sought to propound.

When speaking publicly, humanists attempted to make their images visible to the audience (*ponere ante oculos*), for they felt that human persons were best persuaded by seeing, not by logical thinking. Plato and Cicero had theorized that if one could physically see moral goodness, the sight would awaken love for wisdom (*Phaedr.* 250D; *Off.* 1.5.15). Renaissance humanists felt that they could present the face of moral goodness through oratory. In shaping exemplars, the humanists worked in analogous fashion to ancient Roman artists. They copied standards and modes of expression of works that they ranked as classics. Through that process of imitation, humanists were confident of fostering a rebirth of culture and society.

Humanists were therefore committed to a truth that related to the conduct of life. Rather than argue over general questions, they preferred to immortalize great deeds. After all, the great thoughts had been thought. Humanists approached the philosophical content of truth with the detachment typical of orators. They preferred to work in the realm of the probable and concrete, where historical conditioning and human choice produced unique results. The ethical content of truth engaged humanist energies. Truth for them must affect the way that we live. The funeral orations reflect each of these suppositions: that human persons are convinced by what they see, that antiquity supplied the standards for expression and value, that orators should pursue a style of truth relevant to the conduct of life, and that such a style possessed an inherent element of probability.

Florentine humanists prized epideictic oratory because it best verbalized what we see. They gave examples in their orations of human persons who had been convinced by visible images. For example, Bruni began his panegyric of Florence by asserting that people's amazement at the city's achievements ceased once they had seen it. He then offered a vivid description of Florence, which emphasized its character as ordered and harmonious. Bruni invested his adopted state with sacral qualities by first calling the viewer's attention to its churches. He underlined its imperial mission by leading the eye from the physical mass of Palazzo Vecchio outward to the walls and beyond them to the country.[24]

Florentine control had providentially spread to the surrounding countryside. In Burckhardtian terms the state of Florence for Bruni was a work of art. Florentine eulogists consistently used the aesthetic dimension to symbolize and spur their program of moral reform. Respect for the environment and urban rebuilding witnessed to one's public spirit. Humanists especially applied the principle to the question of religious reform. The orators affirmed that *religio* in their day had collapsed. A committed bishop like Bartolomeo Zabarella helped to revive piety by rebuilding sacred edifices.[25]

Visual objects played a critical role in Bruni's vocation as a humanist. Giannozzo Manetti and an anonymous eulogist narrated that Bruni had been imprisoned in the castle of Quarrata as a child. The boy was an innocent victim of civic strife in his native Arezzo. His father had supported the Guelf alliance in the wars of the late Trecento. By chance Bruni was kept in a room, which had a portrait of Petrarch on its walls. The sight of Petrarch inflamed the young boy with a desire for the poet's studies and virtues.[26]

The language of this tale consciously reflects the vocabulary used by the Roman historian Sallust, who had described how Publius Scipio and Quintus Fabius Maximus were inflamed to perform great deeds for Rome by the constant sight of their ancestors' death masks (*Iug.* 4.5–6). Moreover, it indicates that persuasive truth engaged the affections as well as the intellect. The eulogist for Ioannes Hunyadi stated that he would place an image of the deceased hero before his listeners' eyes and thereby arouse love for him and a desire to be like him.[27] Episodes like these remind us that humanists did not identify education with schooling. To enhance physical space by works of visual art helped to stir the pursuit of virtue.[28]

The source for the story about Bruni was Bruni himself, who included it in his "Journal" of 1440. The chancellor made it clear in the same work that his conversion to the humanities was not yet complete. He only abandoned the study of law for letters after he had moved to Florence and had the possibility to study Greek with Manuel Chrysoloras. Bruni's eulogists again chose to repeat this story in their speeches. It reflected a second conceptual construct closely related to their preferred genre of oratory. The rhetoric of praise suggested to them a pattern of decline and rebirth. The worse the state of affairs when an individual appeared on the public stage, the greater that person's achievements would seem. According to Bruni, it had been seven hundred years since the study of Greek letters had been possible in Italy. He therefore abandoned his law studies in order to participate in a historic cultural revival.[29]

Bruni's summary genealogy of Florentine humanism—from Petrarch to Chrysoloras to himself—omits an important person, Coluccio Salutati. Perhaps Salutati's hesitancy about the appropriateness of humanist studies late in life deprived him of a place in the genealogy. Bruni himself had shown no hesitancy when humanism was attacked by respected clerics. In his preface to the translation of Basil's letter, Leonardo ridiculed the ignorance and perversity of the detractors of the humanities.[30] Perhaps the cultural context in which Bruni and his eulogists wrote from 1440–44 affected the choices they made. The presence of learned Greeks at Florence for the church council spurred their interest in that language and its literature.

Whatever their motives, Florentine humanists wished to present their educational program as a revival of classical practice. Greek letters supplied the clearest evidence of rebirth. In general, they emphasized the rhetorical side of Greek learning. Poggio affirmed that Chrysoloras had initiated a renaissance of that age in Greek history when eloquence flourished with wisdom. Bruni's eulogists even celebrated the chancellor's translations of Aristotle, which restored the eloquence that Cicero had praised in those texts. Once again eloquent, Aristotle went from educational rival to ally.[31]

The heuristic construct of rebirth pointed humanists toward their cultural task. Truth was to be recovered and conserved. Learning was not a function of empirical research or creativity. Though Florentine orators continually emphasized the value of letters, they themselves produced little great literature. Alberti's dog was well-endowed for humanist learning, given his prodigious memory. A library visibly expressed this conviction about the search for truth. Poggio stressed that Niccolò Niccoli had performed a new public service by bequeathing a storehouse of antiquity's treasures to Florence for the use of her lettered public.[32]

Orators have always worked in the realm of probable truth. By approaching truth as probable, humanists could blur distinctions and harmonize ideas from various sources. Their fundamental act of harmonizing united the orator's obligation to serve the commonweal with Christian imperatives to perform charitable works.[33] In a preface to his translation of Plato's *Phaedo*, Leonardo Bruni used the technical, Stoic language of Cicero to describe an agreement (*convenientia*) among pagan and Christian thinkers on basic issues. He used a rhetorical form of argumentation, the "how much the more" of a fortiori logic, to make the same point before the papal court in his first public speech, a funeral oration in 1405 for Otto Cavalcanti, the nephew of Cardinal Angelo Acciaiuoli.

Bruni's strategy in that oration was designed for Christendom's leading court at a moment when learned clergymen were challenging the use of pagan authors for instruction. The speech emphasized how much more important the gifts of God were for Otto than the external goods of wealth, ancestry, and good health valued by Plato and the Greeks. Bruni's idea is banal at best. The form of argumentation, however, became a favorite of humanists, for it allowed them to express appreciation for pagan culture and still uphold the superiority of the Christian message.[34]

That meant that Florentine humanists were free to be eclectic. Matteo Palmieri credited Carlo Marsuppini with rediscovering the Ciceronian "bond of a mutual relationship" (*Arch.* 1.2) that unites the divine and human arts. Like Alberti's dog, these orators tested a variety of schools of thought, scrutinizing with special care their ethical doctrines. Whether one harmonized Plato and Aristotle by emphasizing Aristotle, as Argyropoulos had, or Plato, like Francesco Cattani, mattered little. It was critical that one seek to appreciate the merits of both. At their best, Florentine humanists bred a sense of intellectual tolerance.[35]

The blurring of distinctions among intellectual currents is apparent in the way that humanists described one another. They praised fellow humanists for being eloquent and wise, orators aware of the Platonic criticisms of sophistry and concerned for breadth of culture. They urged that one combine oratory and philosophy and achieve the cultural *copia* that Cicero had advocated in his *De oratore*.[36] The Florentine republic honored its humanist chancellors by posthumously awarding them the laurel crown. That ceremony reflected the nickname of "orator et poeta" applied to humanists early in the Renaissance.

To justify a laurel crowning for Leonardo Bruni challenged Giannozzo Manetti's inventive ability. After a long digression on the history of honorary crownings in antiquity, Manetti was forced to fall back upon two quotations from the *De oratore*, where Cicero presented the orator and poet as next of kin. He then lamely contended that Bruni was preparing to publish his own poetry and commentaries on that from antiquity just before he died. Manetti concluded his speech by conferring the laurel, an act immortalized in Rossellino's tomb sculpture. Manetti's difficulties are understandable. Bruni was an orator but hardly a poet. His constant activity in the forum left no time to retreat to what Petrarch described as the poet's most pleasant solitude.[37] Piazza della Signoria and Vaucluse symbolize two different arenas of culture. Florentine eulogists typically tried to harmonize them.

In 1475 Alamanno Rinuccini affirmed that Matteo Palmieri successfully combined the contemplative and active lives. Palmieri had served the Florentine republic in a variety of offices and wrote scholarly works that supported the revival of the humanities. For Florence's humanists neither the unexamined nor the uncommitted life were worth leading. In the peroration to his eulogy for Leonardo Bruni, Poggio urged that one never use learning for selfish ends nor to harm the commonwealth.[38]

These affirmations point to the final and central quality of truth for Florentine humanists. They consistently praised those who pursued a truth relevant to the conduct of life. In fact, that was the only truth worth pursuing, and it grounded the value of an education in the humanities. The humanist program of learning sought to perfect one in "the arts appropriate to humanity" (Cicero *Rep.* I.17.28). Poggio recounted that Niccolò Niccoli upset his father by choosing to study the liberal arts instead of commerce. The good arts supplied a healthy antidote to the vice typical of adolescence, identified by Aristotle and Cicero as "libidinous desire."[39]

Florentine funeral orators used various schemata to define the disciplines essential to a humanist education. Giannozzo Manetti, in his eulogy for Bruni, repeated the five studies—grammar, rhetoric, poetry, history, and moral philosophy—that his friend Tommaso Parentucelli had used to organize the humanities section of Cosimo de' Medici's library. Manetti made that canon part of the public domain. The anonymous eulogist for Bruni instead categorized Bruni's scholarly achievements under the three headings of moral philosophy, history, and eloquence. Those were the three liberal arts that Pier Paolo Vergerio had isolated as essential in preparing one for public service. Like Cicero, Florentine humanists prized the arts that made one useful to the state (cf. *Rep.* I.20.33).

Antonio Pacini described the humanities in a more generic way in his eulogy for Cosimo's brother, Lorenzo. He noted that Lorenzo decided late in life to acquire training in the arts of speaking and living well. Though generic, Pacini's description epitomized the value humanists assigned their educational program. It would revive the best aspects of Roman instruction by producing "good persons skilled in public speaking."[40] To achieve that goal, Florentine orators urged students to select an ethical teacher, one like Luigi Marsigli or Manuel Chrysoloras or Carlo Marsuppini who exemplified the excellence of character he advocated.[41] Humanists evaluated education and scholarship in terms of its ability to promote life's crucial art, that of "good and holy living" (Cicero *Off.* I.6.19).

How Florentine, then, was the humanism of Alberti's dog? He probably spent too much time on Tuscan at the expense of Latin and especially Greek. His decision to spurn arms and concentrate on letters set a noble precedent that Florentine humanists followed shortly thereafter. They abandoned an ideological stance that had made them propagandists for wars, which embroiled Italy in conflict for half a century. The little pet did well to go and study with Alberti, who offered a style of learning that shaped the conduct of his life. He rightly placed his learning at the service of the commonwealth, avoiding scholarship for its own sake. Florentine humanists shared with Alberti's dog the conviction that society would improve were its important citizens (*principes*) to live the ideals they publicly professed. They all sought to reform people's lives by exploiting the persuasional power of ethos and the rhetoric of praise and censure. Like most orators, Alberti's dog in the end chose a cautious, Roman path to immortality.

THE ORATIONS

Florence

ca. 1403–4   Leonardo Bruni's Panegyric of Florence
"Laudatio Florentinae urbis," ed. Hans Baron in *From Petrarch to Leonardo Bruni: Studies in Humanistic and Political Literature* (Chicago and London: University of Chicago Press, 1968), 232–63.
1420   Anonymous on Baldassare Cossa
"Sermo factus in exsequiis . . . Balthasaris Cossae cardinalis

Florentini . . . ," Milan, Bibl. Ambrosiana, MS P 259 sup., fols. 53–56.

1428 Leonardo Bruni on Nanni Strozzi
"Oratio in funere Ioannis Strozzae," in E. Baluze, . . . *Miscellanea novo ordine digesta et aucta*, ed. G. D. Mansi (Lucca: V. Junctinius, 1761–64), 4:2–7.

1437 Poggio Bracciolini on Niccolò Niccoli
"Oratio in funere Nicolai Nicoli civis Florentini," *Opera omnia*, ed. R. Fubini, 4 vols. (I = Basel, 1538; rpt. Turin: Bottega d'Erasmo, 1964–66), 1:270–77. The speech was written at Bologna and sent to Florence.

1439 Jean Jouffroy on King Albert of Habsburg
". . . oratio funebris pro Alberto rege Romanorum . . . Florentiae in generali concilio habita," Fulda, Landesbibliothek, MS C 10, fols. 51–55, Paul Oskar Kristeller, *Iter Italicum*, 3 vols. (Leiden: Brill, 1965–), 3:537–38. I have not seen the manuscript.

1440 Poggio Bracciolini on Lorenzo di Giovanni de' Medici
"Oratio . . . in funere Laurentii de Medicis," *Opera omnia*, 1: 278–86. The oration is in the form of a letter to Carlo Marsuppini.

1440 Antonio Pacini on Lorenzo di Giovanni de' Medici
"Oratio in funere Laurentii de Medicis senioris," Florence, Bibl. Riccardiana, MS 928, fols. 2–14v.

1444 Anonymous on Leonardo Bruni
"Laudatio Leonardi historici et oratoris," in Emilio Santini, "Leonardo Bruni Aretino e i suoi *Historiarum Florentini populi libri XII*," *Annali della R. Scuola normale superiore di Pisa*, 22/4 (1910): 149–55.

1444 Giannozzo Manetti on Leonardo Bruni
"Oratio funebris in solemni Leonardi [Arretini] historici, oratoris, ac poetae laureatione," in *Leonardi Bruni Arretini epistolarum libri VIII*, ed. L. Mehus (Florence: Paperinius, 1741), 89–114.

1444 Poggio Bracciolini on Leonardo Bruni
"Oratio funebris in obitu Leonardi Arretini," in *Leonardi Bruni Arretini epistolarum libri VIII*, ed. L. Mehus (Florence: Paperinius, 1741), 115–26. This published redaction of the speech indicates that Poggio was writing the *History of Florence* and probably represents a final revision made after 1453.

1445 Girolamo Aliotti on Bartolomeo Zabarella
"In funere . . . Bartholomaei Zabarellae archiepiscopi Florentini oratio," *Epistolae et opuscula*, ed. G. M. Scarmalius, 2 vols. (Arezzo: M. Bellottus, 1769), 2:311–16.

1453 Matteo Palmieri on Carlo Marsuppini
"Dicta in coronatione Caroli Aretini poetae cancellarii Florentini . . . ," Florence, Bibl. Riccardiana, MS 660, fols. 69–70.

1455/1456   Benedetto Colucci on Antonio Partini
". . . funebris oratio in mortem Antonii Partini," in L. Manicardi, "Di una *oratio funebris* inedita di Benedetto Colucci," *Bullettino storico pistoiese*, 15 (1913): 67–74 (fragment).

1456   Anonymous (Donato Acciaiuoli?) on Ioannes Hunyadi
"Oratio funebris acta in funere . . . Ioannis Vaivodae," Florence, Bibl. Nazionale, MS Magl. IX.123, fols. 83–86.

1456   Giannozzo Manetti on Giannozzo Pandolfini
". . . funebris oratio in funere . . . Iannotii Pandolfini equitis Florentini," Florence, Bibl. Riccardiana, MS 3903, fols. 1–20v. The speech was written at Naples and sent to Florence.

1463   Andrea Alamanno on Giovanni di Cosimo de' Medici
"Oratio in funere Ioannis Medicis Cosmi filii . . . ," Florence, Bibl. Laurenziana, MS Plut. LIV.10, fols. 86–89.

1465   Donato Acciaiuoli on Cosimo de' Medici
". . . oratio habita quando Cosmus Medices . . . factus fuit PATER PATRIAE," in Angelo Fabroni, *Magni Cosmi Medicei vita*, 2 vols. (Pisa: A. Landi, 1789), 2:260–62.

1475   Alamanno Rinuccini on Matteo Palmieri
"In funere Matthei Palmerii oratio . . . ," in *Lettere ed orazioni*, ed. V. R. Giustiniani, Nuova collezione di testi umanistici inediti o rari 9 (Florence: L. Olschki, 1953), 78–85.

1478   Cristoforo Landino on Donato Acciaiuoli
"In funere Donati Acciaroli oratio incipit," BAV, MS Vat. lat. 13679, fols. 11–18. Landino's Italian translation of the oration was published by Francesco Sansovino, *Delle orazioni volgarmente scritte da diversi uomini illustri*, 2 vols. (Lyon: G. and V. Lanais, 1741), 1:286–94.

1513   Marcello Adriani? on Cosimo de' Pazzi
"Orazione funerale in morte di . . . [Cosimo] de' Pazzi arcivescovo di Firenze," Modena, Bibl. Estense, MS Gamma I.1, 48, [fols. 1–3 (frag.)]. The text is in Latin.

1516   Marcello Adriani on Giuliano de' Medici, duke of Nemours
"Oratio . . . habita in funere . . . Iuliani de Medicis . . . ducis Nemursiae," Florence, Bibl. Riccardiana, MS 811, fols. 71–78.

1519   Francesco Cattani on Lorenzo de' Medici, duke of Urbino
". . . oratio in funere Laurentii Medicis Urbini principis," Florence, Bibl. Nazionale, MS Naz. II. IV.34, fols. 326–67.

1519   Stefano Sterponi on Lorenzo de' Medici, duke of Urbino
". . . oratio funebris in parentalia Laurentii Medicis Urbini ducis . . . ," Florence, Bibl. Riccardiana, MS 911, fols. 12–19v.

1523–1534   Stefano Sterponi on Alessandro Pucci
". . . oratio funebris in parentalia Alexandri Pucii equitis aurati . . . ," Florence, Bibl. Riccardiana, MS 911, fols. 20–26.

Pistoia

1473   Antonio da Montecatini on Niccolò Forteguerri
       "Oratio habita . . . in funere . . . cardinalis Theanensis . . . ,"
       Florence, Bibl. Nazionale, MS Magl. VII.1095, fols. 140–42v.

Rome

1516   Battista Casali on Giuliano de' Medici, duke of Nemours
       "In funere Iuliani Medicis," Milan, Bibl. Ambrosiana, MS G 33
       inf., II, fols. 62v–68v.

Viterbo

1405   Leonardo Bruni on Otto Cavalcanti
       "Laudatio in funere Othonis," in Emilio Santini, "Leonardo Bruni
       Aretino e i suoi *Historiarum Florentini populi libri XII*," *Annali*
       della R. Scuola normale superiore di Pisa, 22/4 (1910): 142–45.

The Art of Dying Well and
Popular Piety in the Preaching and Thought
of Girolamo Savonarola

▼

Donald Weinstein

In his famous 1957 book, *The Sense of Death and the Love of Life in the Renaissance*, Alberto Tenenti showed how death became an important theme of religious reflection in the late fourteenth century and a pervasive form of popular devotion in the fifteenth-century. Contemporaries as distant from each other geographically and culturally as Francesco Petrarca and Heinrich Suso contributed to the new sensibility with their meditations upon death as a reflection of concern for life. The general European malaise brought on by plague, economic disaster, and endemic warfare made life seem more precious as it became more precarious, with both moralists and contemplatives studying how to make the best of the brief span of earthly existence.[1] For both Petrarca and Suso meditation upon death was the beginning of wisdom about life, but where the successors of the humanist used this insight to promote their cult of fame through moral and intellectual excellence, the heritage of the German mystic was that famous devotional doctrine, the art of dying well. *Ars moriendi* treatises in Latin and the vernaculars multiplied in the fifteenth century, and preachers and artists took it for their subject matter. Savonarola preached his great sermon on the theme on November 2, 1496, All Souls' Day. As *Predica dell'arte del ben morire,* it was printed at least three times before he died in 1498, with woodcut illustrations of unusual power (see figure 1).[2]

Because the *Predica* deals with some of the fundamental themes of the Christian life as well as death, I will use it as my main text in ex-

Figure 1

amining Savonarola's ideas about popular religion. Whether it is meaningful to describe as "popular" the religious beliefs and practices of the multitudes who crowded into the Dominican church of San Marco and filled the vast hall of the Florentine cathedral of Santa Maria del Fiore to hear Savonarola preach is part of a much larger, much debated problem. They were a heterogeneous audience, men and women of all ranks and conditions, although assuredly most of them were lay people of modest station and education. Did such people hold religious beliefs and engage in pious practices that were significantly distinguishable from those taught, authorized, or sanctioned by the magisterium of the church? Were there two religious levels, one elite, intellectual, and clerical, the other popular, credulous, and lay? The "two-tiered model," which projects a horizontal fault line right through the medieval Christian community, a model which has informed so much of the recent work on the social history of medieval religion, has come in for some justifiable criticism.[3] Exaggerating the credulity and disaffection of the masses on one hand and the rationalism and intellectualism of the elites on the other, it ignores a considerable amount of evidence of a shared religious culture.[4] The two-tiered model tends to assume that all religious innovation comes from above, while the primordial religion of "the people" remains fixed and passive.[5] Besides, its categories of elite and popular are imprecise. The new paradigm of medieval religion is not yet visible, at least not to me, but it will have to be multidimensional and dynamic, rather than dualistic and static, pluralistic rather than hierarchical. It will also have to incorporate what medieval people themselves thought about the matter.

My aim here is to consider this last facet of the problem, namely, what one particular religious specialist of the late fifteenth century thought about popular religion. What were Savonarola's expectations regarding the religious capacities of the *donnicciole, idioti, mercatanti, secolari, caldi, and tiepidi* (all his words) whom he looked down upon from his pulpit? How did these expectations influence the sermon that he preached? I will try, also, to say something about another question, one that admits of no simple answer, and that is: were the preacher's expectations adequate to the needs of his audience?

The sermon on the art of dying is a particularly good text for examining how Savonarola dealt with the problems of preaching to the people. In preparing it he borrowed heavily from the existing *ars moriendi* literature, particularly from Gerson and an anonymous fifteenth-century treatise then attributed to the Roman curialist Domenico Capranica, as well as from Suso.[6] In other words, in the sermon we have an excellent case of dissemination and adaptation from a clerical community to a wider reading public to a still broader oral community, some of whose members were illiterate according to Savonarola's own estimation.[7] Moreover, in Savonarola we have a case of a preacher—a spectacularly effective preacher—who, notwithstanding the heavy demands of almost daily sermons and religious and political mentoring, also wrote moral formal theological works and devotional treatises for clerics and Latin-reading laypeople. We will see what differences there may be between these two kinds of material.

First I will analyze the sermon on the art of dying, considering its doctrinal features as well as its principal images and examples. Savonarola begins by noting a human dilemma: we know we are going to die, but we don't want to think about it.[8] He explains this as a case of the natural appetite following an erroneous cognition (the only scholastic terminology in the entire sermon, it should be noted), and he illustrates it with a lurid analogy: just as the sight of a beautiful woman turns a man's thoughts and fixes all his desires on her, so our love of life draws us and blocks the thought of what is opposed to life, namely death. Unlike the ancient philosophers, Christians know that God has prepared a life beyond this world and that he rewards us with heaven or hell according to our just deserts. We will be blessed if, imitating the saints, we keep death constantly in mind, but this is easier for the humble, the simple little woman or peasant whose demands are modest than for the merchant or great prince or prelate.

By thinking about death we come to realize that it pays us to live a good life (or, as Savonarola usually put it in this sermon, to avoid sin). Since we sin either from ignorance or from failure to consider the implications of our actions, we must pray that God will enlighten our understanding so that it can properly guide our will. But there is a complication: while our success in avoiding sin will determine whether or not we will be saved, we cannot know if we have made ourselves worthy of God's love, and without it we go straight (*subito*) to hell. Life is a game of chess with the Devil who is constantly trying to catch us unprepared and deliver checkmate at the moment of our death.

In this dangerous game it should be the strategy of Christians to keep the thought of inevitable mortality ever in mind, to do everything we can to order our lives so that we will be in God's grace when death comes—in other words, to keep uncertainty at the minimum. Thus, the art of dying well is primarily an art of Christian living, and it is to those who still have life and health, who are reluctant to think of dying, that Savonarola directs his sermon. Those who fall sick with what they think is a passing illness have a little less need to be reminded of death, he says; those who are dying and know it have still less.

Fra Girolamo advises everyone to have three pictures in their houses where they can see them constantly.[9] The first, to be hung in their private chambers, (la camera tua) should show Heaven above and Hell below (see figure 2). We should look at it often, thinking that we could die this very day and imagining Death calling upon us to make our choice, whether to go to Paradise or to the Inferno. Such has been the practice of all holy men and women, and we should do likewise. Two things govern all our actions, love and fear. If we love eternal life, we will make every effort to achieve it, and we will refrain from sin. If we fear Hell, we will do the same, reminding ourselves that all the pleasures that tempt us are ephemeral and not worth the loss of Paradise. We need to pray God to illuminate us with this understanding, so that we do not sin, either from ignorance or inadvertence.

To help Christians avoid sin by distinguishing between temporal and eternal goods, Savonarola introduces his image of occhiali di morte, eyeglasses of death. By looking at life through these spiritual spectacles, Christians will see that death colors everything they want in the world, and they will ask themselves whether these worldly things are worth the risk of losing Paradise and earning hellfire. So when men enter the chambers of their [civic] councils, their eyeglasses of death will remind them to speak the truth in the business they conduct there. Those who heap up property and riches and make dishonest contracts will see with the help of their spectacles that they will have to settle their accounts in Hell. Should a woman take a notion to pamper her body and run after pleasure, let her put on her occhiali

Figure 2

di morte; she will not want her pleasures to lead her to damnation. Likewise, boys aroused by temptation, with the help of their death spectacles, will give themselves instead to Christ's service in body and mind. Even priests and the religious may find the *occhiali di morte* proof against every temptation.

Just as real eyeglasses need a clasp to keep them from falling, so our imaginary glasses need something tangible (*sensibile*) to fix them in place. To fix death with concrete images we should make it a habit to visit friends and relatives who are dying, to observe them as they die, to see them buried, and visit their graves. People who are especially weak in the face of temptation should have a picture of death in their house and carry about with them a small token of death (*morticina d'osso*) to look at. These constant reminders will make us wish to die well, and we will find some good counselor who will urge us to make our confession immediately and order our affairs so that we will always be ready if death takes us unawares.

From this advice for the healthy, Savonarola turns to counsel those who fall ill. The second of the three paintings is for them: a man lies on his sickbed while Death knocks at the door (see figure 3). This is the Devil's cue. Neither the Devil nor the invalid knows whether this is the final illness, but the Devil misses no chance, using every trick to divert the invalid from thinking about Death and leading him to perdition through inadvertence. When you fall sick, the Devil will send you thoughts about your house, your shop (*bottega*), your farms (*poderi*), and about politics (*di Stato*) and cause you to persuade yourself that you will do this or that as soon as this touch of fever passes. Against these diabolical tricks your remedy is to gaze at the crucifix and recite Psalm 37 "Rebuke me not, o Lord, in thy indignation, nor chastise me in thy wrath."[10]

When the Devil sees that he cannot persuade you to take your illness lightly, he will try to get at you through other people. Your wife and relatives or your doctor will reassure you that you will recover; then he will try to persuade you that you are not ready to confess until you have examined your conscience; you will do it tomorrow. If this does not work, the Devil will round up your peasants and shop foremen, and they will present you with a thousand business details and a thousand obstacles to delay you from confessing. Then you must concentrate hard and remind yourself that confession is the most important business you have. When the Evil One sees you at

Figure 3

your confession, he will try to distract you by setting your wife and children on you, first, to nag you about your property and to tell you stories to cheer you up. At such a time everyone needs a spiritual helper. Choose some pious man or woman, priest or layperson, who will stay at your bedside and keep reminding you that your illness may be fatal and that you had better confess and settle your accounts with God.

Finally, Savonarola turns to consider the state of those who, having put off confession, are at the point of death and ready at last to do penance. His third picture shows the dying man surrounded by family, friends, confessor, and demons (see figure 4). Death, a skeleton with a scythe, sits at the foot of the bed. Angels and the Madonna and Child appear over head. Unhappily, such a person has little hope of salvation. In life we are free to turn to God, and he will help us. But if we wait until we are on our deathbed, our hearts will be so hardened as to be almost beyond change, and if we die in that state, God will no longer intervene. Besides, the soul is in terrible pain as it leaves the body, and this distracts us from thinking about our sins. Even if we do think about them on our deathbed, it will be only from fear of Hell, an inadequate emotion for true conversion for which, according to St. Augustine, we also need love.[11]

As if this were not trouble enough, enter our family again, jostling one another to tell us that we are not really dying—because the sick should not be frightened!—joking, pressing our hand and asking if we know them, and chortling, "He recognizes me!" and saying anything but what they should say for our salvation. And again comes the Devil, this time to bring us to despair. By enumerating our sins of sense and mind (speaking evil, staring at indecent sights, listening to idle and wicked talk, hunting for exquisite tastes and scents) the Evil One convinces us to give up all hope of forgiveness and finally to doubt our very faith by telling us that the soul dies with the body. Savonarola makes no effort to meet this final diabolical thrust with counter arguments for the immortality of the soul; instead, he advises the dying to have someone about them to recite the Credo repeatedly, as friars do, and to have great faith in the goodness of him who was crucified for their sins, to be contrite, confess, and take communion. He concludes the sermon with two exempla from the *Dialogues* of Gregory the Great. One shows that we should not wait until we are

Figure 4

on our deathbeds to prepare ourselves. The other demonstrates that the prayers of the community may save even a hardened sinner from the clutches of the Devil.

This synopsis conveys only faintly the color of Savonarola's sermon on dying and does little justice to his preaching genius. His language could be vivid, as in the image of lusting after a beautiful woman, dramatic, as in the representation of life as a chess game with the Devil,[12] and original, as in his metaphor of looking at life through the eyeglasses of death.[13] He achieved intimacy with his listeners by pretending to engage in direct dialogue with them and even addressed God directly, although he reserved all the spoken parts for himself. Following good mendicant tradition, he employed homely images with which his audience could identify. References to shops, farms, tenants, and stewards and his shrewd description of the grieving and scheming family in the sickroom suggest that Savonarola observed his world closely and used his experience to plumb the *borghese* conscience with such commercial metaphors as the keeping of moral accounts in the afterlife. We know of one famous deathbed scene Savonarola himself attended. Four years earlier he had visited the dying Lorenzo de' Medici. Savonarola exhorted him to have faith and, should Lorenzo survive, to live a virtuous life; if not, to accept his death with resignation. Lorenzo asked for Fra Girolamo's blessing and received it. Perhaps there is something in this sermon that was inspired by the elaborate Medici death scene as described by Angelo Poliziano, with its goings and comings of doctors and family and the conversations with grieving friends, although he could have found little to criticize in Lorenzo's deathbed gravity and readiness to confess.[14] While most of Savonarola's references could have been inspired by observations of life in any fifteenth-century Italian city (for example, amidst his own family in Ferrara), some of them, such as the moral problems of a citizen attending Council meetings who thinks about politics even on his deathbed, speak directly to the intensely political Florentines.

The content of Savonarola's religious message was as carefully tuned to his sermon audience as were his rhetoric and language. I will try to show this by comparing some of the ideas of the sermon on dying with those of his theological and devotional writings. Not that the preacher and the theologian were strangers to each other. In the treatises he is preoccupied with many of the same concerns as in the sermon, repentence, for example, and displays similar attitudes, such as a rejection of philosophy and worldly science. But in his treatment of such major themes as faith, grace, and the Christian life, there are certain revealing differences.

In the sermon Savonarola has little to say about faith. Faith is mainly taken for granted: it is that belief in God's redemptive plan which leads us to worship him and to try to live the good life so that we may be worthy of his love and grace. By contrast, in the *Triumphus Crucis* his most ambitious doctrinal work, faith has an active role and a spiritually creative effect: it is not only cognitive but regenerative. As he put it: "the principal cause of the good Christian life is faith in Jesus Christ crucified, formed by love; that is, it works (*operatur*) by love, or, as Scripture puts it: the justice of God is through faith in Jesus Christ *in* all and *over* all who believe in him, and without faith it is impossible to please God."[15]

This is, of course, a paraphrase of St. Paul's Letter to the Romans 1:17, the very text that would be the cornerstone of Luther's reformation just twenty years later. The similarity with Luther is even more striking in several passages where Savonarola writes that faith is the gift of God's grace. I don't propose to debate here whether Savonarola was a forerunner of evangelical doctrine,[16] only to point out that in writing for what he must have perceived as a more sophisticated, Latin-reading public, Savonarola put forth an active, regenerative view of faith that fits awkwardly with the moralistic piety and cognitive notion of faith in the sermon.

In the sermon, as we have seen, Savonarola has a great deal to say about right conduct, or *ben fare*, but he deals with the problem of the moral life largely in negative terms—Christians should strive to avoid sin. He enumerates the sins repeatedly: pride, lust, untruthfulness, greed, and the pursuit of other sensual and material pleasures—(the Seven Deadly sins and a few others). This is, however, a routine list wherein, as is the case with faith, Christian virtue remains largely undefined and taken for granted; presumably it is the state we achieve when we refrain from those sins. While he refers to *carità* as the foundation of the Christian life, this is undeveloped and overshadowed by the sermon's commonplace moralism.

In his theological and devotional writings, however, the Augustinian side of Savonarola's piety takes over. Love, not the avoidance of sin and not the fear of death, is the inspiration of the good Christian life. Here is a typical passage from the *Triumphus Crucis:* "the Christian life consists entirely of this, that once having freed itself from everything created, mental as well as physical, it turns through contemplation and love entirely to God and becomes one with God in spirit."[17] Similarly, while in the sermon conversion is the abandonment of one's sinful ways, in Savonarola's meditation on Psalm 50 to convert is to exchange the wisdom of the world for God's true wisdom.[18] And while in the sermon the act of meditation leads the Christian to dwell on death and the need to be in God's grace, in his writings meditation and contemplation receive a far richer treatment. For example, in his *Expositio orationis Dominicae* Savonarola writes that the principal effort of the Christian life ought to be to worship God through interior means: "to read, to pray, to meditate and to contemplate: for these pertain to the intellect and awaken faith, hope, and charity, devotion, and all the other affections that perfect humans in the knowledge and love of God."[19]

Such is the Christian piety—call it spiritual, Pauline, Augustinian, caritative, or contemplative, it is all these—that informs Savonarola's written discourse. These themes of the inner religious life appear only fitfully and weakly in his preaching, at least in this sermon, where his emphasis is on avoiding sin, earning merit, and taking confession. What accounts for the differences? Undoubtedly, a sermon on dying would emphasize penitence and confession, but since the sermon is at least as much about living as about dying, this explanation will not take us very far. We will do better to return to our original question: what did Savonarola think about popular religion? The answer to this question mainly turns on the difference between the life of the clergy and the life of the laity which he equates with the difference between the active life in the world and the contemplative life of prayer and meditation. Talking to a congregation of cloistered women, Savonarola said that while he could give *them* the solid food of contemplation and spirituality, lay people, (*secolari*) like children, need milk to fill and nourish them.[20] St. Paul's Letter to the Hebrews 5:12–14 is the source of this image, but where Paul was differentiating between those who were strong and those who were weak in the faith, Savonarola was making a distinction between clerics, who were capable of an interiorizing piety, and laity, who needed something more elementary. He explains this further in his treatise on mental prayer, writing that true cult, which is interior, had been established in the primitive church for all Christians. Ceremonies had come to be adopted as a concession to the decline of religious ardor (*fervore*), a medicine for weak minds. Through ceremonies people may in some way come to love divine things, but nowadays with the total absence of piety they are not very helpful. Laypeople are so involved with worldly matters, so blocked by avarice and ambition, that they have great difficulty in turning from outward ceremony to raise their minds to God. Yet, he goes on to say, meditation is not only for monks and the religious, but for everyone.[21] The *vita attiva* cannot be separated entirely from the *vita contemplativa*. Rightly used, ceremony and vocal prayer can lead laypeople inward to true prayer and to God.

There is in these passages more than a little of the clerical ascetic's traditional misgivings, if not contempt, toward the lay condition. For Savonarola worldly materialism was the greatest obstacle to the religious life, far greater than ignorance or stupidity or the fragilities of the weaker sex. Indeed, these, being the disabilities of the simple and humble, could even be turned into assets, since they were protections against ambition for power, riches, and knowledge.

And yet, laypeople of every condition were redeemable; that was the premise of the friar's whole career as a preacher, prophet, and reformer. Savonarola gave his considered view of his religious mission—and of his preaching strategy—in one of the very last things he wrote, the Latin meditation on Psalm 50, as follows:

> Of course there are different roads as there are different kinds of lives: clerics follow one route, monks another, mendicants still another; married people take one route, worthy and continent widows another, and maidens yet another; princes follow their way, professors theirs, merchants theirs; each status follows its own route to the heavenly homeland. I will teach the wicked your [God's] way, according to their various conditions and their capacities; and the impious will convert to you because I will preach to them not myself but Christ crucified.[22]

This conception of the preacher's task must have guided Fra Girolamo as he labored over his sermon on the art of dying for that Day of All Souls, 1496. Preaching to the impious and wicked of every condition and capacity required a different strategy than what was appropriate in preaching to religious sisters or writing for a Latin-reading, and presumably already safely converted, public. For the ordinary laypeople who made up the bulk of his congregations the Christian message had to be radically simplified and externalized, with the emphasis upon the fear of punishment, avoidance of sin, frequent resort to the sacraments, especially Penance, and to pictures, crucifixes, and death's heads. Yet, the message was the same, however simplified: salvation through faith in Christ crucified, love, repentence, prayer, and reform of life. Savonarola's own model of religion was two-tiered only in the sense that it drew a horizontal line between clergy and laity. A more accurate description of his model would be an ascending but continuous pathway that starts out amid the hum of vocal prayer and the flash of ceremony, in full view of the external world, and gradually becomes silent and invisible as it moves into the realm of contemplation and the spirit. So, if it seems that in his writings Savonarola takes up the problems of faith, grace, love, and contemplative prayer at the point where the sermon on dying leaves off, that is exactly the case. Savonarola the preacher catches the attention of sinners by means of threats of hellfire and such vivid imagery as the Devil's chessgame, and gives them a simple formula for avoiding sin, and from there Savonarola the writer takes over to pursue a more subtle and demanding, but ultimately more fulfilling, message of love and faith.

How well Savonarola's congregation was served by this somewhat condescending view of lay interests and capacities remains as much a question for us as it seems to have been for him. Having brought his *secolari, indotti,* and *illiterati* in through the wide gate of fear, moralism, and "externals," was he ready to lead them on the ascent into true spirituality? Even if for Savonarola the answer is yes, the more important question is whether mendicant preachers in general, trained as they were to preach the formulaic piety represented by this sermon on the art of dying, did not underestimate the religious capacities and misunderstand the spiritual needs of some of the laypeople in their charge. The following case, involving Florentines at least tangentially connected with Savonarola, may illustrate my point.

In 1513 two well-born Florentines, Pietro Paolo Boscoli and Agostino Capponi, were condemned to death for conspiring to kill three members of the Medici family. The Medici had recently returned to power, ending the republican interlude that had opened in 1494 under Savonarola's guidance. We have a minute account of the thirty-four-year-old Boscoli's spiritual struggle during the night before his death. It was written by his friend the humanist Luca della Robbia (not the artist of the same name), who was at his side during the ordeal.[23] Luca's meticulous and self-revealing chronicle of these final hours, painful for him as well as for Boscoli, may be read as a pathetic, and ultimately ironic, commentary on Savonarola's death sermon, for it demonstrates the inadequacy of the sermon's conventional piety when applied to the religious agonies of one worldly but sophisticated Florentine layman.

The scene as Luca described it might have provided another illustration for Savonarola's printed sermon. Also, Savonarola's preparation for his own execution in 1498 was much on the minds of Boscoli and Luca della Robbia.[24] Boscoli chose Luca as his spiritual counselor and was concerned to find a confessor "dotto e buono" from San Marco. His first choice was the Savonarolan Zanobi Acciaiuoli, but Fra Zanobi being unavailable, he finally accepted another Savonarolan, Fra Cipriano da Pontassieve, prior of San Domenico in Fiesole. No members of the families of the condemned were admitted, but there were several others in attendance, including members of the Confraternity of the Tempio, whose office it was to recite prayers and to hold up the Tavoluccia, the devotional image which they offered to condemned criminals to look at and to kiss.[25]

While the setting was reminiscent of Savonarola's death scenes, the script diverged in some critical places, for none of the consolations or assurances of friend, confessor, or confraternity brothers spoke to Boscoli's need. Boscoli was contrite, he confessed, and fervently recited the Credo; the brothers of the Tempio repeated their Paternosters; Luca and Fra Cipriano helped him to stop comparing himself to Brutus and to prepare to die as a Christian, but while his intellect accepted God's will and assented to his impending death, his feeling would not be moved: however much he desired it, he did not feel the "dolce affetto" for Christ's humanity that conscience told him he should have in order to die in peace.

Neither Luca nor Fra Cipriano could understand this; they insisted that such feeling might be desirable, but it was not required for salvation. As Luca put it, the desire is enough; the sweetness is not essential. Misunderstanding Boscoli to mean that he wanted to perceive Christ with his senses, Luca warned that this was not possible in this life, and that Boscoli's desire might come from the Devil. When Boscoli disclosed his fears to Fra Cipriano, his confessor replied that he might induce the intense feeling he missed by repeating Psalm 69, but in any case it was enough that Boscoli accepted his death knowing that his sins merited it.

Dawn came and the two conspirators were brought down the passageway to the place of execution, Boscoli accompanied by his friend reciting from the Psalms. As he climbed the stairs of the scaffold to the block, he confessed that he still felt some *combattimento,* and he asked the executioner to give him another moment because the union with God that he had been seeking all night still eluded him. It was granted, but whether Boscoli found the "dolce affetto" before he died is unclear.

Some weeks later, Luca della Robbia encountered Fra Cipriano, and the two talked about the good death that Boscoli had made. The friar was confident that Boscoli was among the blessed and not in Purgatory, for he had never seen such intelligence in confession and such strength of purpose. Fra Cipriano even suggested that they may have been wrong to discourage Boscoli from comparing himself to Brutus, for St. Thomas had said that conspiracies against tyrants who ruled by force were meritorious; thus Boscoli was right in thinking that he died a martyr. (And, added Luca, I confirmed this later in the *Summa Theologica* and *De regimine principum.*) But of Boscoli's last spiritual agony, they spoke not a word.[26]

A Renaissance Artist in the Service
of a
Singing Confraternity

▼

Cyrilla Barr

Renaissance exempla abound in illustrations of the close interaction of religious and secular values. Private domestic patronage of art and music in fifteenth-century Florence is no exception. With the entry of the working class into the arena of the consumer-collector-patron, the social level and economic resources of the purchaser-patron begin to be reflected in the quality of the art and music produced, resulting in what has been described in suitably condescending language as "a pervasive mediocrity of taste" which alone could account for "workshop productivity" in art.[1] In music the phenomenon is characterized by the emergence of the amateur musician, the cobbler, weaver, tanner by trade whose modest musical talents earned for him a small stipend in return for singing the services of lay religious companies of *laudesi*.[2] This study looks at the phenomenon through the specific example of a painter designated by art historians as a lesser artist of the workshop tradition and a prominent singing confraternity in Florence's *Oltrarno*: the artist Neri di Bicci (1419–91) and the singing confraternity the Compagnia di Santa Maria delle laude in Santa Maria del Carmine, hereinafter identified by its more popular title the Compagnia di Sant'Agnese (the Company of St. Agnes).[3]

This company is perhaps best known as the producer of the famed Ascension play that it presented annually throughout most of the fifteenth century and which is well chronicled in the extensive *filze* of the company deposited in the Archivio di Stato.[4]

An examination of the pattern of expenditures recorded in the account books of the company reflects a growing tendency away from the preoccupation with charity and poor relief in earlier times to a greater emphasis upon display and pageantry in the Quattrocento—a characteristic to be observed in other *laudesi* companies of Florence as well.[5] The very name *stendardo*, which later came to replace *laudesi*, denotes the more public orientation of company activities that emphasize the material trappings of their devotion as the standard is carried in procession.[6] The rood screen in the mendicant churches in particular might be said to be symptomatic of this change in the *laudesi*: once a barrier between clergy and congregation, it now became the stage for mounting the religious spectacle.[7]

Documents of the Company of St. Agnes reveal that as early as 1425 expenditures for the production amounted to more than 61 percent of the company's budget for the year.[8] The financial burden of representations later resulted in a succession of deficit budgets until 1467, when, after a series of subsidies from the Signoria, the budget balanced exactly.[9] This was due largely to the subvention of the city government, but it may also reflect at least in some degree the careful management of Neri di Bicci who assumed office as *sindaco* that year.

Neri's association with the company and its play is central to this investigation. His *bottega* (workshop) was located near the Carmine,[10] and evidence of his stewardship of the company is attested by the frequent recurrence of his distinguished handwriting in its financial records (see figure 1). As *sindaco* he brought a certain business acumen, undoubtedly learned as the manager of his own atelier, to the service of the Company of St. Agnes and by extension to the service of modern musicology as well. For since the repertoire of the *laudesi* was for the most part a popular and unwritten one, music historians are more and more recognizing the importance of exploring nonmusical documents, archival records such as these, in pursuit of information concerning performance practice.[11]

The same meticulous record keeping which characterized Neri's well-known *Ricordanze* (Workshop Records) may be observed in the confraternity accounts.[12] The *Ricordanze* reveal a good deal about the nature of supply and demand in the business of art as well as insights into Neri's personal style. Clearly, he was versatile and industrious, producing on commission such diverse items as devotional objects for the home, domestic interiors, altar frontals, covers for musical instru-

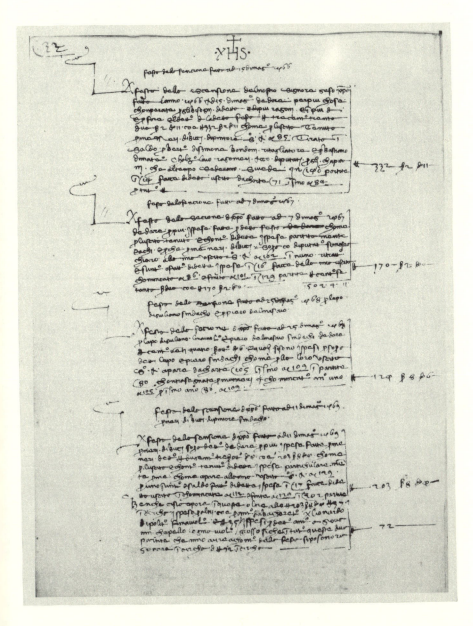

ments, and mandorlas for allegorical and religious spectacles. Although the *Ricordanze* cover only the period from 1435 to 1475, they record over 275 commissions. Bruno Santi, in his edition of the *Ricordanze,* alludes to the existence of some of Neri's records for the Company of St. Agnes, specifically an inventory, but he seems not to have examined the many other entries in Neri's easily recognizable hand which are scattered throughout several other documents.[13] While these do not reflect the activities of his workshop for the years omitted from the *Ricordanze,* they do reveal a significant amount of information relative to life within the company and the nature of its musical activities.

It is not known exactly when Neri joined the Company of St. Agnes. His father, Bicci di Lorenzo, had been one of the captains in 1448;[14] and the first mention of Neri occurs in 1454 when he is listed among the *capitani.*[15] The earliest example of his script in the surviving records is found in July 1466 when Neri was *sindaco* and *camarlingo* (chamberlain).[16] He was reelected the following January and immediately took up the task of compiling in his own hand a detailed inventory of "all the things found at this present day [January 17] belonging to the said Company [of St. Agnes] both in our place and outside our place."[17] The document is divided into twelve sections, all having descriptive titles, and it can best be examined by grouping the sections according to the kind of information contained in them.[18]

The eye of the artist accustomed to making measurements, distinguishing the quality of colors and decorative elements, and explaining the intricate mechanism of theatrical machines serves the researcher rewardingly with an abundance of detail which embellishes the general outlines of what has long been known of confraternal life from surviving statutes. It is significant that the first two categories of materials inventoried are concerned with affairs known to be of high priority to *laudesi* companies, the burial of their dead and the singing of *laude.*[19]

As early as 1281 the Commune had enacted sumptuary laws forbidding the use of excessively large candles or elaborate palls for funerals, but confraternities were exempt from these laws.[20] Indeed, one of the advantages of being a member of a lay religious company was the assurance of a larger and more elaborate funeral and the possibility of being laid to rest in the company's tomb inside a church where in

successive decades commemorative vigils and masses would be celebrated. There was an added incentive when that church was a mendicant church. The Company of St. Agnes was no exception; the primitive ordinances are replete with references to such suffrages as well as
to the company's tomb in the Carmine.[21]

The exempt status of this confraternity is clearly reflected in Neri's
enumeration of items needed for burial of the dead in part one of the
inventory. No funereal black is to be found here. Instead he describes
a pall of red fabric lined with red linen and adorned with the figure of
Christ and a taffeta drapery with a painting of the Ascension ornamented with red and gold tassles. A second pall of yellow and blue
striped taffeta seems to have been used at the home of the deceased
(in chasa). There were cushions of the same material filled with down
and decorated with tassles and an older pillow described as ispogliato
which was used beneath the head of the corpse.[22] In addition, there
is mention of large torches to carry in the procession accompanying
the corpse to the place of burial while appropriately mournful laude
were sung.[23]

The exact manner of performing laude has been a matter of speculation among musicologists for some time.[24] Although the items listed
in the second category of the inventory do not reflect upon the actual
performance, they do suggest much about the circumstances and the
material objects necessary. Foremost among the required accoutre-
ments is the lectern which seems to have been on wheels and had
attached to it a storage area with a lock and key, in which were kept
the candles and other necessary items.[25] It is apparent that sundry
ornaments could be attached to the top and sides of the lectern, thus
changing it from its simple, unadorned state for ferial days to a more
elaborate state appropriate for festive occasions—more ornate candle-
holders were attached and a carved wooden relief of the Virgin and
angels adorned the top.[26] Here, as well as in the description of the
books of laude themselves, some vestiges of liturgical influence are
perceivable in the semblance of ritual arrangement, a sense of classifi-
cation and hierarchy of feast days, and the changing of the color of
liturgical trappings. The cloths used to drape the lectern reflect the
occasion, ranging from black taffeta lined with white linen and edged
with gold fringe, used when laude were sung on the day of the death
of a fratello,[27] to cloth of changeable striped silk lined with linen and

emblazoned with painted figures of Our Lady and the ascending Christ, used on feast days.[28] On high festal occasions bookmarks of red and green silk, ending with crystal pendants and brass fastenings were used.[29]

Most importantly, the books of *laude* themselves (five in all) are described in detail with attention (not surprisingly) given to the fact that several were illuminated and contained musical notation.[30] The mention of music is valuable confirmation of what up to recently has been only speculation, namely that the Company of St. Agnes must have owned an illuminated *laudario*. Remnants of several such manuscripts of fourteenth-century Florentine origin have surfaced in various European and American libraries, and there is reason to believe that several of these fragments originated with the Company of St. Agnes.[31]

The last two books enumerated, the Gospel in rhyme and the Passion in rhyme,[32] are of particular interest and raise a question relative to several entries in the financial records notably one to Nicholò Mascalzoni, a tenor, for "singing this past Lent from the pulpit as is customary," and another to an unidentified singer "for helping him."[33] This could suggest either a kind of semidramatic rendition of the Passion or possibly the singing of Passiontide *laude* in church at a time when Latin was still the norm.

The records of penitent confraternities of *disciplinati* from the fifteenth century often describe the act of flagellation and the exact manner in which the singing of *laude* was incorporated into these private offices,[34] but contemporary records of *laudesi* companies tend to be more vague.[35] It is therefore illuminating to read the sections of Neri's inventory which deal specifically with the company's activities in its oratory and in church. It is known that the company did own an oratory as well as a chapel in one of the bays of the left aisle of the church.[36] It is obvious from the contents of part three of the inventory that the *luogo* referred to in the title was the locus of both administrative business and private devotion. Its contents include such essentials of accounting as desks, inkwells, locked chests, a table where the officers sat when collecting dues, a dish for the money, and a throne where the *capitani* sat when with the company.[37] To this throne was chained the book containing the rule and the company roster,[38] but there were devotional objects as well, such as an altarpiece—a triptych of Our Lady with four scenes from the life of John the Baptist—which was placed above the throne of the captains.[39]

The seventh part of the inventory, entitled "Furnishings and Equipment for the table which is prepared for our Company," contains almost exclusively things needed for administration. One entry in particular, however, deserves some consideration for its implications. The last item reads, "fourteen kneeling, painted wooden figures, that is, twelve apostles, Our Lady and Our Lord, which are placed on the table on Holy Thursday."[40] An entry in the accounts from the previous year reveals that a certain Albizo di Dino was paid for his work of "putting the apostles on the table."[41] Judging from his salary, which was more than twice that received by a *lauda* singer for an entire month, the arrangement of these curious kneeling figures must have been a considerable task. Were they possibly large statues which had to be toted up from the vault? And what was the significance of this assembly of apostles? Was it perhaps intended to replicate the *lavanda dei piedi* at the Last Supper, which we know was commemorated by another company active in the Carmine at this same time, the *disciplinati* of St. Nicholas of Bari.[42] Like much archival evidence, such entries often raise more questions than they answer.

Fortunately, parts four and six of the inventory offer somewhat more tangible signs of the company's outward comportment in the devotional exercises held in the chapel. Part four is given entirely to a description of the *stella*, a star-shaped object which was hoisted prominently in some part of the church. Various other *laudesi* companies of Florence owned such *stelle*, perhaps inspired by the well-known star used in the procession of the company of the Magi for whom it would have had obvious symbolism.[43] Its significance here is not entirely clear, but its function was to support various devotional items which were suspended from its rays and could be changed to be appropriate to the particular observance. Among the decorations, Neri enumerates richly painted angels, seraphim on one side, cherubim on the other, as well as little clouds with representations of Our Lord ascending and other symbols of the company.[44]

Part six speaks specifically of "our altar," the location of which is clarified beyond doubt by several references to objects needed for the celebration of mass—a bell used to announce the beginning, the offertory and the elevation of the host, and candles or torches to burn on the altar.[45] Here again Neri mentions a lectern for the *laude*, thus establishing that *laude* were by now being sung not only in the oratory and in outdoor processions, but also inside church—though there is no way of knowing if they were actually incorporated into the liturgy (as in San Zenobio at this time) or if they were limited to private and para-liturgical usage such as the numerous vigils kept by the company in its chapel.[46]

Parts five, eight, nine, and ten of the inventory all enumerate materials needed for the Ascension play and have been dealt with at least in part in an earlier study, which seeks to document the description of the play left by Abraham of Suzdal, the Russian bishop who saw it in 1439 while attending the Ecumenical Council in Florence.[47] Among the entries not addressed in that study are the references in part five which establish that somewhere in the church, "*mezza di chiesa*," there was a storage place referred to as the *volta*. Besides various small items such as costumes and properties consigned to this vault, it seems that entire units of the set were stored more or less intact. Item nine, for example, lists "one painted wooden castle" and item ten, "one mountain in the vault." It seems likely that this was a kind of scaffolding later covered with fabric, for item thirteen is "one piece of linen cloth used to make the mountain from which the angels of paradise ascend."[48] Although the dimensions which Abraham gives are undoubtedly eye measurements, his mention of the mountain as being "ten feet high at its apex" indicates that the storage vault was a sizable space—suggesting possible location in the undercroft.

One other item of particular interest mentioned in part eleven of the inventory is described as "a relief of a cloud with rays coming out of it . . . and in the middle is a lamb in relief holding two palm branches and a branch of lilies in the center, colored blue with rays of gold."[49] The description conforms to a payment registered that same year in Neri's hand "to Simone, an engraver and disciple of Donatello, for making a relief of a lamb and other things for the little cloud that is placed above the door."[50]

The sole remaining portion of the inventory is part twelve which contains a listing of the account books belonging to the company. These, without a doubt, are some of the records now in the archives upon which this study is based. One specifically mentioned as "Campione A" is bound with the inventory. In addition, folios one through sixty-six are largely in Neri's hand and contain among other things a summary of expenses for the Ascension feast for the years 1466 through 1469.[51]

In his capacity as syndic it was Neri's responsibility to transact business and maintain the company's records, a task which he diligently fulfilled not only when he was in office but at other times as well, as may be observed from the third entry in the above-mentioned summary of expenses, dated May 25, 1468, which specifically states that Lapo di Giuliano was *sindaco*, assisted by another artist whose name appears frequently in the company's records, Piero del Massaio.[52] Neri's bookkeeping skill must have been in demand, and not surprisingly, for the records that he has left are meticulous, itemized, numbered, clearly dated, and are frequently cross-referenced with other records.[53]

These, as well as later entries not in Neri's hand, document the company's tendency toward a more public manifestation of devotion in the form of religious plays which were invariably embellished with music, both vocal and instrumental. Coincident with this transformation is the change in the function of the *lauda* itself which now tended to lose its participatory value as a religious expression in which all might join and instead became a performance to be listened to or, in the case of the *rappresentazione*, to be watched as well. This tendency is reflected in the documents of some of the wealthier *laudesi* companies of Florence at least a century earlier when, for example, the companies of Orsanmichele, San Piero Martire, and San Zenobi were already hiring salaried singers to perform their functions.[54] Curiously the first records of employment of "professional" musicians for the *laudesi* in the Carmine are for instrumentalists to play for the feast of the Ascension in 1425, 1427, and 1428.[55] The earliest surviving record of payments to singers occurs nearly twenty years later in 1447; entries throughout the next decade are only intermittent and are usually for special occasions.[56]

Beginning with Neri's assumption of office, the records of payments to musicians tend to be more complete, and by the latter part of the century the deliberations of the *capitani* reveal that singers were systematically hired for six months at a time. Documents record both the statement of salary and identification of the singer, usually by name as well as trade. Debits confirm that they were generally paid at the end of that six-month period, and if services were satisfactory, the singer might expect to be, and generally was, reappointed. Instrumentalists seem to have been hired on an "ad hoc" basis for a particular occasion.

It becomes apparent in studying Neri's records that he must have applied the same entrepreneurial talents used in his workshop to the administration of the company, for the records reveal a distinctly businesslike approach to remuneration for services rendered. We find, for example, that in 1467 the barber, Guelfo di Bartolomeo, was hired as *laudieri* and had the added responsibility of coming to church between eleven and midnight to prepare the lectern and other things necessary for the vigil service. For this he was paid every two months, with the stipulation that "he shall have 5 *soldi* deducted from his salary every time he misses through his own fault or out of negligence."[57]

Somewhat later the salary of Giovambattista di Currado (who sang for many years for the company) was reduced for a reason expressed with incontrovertible logic, because "he is singing at Santa Croce, and he cannot be there and here at the same time."[58]

Not all were paid equally, and there is evidence that length of tenure and quality of performance were rewarded. A certain Giovanni di Francesco, identified as a linen weaver by trade, was consistently paid less than the other singers for what we may only conclude must have been the inferior quality of his performance, for later the *capitani* voted to raise his salary by two *soldi* because "he improved his voice and sang better."[59]

The absence of payments prior to about 1450 suggests that the company members were themselves still doing the singing. When paid singers were finally employed by the Company of St. Agnes, their salaries were less than half those received by the singers from Orsanmichele,[60] undoubtedly reflecting in part the strain on company finances caused by the elaborate Ascension plays. But coinciding with Neri's assumption of office and throughout the following years the expense accounts reflect more frequent use of paid singers, still, however, referred to by the general designation of *laudesi* or *laudieri*. The first entry to suggest a distinction in voice types, thus implying singing in harmony, is therefore significant and occurs on March 22, 1478, when a singer identified only as "uno amicho che teneva il tenore alle nostre laude" was paid for one month's services.[61] To "hold the tenor part against the *laude* (the melody)" certainly implies the creation of harmony or heterophony and must have been a successful experiment, for exactly two months later two singers were hired and identified as "nostri tinoristi."[62] The taste for harmonious rendition must have endured, for by the late 1480s the company was regularly employing an average of five singers simultaneously, with the balance generally being three singers designated as *laudieri*, that is singing the melody, and two as *tinori* or *tinoristi*, who would have sung the added part or harmony. Entries around the time of Neri's death in 1491 refer to sopranos, and it is almost certain that even earlier trebles had been singing with the company, for the *laudesi* of St. Agnes had a close association with at least two *fanciulli* companies, Sant'Alberto and San Giorgio.[63]

It seems noteworthy that the names of tenors recorded reflect that certain families are represented here repeatedly, three from the family dal Radda alone sometimes referred to as "nostro familia tinori."[64] It is possible that the knowledge of these added parts, which were never written down, was cultivated within a family and passed on to its male members. Such practice would not have been unprecedented, for it is known that in the commedia dell'arte, coeval with the *sacre rappresentazione*, a family might specialize in developing a repertoire of *lazzi*, *burle*, and improvised repartee of a particular character of the commedia, which then passed on from father to son so that a given family became identified, for example, as the family of Pantalone or Arlecchino.[65]

Evidence of instrumental participation in the performance of *laude* either for prayer services or for the Ascension play is much too sketchy to enable even reasonable speculation. A few entries of payments to pipers occur as early as 1425, but no more are to be found until Neri's records for the Ascension feast of 1467. Although he mentions specific names, it is not possible to ascertain how many players were employed at a given time since payments are usually designated for an individual "and companions."[66] One entry in particular suggests that the angel musicians described by Bishop Abraham may have been more than merely a *tableau vivant*. The disbursements for the play in 1467, which identify a certain Gualberto as "suonatori di suoni grosi del paradiso,"[67] bring to mind the Russian bishop's remark that God the Father high above in Paradise was surrounded by "a large number of children with flutes, lyres, and bells" and that these angels "moved around him while harmonious music and sweet song resound from afar."[68]

The absence of references to players between 1428 and 1467 might be accounted for by the loss of some documents, but there is a slim possibility that it may indicate that players were paid from some other source. That interval of time is roughly coincident with the period when the Ascension play was financed by the subsidy from the Signoria which was renewed three times at ten year intervals. This, as well as the fact that the spectacle was known to be a kind of showcase of Medici grandeur and civic propaganda, may suggest that the instrumentalists of the Signoria participated in some fashion.[69] Records of the Camera del Commune from this time reveal the employment of a substantial number of instrumentalists, *pifferi*, *tromboni*, *trombetti*, *nacherini*, and *cennemelle*, with a marked preference for German brass players.[70]

Neri di Bicci died at the beginning of the same decade that saw the expulsion of the Medici and the demise of Savonarola. The Ascension play did not cease to be presented during this last decade of the century, but it was not maintained with the same verve, perhaps now eclipsed by the burning of the vanities instigated by the Dominican ascetic. Although the Ascension spectacle declined, the singing of *laude* continued, and account books reflect payments entered with regularity throughout most of the remainder of the decade.[71] It is unlikely that Savonarola would have objected to these since he himself penned *lauda* verses, and *laude* were sung in the procession leading to the Piazza della Signoria preceding the famed bonfire of 1497.[72]

By 1493, however, the Company of St. Agnes found it necessary on occasion to hire singers from Orsanmichele,[73] and musical services were thereafter confined mainly to vigils, which reflect the growing number of testamentary obligations of the company resulting from one of its main sources of income, the bequests of money and property for which the testator in turn required a given number of prayer services with *lauda* singing and candles.[74]

By a special deliberation of the *capitani* the feast of the Ascension was observed with some solemnity in 1503, and the play was again refurbished in 1515.[75] But the halcyon days had passed, and the sad state of disrepair is reflected in the entry from 1515 which states that because these things were "ruined and in disorder" (*guasto e in disordine*), a certain Amadeo who had been appointed to renovate the set had to refashion it from a model which was based upon a painting in the Carmine.[76] Furthermore, the deliberations permitting the performances of 1503 and 1515 make it clear that money for the production could not be taken from the treasury of the company but had to be solicited by means of a forced loan from the members themselves.[77]

It is fortunate that the years of Neri's stewardship coincide with the period of most vigorous musical development and with the major renovations of the play, both of which he so scrupulously chronicled. There is a certain irony in the fact that of the hundreds of commissions fulfilled by him and noted in his *Ricordanze*, only a few surviving works are identified. Perhaps that is confirmation of the inferiority suggested by the deprecatory label, "workshop artist." But the voluminous records of the confraternity inscribed in his hand and beginning with that familiar introduction, "Io, Neri di Bicci di Lorenzo Bicci, dipintore," not only identify him as artist, devoted *fratello*, and capable administrator, but remind us that just as not all patrons of Quattrocento Florence were Medici or Pitti, so also not all artists were Leonardos. For Neri, living in fifteenth-century Florence must have been comparable to playing Salieri to the multiple Mozarts of his lifetime—a role which he nevertheless fulfilled with dedication, undoubtedly bringing satisfaction and pleasure to the many who go down in history unnamed and thereby witnessing that art and music in Quattrocento Florence were not the exclusive delectation of the wealthy.

APPENDIX A

THE INVENTARIO OF NERI DI BICCI, 1466–67

Part

1 Things needed for the burial of the dead
2 Furnishings and materials for the lectern for saying the *laude*
3 Things found at this time in our company, for services proper to our place
4 Material and equipment for the star which is placed in church many times a year for the feast
5 Materials in the vault in the middle of the church which are used for the feast
6 Materials and equipment for our altar

7 Furnishings and equipment for the table which is prepared for our company

8 Materials and equipment for use in the heaven and in the cloud when the feast of the Ascension is celebrated

9 Goods and furnishings used in the Paradise when the feast is observed

10 Goods found in the little vault under the company oratory needed for the feast and other things

11 Goods for the use of the company, for the feast and other needs

12 Books found in the possession of the company in which are recorded the debits and credits, and other books

APPENDIX B
SUMMARY OF EXPENSES FOR THE ASCENSION PLAY
1466, 1467, 1468, AND 1469

ASF CRS 115, Libro Campione A, 1466–1510, fol. 33, left side

Festa dell'Asencione fatta adì 15 di maggio 1466
La festa dell'Asensione del nostro Signore Gesù Christo fatta l'anno 1466 adì 15 di maggio de' dare per più chose chonperate per gli bisogni di detta, e di più rag[i]oni e in più dì, et per fare el detto dì la detta festa, lire trecentotrentadua s. 2 d. 11, c[i]oè, L. 332 s. 2 s. 11, chome per l'uscita tenuta per me, Neri di Bicci dipintore, segnata A, a c. 85 ——— L. 332 s. 2 d. 11

Festa dell'Asencione fatta adì 7 di maggio 1467
La festa dell'Ase[n]cione di Christo fatta adì 7 di maggio 1467 de' dare per più ispese fatte per detta festa, chome per l'uscita tenuta e chonto di dette ispese partitamente e a chi e per ché, per me Neri di Bicci sopra c[i]o' diputato, si mostra chiaro alla mia uscita segnata A, a c. 102, in uno ritratto e sunto ò fatto di dette ispese in 16 facce della mia uscita, chominc[i]ata a c. 86 e finita a c. 101, in 129 partite, lire centosetanta s. dua, c[i]oè L. 170 s. 2 d. O ——— L. 170 s. 2 d. —

Festa dell'Asensione fatta adì 25 di maggio 1468 per Lapo
di Giuliano, sindacho, e per Piero del Massaio
La festa dell'Ase[n]cione di Christo fatta adì maggio 1468 per Lapo di Giuliano, linaiuolo, e Piero del Masaio, sindachi, de' dare lire centoventiquatro s. otto d. 6, e quali si sono spesi per sopradetti Lapo e Piero sindachi, chome per la loro uscita segnata A apare, da charte 105 insino a 109 in partite 80 ——— L. 124 s. 8 d. 6

Festa dell'Asensione di Christo, fatta adì 11 maggio 1469 per Neri di Bicci,
dipintore, sindacho
La festa dell'Asensione di Christo, fatta adì 11 di maggio 1469 per Neri di Bicci sopradetto, de' dare per più ispese fatte per me, Neri detto, lire dugentatre s. otto d. 4, c[i]oè [L] 203 s. 8 d. 4 chome per l'uscita e chonto tenuto di dette ispese partichularmente per me, chome apare alla mia uscita segnata A a c. 129,

per uno sunto e saldo fatto di dette ispese in 17 facce di detta uscita, inchominc-
[i]ate a c. 112 e fin[i]te a c. 129, in 202 partite ———— L. 203 s. 8 d. 4 Benché ci
sia a pore in questa, oltre alle L. 203 s. 8 d. 4, lire 37 in circha ispese per altri,
cioè per Antonio da Bachereto a Lionardo di Polito, funaiolo, e L. 35 ispese per
detto Antonio a Giovanni Chapello, legniaiuolo grosso. Siché in tutto queste due
partite che à nno a ire a chonto della festa si posono rag[i]onare in circha di L.
72 in circha ———— L. 72 ————

Death Rites and the Ritual Family
in Renaissance Florence
▼
Sharon T. Strocchia

The subject of this essay is not the art of dying well but rather the art of being buried honorably. The demand for honor in Renaissance Florence was an important social and political need that justified a variety of investments. As a form of both social and moral authority, honor acted as one of the major organizing principles of Florentine social life. To Leon Battista Alberti honor was quite simply "the most important thing in anyone's life."[1] In recent years historians have pointed to wealth, political involvement, building programs, and well-crafted strategies for marriage and patronage as the primary routes to honor and reputation.[2] To this inventory we must now add ritual expressions of honor, both public and domestic, that reveal how Florentines organized and defined themselves.

Among these ritual expressions of honor, death rites occupy a central place. In the Mediterranean economy of honor and shame, to bury honorably the dead was an essential part both of one's social and human obligations.[3] Yet, beyond this deeply Mediterranean sensibility toward the care of the dead, late medieval and Renaissance Florentines positively encouraged a high profile for funerary rites. For Manno Petrucci, writing about the burial honors paid to his brother Giovanni in 1443, such celebrations were not only visible expressions of loss but also what "our status required."[4] Clergy as well as laity shared a similar emphasis on honor. When the Vallombrosan abbot and general of the order, Bernardo Gianfigliazzi, died in March 1422, for example, "the prelates of the order, together with the Gianfigliazzi family, deliberated that for [the family's] consolation and honor, the funeral ceremony would be made in the church and monastery of Santa Trinità," the focus of heavy Gianfigliazzi patronage.[5] Sumptuary laws notwithstanding, the ceremonies surrounding burial offered Florentines a singular opportunity to crystallize the honor won through other social strategies, and they seized this chance with characteristic gusto. Despite the inevitable loss in human terms, death unleashed the same social energies that gave Florentine daily life its heady and competitive atmosphere.

In the late fourteenth and fifteenth centuries Florentines used the occasion of death as a way to narrate their personal and family histories to their parishes, neighborhoods, and the city as a whole. Within the space of a few hours Florentines of middling to upper rank summarized in a single ceremony the strength of their social standing. After three generations of ancestral activities aimed at building family alliances and political networks, Piero Parenti remarked that on the occasion of his father's death in 1497 he proudly staged "a public celebration in keeping with the rank he and I merited."[6] Likewise, the impressive funeral of Giuliano de' Medici in 1516, whose death robbed the Medici house of a powerful dynastic hope, capped several decades of strategic family maneuvers.[7]

What Florentines meant by an "honorable burial," however, was subject as much to family projections and expectations as to economic capability. Unlike Venetians, who enjoyed an official patrician class, Florentines made and remade reputations based on common opinion. In this assessment the present ambition of the living figured as strongly as the past achievements of the dead. Parvenus like the Ginori, who sought to establish themselves among the social elite primarily as Medici satellites, viewed funeral ceremonies as yet another way to buy social respectability by mimicking the habits of the upper class.[8] To some extent this strategic use of ceremony cut across class lines. The list of buyers who sought exemptions from sumptuary controls on late Trecento funerals, for example, was not restricted to established patrician houses but also included a mercer, knifemaker, shoemaker, coppersmith, keymaker, and *pezzaio*, as well as several doctors and notaries.[9]

For those interested in enhancing their social mobility, funerals offered a way not merely to narrate but also to embellish their family histories. As a social strategy, funeral ceremonies both stabilized and created social myths about individuals, households, and lineages. Instead of offering a straightforward depiction of social hierarchy, death rites paint a social portrait nuanced by ambitions and lost hopes. Happily for Florentines, death rites achieved their assorted aims while largely escaping the dowry wars that plagued the Florentine marriage market.[10]

Given that death rites represented such a dense strategic nucleus for Florentines, they offer a fresh and complex source for the modern social historian that helps offset the bias of family records. By the end of the fifteenth century scores of Florentines had compiled genealogies, records of public officeholding, and other family memorabilia that served to celebrate their lineages.[11] Yet these were documents written from a specific point of view. Used as a foil to this rich but imbalanced fare, death rites offer a perspective on economic and affective relationships between family members that are either hidden from historical view or that are severely distorted in family diaries. On the most basic level of household organization death rites describe types of domestic arrangements and affairs that are commonly masked by the heavy lineal concerns of Florentine diarists, whose accounts are geared as much toward an idealized representation of persons and events as to their accurate description.[12]

On a more complex level of social organization burial rites help document modes of collective behavior in which relationships between the family and community become more transparent. What a family considered it could rightfully do with its dead acted as an arena in which tensions both within the domestic unit itself and in the larger community could be played out.[13] Here the conclusions drawn in family records by observers partial to their own cause can be checked against the wide variety of Florentine sources, such as tax returns, ecclesiastical and communal accounts, wills, and assorted legal proscriptions and disputes. Moreover, in addressing concerns about the nature and structure of the afterlife, Florentine death rites offer a useful perspective on piety that argues against pre-Tridentine Catholicism merely as a cult of the living in the service of the dead.[14]

Bearing in mind both the social and symbolic nature of ritual, we can productively view burial episodes as practical occasions that meshed actual with idealized social relations. Ritual episodes were entangled in the web of daily life, not exempt from it, and they reveal far more than purely normative expectations and behavior. In the frictions and conflicts generated by such events, death rites highlight areas where social practice challenged, rather than conformed to, social ideology.

Amid the wealth of information that death offers about life, my objective here is to evaluate what death rites tell us about the Florentine family in the late fourteenth and fifteenth centuries. While students of Florentine life have become familiar with the formula of "kin, friends, and neighbors" ("parenti, amici, vicini"), there remains considerable controversy about how to define the most fundamental of these terms.[15] If fifteenth-century Florentine families seem to have been continually at odds with one another, the historians who study those families have reached no greater consensus about the nature of Florentine family life. Historians have disagreed not only about the tenor of affective bonds, which are understandably difficult to assess, but also about such basic data as domestic structures and the core of family organization.[16]

Rather than simply reviewing the relevant historiography, I want more importantly to argue from these composite views of the Florentine family to suggest how several interpretations might effectively complement each other. My primary aim is to examine how death rites both played on existing bonds of kinship and created new ones that helped define the "family" in new ways. In pursuing this goal, I will be less concerned with the level of events than with drawing an ethnographic portrait delineating several important structures of fifteenth-century Florentine society. This is not to say that the Florentine family escaped the profound changes that reshaped Florentine society in the fourteenth and fifteenth centuries. But an ethnographic approach against which more traditional methods and evidence are judiciously posed is particularly valuable at this point in our research agenda, for it permits us to reformulate and redirect the issues and problems involved in recovering Florentine family life.[17] Moreover, one might argue that such a long-range and ethnographic view is not only useful but also crucial, since many goals of death rites can only be understood in the context of the long evolution of Florentine and European family structures.

In order to understand the part played by death rites in constructing a sense of kinship in Renaissance Florence, we need to look first at the major features of the ritual process surrounding death. Florence was a society that described itself through ceremony; in this world commentators looked to public rather than to private or domestic rites as the center of the ceremonial complex they defined.[18] The authors of diaries and chronicles focused their attention on two public occasions: the funeral and the requiem. The funeral, which normally took place within twenty-four hours after death, began with a gathering of mourners at the deceased's house; from there the cortege proceeded through the neighborhood or quarter to the burial church. Normally a requiem mass immediately followed the procession, although in some instances the requiem was delayed for one or more days after the actual burial. Set in the public spaces of streets, piazza, and churches, both the funeral and requiem were occasions for public recognition. In narrative sources these public scenes totally eclipse domestic death rites such as the vigil, lamentations by women, and mourning banquets.

This emphasis on public rites should not be surprising in an environment as competitive and publicly oriented as fourteenth- and fifteenth-century Florence.[19] Nor should it be surprising given the orientation of diarists toward the designs and purposes of male kinsmen, who dominated public proceedings. The repeated focus on the funeral and requiem only underlies what was at stake in public funerary display: the power to control identity, whether of the individual, family, or commune.

What was also at stake in the funeral and requiem was the assertion of order over disorder, and it is here that the varying objectives of death rites provide a reading of multiple family identities. The way the family was represented in each of these rites was linked with particular ritual objectives, so that the activity's intention to a great extent determined its participants. In reconstructing family structures and identities, it is critical to recognize, as we have not sufficiently done, that the fluid, overlapping, and often competing definitions of the family depended to a high degree on the activity pursued. Even that master of family mythmaking, Leon Battista Alberti, recognized that family members were variously linked according to the domain of organization and decisionmaking involved. The realities of diverse bonds and interests in a variety of arenas created family structures of considerable complexity.[20]

Because the two major ritual episodes diverged in their aims, the sense of kinship established by the funeral was fundamentally different from the concept of family that operated in the requiem. As its major social objective, the funeral procession aimed at achieving order through essentially political means in that it revealed relationships of power between individuals and groups. The funeral's major concern was to separate persons on the basis of status and to legitimate those distinctions by recreating them in the processional order.[21] In establishing the priority of mourners, for example, the funeral effectively combined elements of family organization with a larger set of social ideals.

By contrast, the requiem, which aimed at achieving order through incorporation, drew together a much wider range of civic and family participants into a cohesive community. Those family members purposely excluded from the procession, or relegated to its periphery, found an accepted place in requiem proceedings, since it was this gathering process that renewed and strengthened social, communal, and spiritual bonds.[22] The requiem emphasized broader political as well as domestic networks. When appropriate, officials of the Signoria attended requiem rites, such as those held for the cardinal of Portugal in 1459, even though the priors were conspicuously and necessarily absent from the funeral itself.[23] Thus in assessing the way death rites played on and contributed to existing bonds of kinship, it is necessary first to distinguish the objectives of each episode and to examine how these aims were achieved.

In differentiating persons at both the domestic and social level, the procession relied not only on social class but also on gender as a criterion for separation. One of the most powerful distinctions the funeral made revolved around the appropriate place of women, especially kin relations, in formal proceedings. The task of fully reconstructing women's role in Florentine funerals is rendered difficult because descriptive sources make virtually no mention of women's processional participation. This silence, however, is no inadvertent omission; judging from sumptuary rulings, customary advice, sermons, and descriptions of other ceremonies, Florentine women were formally excluded from funeral processions in the late fourteenth and fifteenth centuries, largely because of their disorderly yet expected shows of grief. Writing to Francesco da Carrara in 1373, for instance, Petrarch advised him to "order that wailing women should not be permitted to step outside their homes; and if some lamentation is necessary to the grieved," he continues, "let them do it at home and do not let them disturb the public thoroughfares." Fifty years later, San Bernardino echoed similar sentiments and advised women to be kept at home until the burial was over, when they could then honor the dead in church.[24]

Regardless of social class, mothers, wives, sisters, daughters, and daughters-in-law did not follow their dead kin to the grave in places of honor in the late fourteenth and fifteenth centuries. Instead, it was only male relations who represented the collective kindred as formal mourners in the funeral processions of both men and women. Widows and other kinswomen walked in the cortege only when the corpse was not physically present, which thereby made the procession a more secular occasion. As one example, the diarist Jacopo Salviati noted that Guccio da Casale's widow and other male and female relatives trailed behind Guccio's bier in 1400; he also noted, however, that this exception occurred in the context of a ceremony performed ten days after the actual burial.[25]

The exclusion or restriction of women at funerals was not unique to Florence. Sumptuary laws in Bologna, first passed in 1276 and followed by several similar redactions, strictly prohibited women from leaving the house and going to the church before the body was actually buried.[26] Similarly, Roman sumptuary statutes enacted in 1471 proscribed women outside the circle of immediate kin from visiting the house of the deceased and further advised them not to show up at the requiem in a wild or disheveled state.[27] While it is always difficult to test the level of compliance with sumptuary proscriptions, descriptive evidence from ducal Milan confirms a similar politics of gender, as the following example makes clear. Writing to Barbara Gonzaga, marchioness of Mantua, on January 22, 1461, the Mantuan ambassador Vincenzo Scalone detailed the lengthy obsequies held the preceding day for Francesco Sforza's mother, Lucia Terziani da Marsciano. Scalone was explicit that the funeral procession had involved no women and that they were also excluded from the domestic hand-washing ceremony that followed in the *saletta del ducato*. Scalone did note, however, that Duchess Bianca Maria Visconti, unspecified women kin, and a large number of women from the duchy performed ritual laments over the body and had assumed mourning garments afterward.[28]

Yet it would not be entirely fair to say that in Florence women were completely excluded from funeral corteges. Rather, as in so much else in Florentine public life, women found themselves on the periphery of formal mourners, set apart as an informal addendum to the procession. While this customary cordoning off has left few narrative traces in the Florentine historical record, the different logistical needs of Venetian funeral ceremonies have left a somewhat firmer mark. A 1421 list of funeral expenses for an anonymous "good woman" of Venice, for instance, documented payment for a separate boat to transport women participants.[29] In Florence women kin, neighbors, and friends may have also taken a different route than the funeral cortege to attend the requiem, at which, by contrast, their participation was deemed essential. Nevertheless, as a reflection of hierarchical concepts as well as the fear of women's disorderliness in the grieving process, the procession, at least in its formal, measured progress, represented a severely truncated form of both domestic and extended family units marked by the absence of women.

Gender played another significant role in structuring the family represented in the funeral procession. The determining factor here was not the mourners' gender, but rather the gender of the deceased. That is, the spatial arrangement of mourners in the cortege differed according to the sex of the dead person, at least for the urban elite. This order of mourners spelled out a divergent set of kin ties for men and women. Simply put, the processional order at men's burials exemplified the strength of the patrilineage in the face of other family claims; women's funerals, however, embodied divisions and tensions between the patriline on the one hand and a more bilateral kindred on the other. Put another way, funerals for men focused on the agnate lineage, while those for women recognized shifting household structures and a kindred that encompassed cognates as well as agnates.[30] Funerals in Renaissance Florence thus brought to the fore, in a highly visible and practical way, the long-term problems and contradictions in the evolution of Florentine family structures in which the patrilineage only gradually supplanted an older bilateral arrangement.[31]

When the Florentine elite buried their kinsmen, the cortege emphasized a decidedly lineal face. The place of honor closest to the corpse was occupied either by household members or by more laterally extended relations, but these mourners were all agnatic rather than cognatic relations. The diarist Pagolo Petriboni, for example, recorded how, at the funeral of Giovanni Bicci de' Medici in 1429, the dead man's sons Cosimo and Lorenzo trailed directly behind the bier, followed by "28 men and boys of the Medici." Similarly, Petriboni noted that, among the great honors paid to the politically active Matteo di Michele Castellani, who also died in 1429, seventeen men of Castellani's *casa* mourned in procession, including his son, brother, and nephews.[32] This structural emphasis on agnates, whose pronounced beginnings can be located in Italian communes of the late twelfth and thirteenth centuries, continued throughout the Quattrocento and intensified in the sixteenth century.[33] Several generations after Bicci de' Medici's death, two diarists recorded the place of honor allotted to Lorenzo, duke of Urbino, at his uncle Giuliano's burial in 1516, at which the Medici triumphally paraded their lineage.[34]

This emphasis on the agnatic lineage at men's burials stood in sharp relief against the other pronounced faces of the Florentine family, the *parentado* and the conjugal unit itself. As an image of both social ties and social distance, the cortege for patrician men measured a perceptible gap between blood kin and those acquired through marriage. Cognatic relations had no special status in the procession but clustered along with friends and neighbors at some physical and social distance from the bier. While the extended social networks created through marriage were indeed represented, as Tribaldo de' Rossi observed about the presence of "tutto il parentado" at Filippo Strozzi's burial in 1491, their role was clearly subordinated to the greater claims of one's agnates and progeny.[35] Thus in a large social sense, one of the goals of men's funerals was not only to assert the reputation of an individual household or lineage, but also to assert the primacy of a relatively new type of kinship organization. As regular occurrences in daily life that could be used in strategic fashion, men's funerals formed

part of a family game that was being reworked along more pronounced patrilineal lines.

In keeping with the agnatic projections of men's funeral processions, the celebration of a conjugal ideal in these episodes was also
severely limited. Florentine widows were called on to display visibly
their grief and loss, to meet yet new marital strategies, to nurture the
conjugal cell with their economic and affective resources, but they did
not formally participate in the cortege itself. Despite the fact that,
according to the 1427 Catasto, one in every four women in the city
was a widow, repeated confrontation with this phenomenon only
served to entrench customary practice rather than to modify it.[36] Such
constraint was no doubt due in part to the thorny question of bilateral
recognition that a patrician widow's presence brought into play. In
fact, there is some evidence to suggest that the tightening exclusion of
women from funerals in the fourteenth century was linked with the
growing assertion of patrilineal claims.[37] Moreover, the increasing
competition between the two faces of the Florentine family system
threw a widow's "honorable" behavior at the funeral into question.
Once widowed, a woman's allegiance to her marital kin was by no
means guaranteed, especially if her birth family envisioned a new
marriage alliance.[38]

Along with an agnatic family model in men's funerals that down-
played a conjugal ideal went a specifically dynastic family orientation.
Showy funeral ceremonies were occasions for a mutual sharing of
honor and prestige between fathers and sons, at which sons demonstrated the responsibility and reverence they owed their fathers. After
all, the controlling image of funeral processions was, as Alberti said,
"the father of a family followed by many of his kinsmen," who was
thus shown to be more eminent "than one who is alone and seems
abandoned."[39] Beyond offering reassurance through sheer numbers,
however, the funeral sought to emphasize the status of a reduced
number of claimants who, as either sons or heirs, shared a particular-
ized bond with the deceased. This link was marked by proximity to
the bier, so that the principal mourners clustered directly behind the
body.

These dynastic claims were also charged with a set of social and
economic obligations that might indeed prove weighty to living heirs.

If honor in death meant social recognition and a chance at family mythmaking, it also meant a potential burden of debt, as Antonio and Ser Francesco Masi learned after their father died in 1405. The two brothers were forced to sell all their household goods, along with their father's and mother's clothes, to pay the 140 florin funeral costs; as late as 1456 Antonio's nephews still owed him the share they had inherited as part of their own father's debts.[40] Even as wealthy a man as Palla di Nofri Strozzi complained in a letter of March 1422, almost four years after his father's death, about the heavy burial expenses that still weighed on his finances.[41] Catasto reports as well as *ricordanze* are littered with examples of sons strapped for funds because they acted "honorably" toward their forebears, possibly playing on the expected sympathies of tax officials as well as reporting fact. The sons of Niccolò di Zanobi Bonvanni, for example, who were Medici partisans resident in the neighborhood of San Lorenzo, claimed a debt of more than 300 florins for the funeral of their father who died just prior to their 1469 report, while in 1427 the five sons of Ser Luca Franceschi split the roughly 250 florin cost of his burial into five more manageable parts.[42] In addition to making a dynastic family claim, restricted proximity to the corpse also indicated that in Renaissance Florence the economic burdens of funeral pomp were not widely shared either among social groups or among the kindred.

While family diaries are rich but somewhat anecdotal, the dynastic claims and obligations seen in these records of funeral processions can be assessed more systematically using the evidence of sumptuary licenses sold by the commune. The commune first began selling exemptions from sumptuary restrictions in 1384 for a fee of 10.5 florins and up.[43] Between 1384 and 1392 the commune sold at least 233 such exemptions that allowed Florentines to surpass the sumptuary statutes governing funeral display.[44] The social profile drawn by these licenses offers an enriching perspective on both social class and on the family definitions and priorities of male kinsmen, especially as embodied in the processional order. While the vast majority of licenses were bought by members of the seven major guilds, this elite group did not represent an exclusively patrician clientele based on antiquity of lineage. Of the 233 exemptions sold, 62 (26.6 percent) were purchased by Florentines lacking surnames. These men included professionals identified by their titles as notaries and doctors, their sons, and lesser silk merchants and tradesmen. In the late Trecento the instrument of funeral pomp was thus part of the strategic vocabulary of a much wider social group than a narrowly defined patriciate. Due to changes in the organization of magistracies and in communal accounting procedures, there is unfortunately no comparable evidence from a later period that would allow us to make precise comparisons based on similar data.

Of the 233 sumptuary licenses sold by the commune between 1384 and 1392, 164 (70.38 percent) were issued for the burials of men, 69 (29.61 percent) for women, indicating the relatively greater social importance of sumptuous displays staged for men as opposed to women. While each person honored by a licensed exemption was recorded by his or her proper name, the identities of the purchasers are somewhat more problematic to determine. In the group of permits bought for men's burials, for example, almost half (80 permits, or 48.78 percent) were purchased by persons designated only as the man's heirs. Since heirs might include female agnates acting through their guardians, as well as grandsons, nephews, or other more distant relations, the lack of precise information hampers analysis of roughly half the permits.[45] Moreover, communal accountants did not report the relationship of buyer to deceased at all in another 27 cases (16.46 percent).

For over one-third of the licenses purchased for men (57, or 34.75 percent), however, communal accountants did specify the relation of the buyer to the deceased kinsman. Of this known group, 26 permits (45.6 percent known group, 15.85 percent of men's total) were bought by sons for their fathers, 17 licenses (29.8 percent and 10.36 percent, respectively) were obtained by the deceased's brothers, 8 licenses (14.0 percent and 4.87 percent) by fathers whose sons predeceased them, and 5 (8.7 percent and 3.04 percent) by persons sharing the same surname but whose precise relation was not given. Only one license was purchased for a dead nephew.[46]

Among this known group of purchasers of sumptuary permits for men, it is clear that the ties of kinship represented were not laterally extended bonds but immediate blood relations. At least fifty-one permits (89.4 percent known group, 31.09 percent of total) were bought for members of one's nuclear group—fathers, sons, or brothers—with whom the purchasers had, at least at one time, shared the same household. That is, a sizable portion of sumptuary transactions in the late

Trecento were designed to honor a closely restricted blood kin. These showy funerals were designed to celebrate the family tradition of a limited rather than of an extended family arrangement. Only one permit, bought to honor a nephew, claimed a male family member outside the nuclear circle. For the purchasers of sumptuary permits, patrimony was not dispensed lightly or frequently in the service of their extended relations. Thus the more systematic data of communal records confirms the descriptive evidence of family diaries and chronicles regarding the primary mourners in men's funeral processions.

The evidence of communal licenses makes clear, however, that the household group celebrated by sumptuary strategies was not strictly dynastic in its orientation. In late Trecento Florence the growth of more than a fledging dynasticism was hindered by two major obstacles: first, by the economic fragmentation created by partible inheritance and, second, by continual, organic shifts in household arrangements. The appreciable number of brothers honored by sumptuous funerals indicates that the Florentine family arrow did not focus on a budding vertical dynasty comprised exclusively of father, self, and son. Lateral ties among those of the same generation also made a strong showing. Not surprisingly, fraternal bonds were most marked among those families with an established tradition, rather than among newer men. Twelve of the seventeen sumptuary permits honoring brothers were bought by members of such patrician houses as the Ridolfi, Rinuccini, Cavalcanti, Capponi, Corbizzi, Orlandini, and Tanagli.[47] Although a family name and tradition were at stake in funeral display, these were nevertheless ill-defined in terms of dynastic success or succession.

From the viewpoint of economic organization, then, late Trecento funeral processions celebrated a rather narrowly defined household unit, dominated by male agnates, as the heart of a patrilinear family tradition. The economic organization of Trecento funerals carved out a family identity for patrician men and their imitators that was primarily centered on the household, either in its current or in a previous configuration. This evidence reinforces Richard Goldthwaite's argument that the Florentine upper class lacked a sustained economic organization for the family, a deficiency which both allowed for social mobility and that mitigated against the establishment of dynasties.[48]

It is only by comparing men's funerals with those staged for women, however, that the full implications of this complex family statement become apparent. While the funerals of Florentine patrician men had a boldly lineal design, the funerals of their kinswomen reflected the more flexible and varied arrangements into which Florentines organized themselves on the household level. One frequently encounters in *ricordanze* accounts of sons burying their "good" mothers who had remained in the household after their father's death, as did Bartolomeo and Francesco Sassetti in 1430; less often, one finds brothers burying their widowed sisters who had returned to the natal fold or, in other circumstances, a woman's nephews or uncles undertaking this charge.[49] For married women, the right of *tornata*, by which a widow might return to her natal family after her husband's death, implied not only continued support and maintenance during her lifetime but also the responsibility for mortuary arrangements upon her death.[50]

When a patrician woman died, the cortege stressed the household in which she lived at the time of her death, whatever its configuration, as the most significant family unit. In his family record book the coppersmith Piero Masi noted how his widowed aunt, Monna Mea, had resided in his father's household for fifteen years prior to her death in 1512, and it was this household that arranged her burial.[51] Masi also recorded the burials of his mother, paternal grandmother, and maternal grandmother Monna Agnola, who had come to live in her married daughter's household when she was widowed.[52] As head of the household, Piero's father Bernardo thus bore responsibility for the funerals of his wife, sister, mother, and mother-in-law, and the processional placement would have acknowledged his care.

Although the household unit cornered processional honors at women's burials, these funerals also reflected the alliances and new domestic contexts women created through marriage. Florentine women were responsible for both reproducing society and extending social bonds through marriage; that women both generated *parentado* and were, to some extent, defined by it found ample recognition in the cortege, in which cognates played a much more prominent role than they did at men's funerals. As evidence for the organization of kinship in Renaissance Florence, women's funeral processions document the simultaneous existence and importance of both the patrilineal and bilateral kindreds, that David Herlihy argues characterized early modern European families.[53]

Moreover, women's funerals stressed not only a greater sense of kin connection but also a greater sense of family continuity than did those of their male kinsmen. Here again marriage and *parentado* played a key role both in defining a sense of family identity and in locating women's place in the Florentine family system. Family and generational continuity was achieved in women's processions by acknowledging those marriage alliances made by their daughters as well as by themselves, so that sons-in-law were distinctly part of the processional order. At men's burials, by contrast, the generational continuity spawned by another lineage went purposely unrecognized.

The well-to-do weaver Guasparre Landini effectively described the priorities and ambiguities of Florentine kinship active in women's funeral rites when noting his mother Lisabetta's burial in September 1521. According to this account (one of the few substantial records describing women's processions), Lisabetta's husband Matteo occupied the place of honor nearest the body, closely followed by their three sons; next came Lisabetta's sons-in-law, identified by name, followed by a man described only as a kinsman (*parente*). After this core group walked a crowd of sixty to seventy men described only as *"uomini da bene."*[54] As the nexus for both nuclear and cognatic kin, Lisabetta mediated a diversified kin group that effectively gave her a more complex social identity than was enjoyed by men of her rank, who were confined at their deaths to a lineal association.

Yet at least one aspect of kinship did not fit smoothly into this family scheme, at least as noted by Guasparre Landini himself. Although a woman's marital kin were widely incorporated into her funeral proceedings, the appropriate place or her natal kin remained a point of conflict, just as it did in daily life. Landini's account never specifies whether his mother's natal kin, the Antinori, formed part of that "lovely crowd of good citizens," or if they even took part in the proceedings. This problematic ambiguity as to a daughter's links with her own lineage represents a thorny phase in the evolution of Florentine and European family systems in which the assertion of patrilineal and conjugal bonds increasingly challenged and competed with the older authority of natal blood ties.[55]

Within the patchwork of domestic arrangements represented in women's funeral processions, there is evidence to suggest that, for women, the scale of funeral pomp depended not only on household wealth but also on the fulfillment of social norms linked with the life cycle. Judging from the frequency of detailed funerary descriptions, it appears that women in two particular statuses were more highly honored than others: first, wives of the urban elite who predeceased their husbands and, to a much lesser extent, "good mothers," that is, widows who had remained with their children after the death of their husbands.[56] Both descriptive and systematic evidence suggests that Florentine women in these two states of the life cycle were rewarded with more costly funerals than were young, unmarried women or those living in other domestic configurations, although even the most sumptuous of these events paled next to those staged for male kin. The burials of sisters residing with their brothers after being widowed, for example, appear in diaries in only a cursory way, so that fathers who made separate testamentary provisions for their daughters may have indeed recognized their potential plight.

While fluctuations in household finances and composition make comparisons of burial costs somewhat imprecise, the following examples help illustrate some of the disparities in funeral costs between men and women, and between women themselves. In the late Trecento and early Quattrocento the Ciurianni household headed first by Barna and later by his son Valorino was visited by death numerous times. When Barna's wife Agnesa died after a three-month illness in May 1362, he responded with a funeral costing approximately seventy florins. Barna himself died in 1380, and his son Valorino spent over twice that sum to honor his father. The following year Barna's mother died, yet this time Valorino mustered only thirty-five florins for the burial. Death claimed a household member once again in 1382, when Valorino's first wife Tessa was honored with a burial costing about thirty-three florins and, later, with an altar cloth valued at 15 florins; in 1428, when his second wife Caterina died, Valorino spent approximately twenty-six to twenty-seven florins. Valorino's "good and lovely" seventeen-year-old granddaughter Tessa died in 1429 but he recorded no figures for the "great honor" the household paid her at Santo Stefano a Ponte.[57]

Fortunately we can test the sporadic evidence of domestic records against the systematic data of sumptuary licenses to assess the relationship between kinship and funeral pomp for women. The great bulk of the communal licenses intended for women's funerals were purchased by husbands for their dead wives (42 licenses, or 60.86

percent), a statistic which confirms domestic descriptions.[58] Ten licenses (14.49 percent) were bought by sons for their mothers, presumably because their husbands were no longer living; whether or not these women shared their sons' households or lived independently, however, remains to be explored. In addition, seven exemptions (10.14 percent) were bought by persons designated only as the women's heirs; the commune sold six licenses to persons whose relation to the deceased was not specified, and an additional two to a relation sharing the dead woman's surname. One license was purchased by the hospital of Santa Maria Nuova, which acted as the woman's executor. In the entire group of 233 licenses only one was bought by a brother for his dead sister.[59]

The predominance of wives in this group probably signals less a sense of conjugal domesticity than the clear claim a husband had to his wife's identity at the time of her death. As part of a family strategy, her funeral pomp was directly focused on the conjugal association. This reading of conjugal strategies is supported by the fact that communal accountants were far more specific in identifying those persons who purchased sumptuary licenses for women than they were for men. Some 80 of 164 licenses (48.78 percent) bought for men's burials designated the purchasers only as the deceased's heirs, as opposed to roughly 10 percent for women. The evidence of sumptuary licenses also suggests that widows were rewarded with sumptuous funerals far less frequently than were wives, who continued to fulfill conjugal purposes in death as in life. These licenses further document a striking lack of domestic and economic ties between brothers and sisters; apparently for brothers marriage was such a powerful transfer of their sisters' family identity that it undermined their own sense of allegiance.

What is apparent in assessing the kin organization embodied in Florentine funerals is the extent to which definitions of kinship revolved around gender. The family projections seen in men's funerals were far more agnatic, patrilineal and dynastic than those evident in women's processions; moreover, recognition of a conjugal ideal was limited to a recognition of progeny. In contrast to the ceremonies made for their male kinsmen, the funerals of elite Florentine women actively celebrated the bonds of *parentado* created through marriage, including the conjugal match itself. Yet this scheme was by no means a tidy one, as it also illustrated that, for Florentine women, kinship was defined by the competition between natal and marital bonds and even by the severance of ties between brothers and sisters. Florentine funerals make clear that how one defined one's "family" was not only related to the vagaries of household shifts but also to the more fundamental fact of gender.[60]

For all its richness and complexity, the funeral was only the first of two public episodes by which Florentines honored their dead and defined their sense of kinship. The major objective of the funeral was to differentiate among persons and to legitimate those distinctions by means of the processional order. By contrast, the requiem rite that succeeded the funeral aimed at incorporating a wide range of kin, social, and civic networks. In bringing together kin of all kinds, friends, neighbors, colleagues, and acquaintances, it was the gathering process of the requiem that played on and extended existing social bonds. Thus there was a dynamic interaction between the funeral and requiem in which the separation achieved by the procession was offset by the integrating function of the requiem.

This divergence in ritual objectives between the two rites projected divergent models of the Florentine family and a very different sense of family identity. While the purpose of the funeral was to emphasize the status of a reduced number of claimants, the purpose of the requiem (as was the purpose of *cognatio* itself) was the enlargement of the kindred. By representing both the group's wealth and numbers, the requiem recognized and reiterated that the biological survival of the kindred was of paramount importance. The ritual family of the requiem included cognates as well as agnates and went well beyond the shifting boundaries of household or lineage. In providing a base for continued social relations among individuals who did not share a common badge of membership, the requiem represented a fundamental restructuring of the family from the one embodied in the funeral. The ritual family of the requiem differed from that of the funeral in another important way. In contrast to the ancestor focus of the funeral, which stressed a common line of descent for participants, the requiem traced out a kin structure from an ego-focus; that is, it represented kin networks as spun out from the dead person himself.[61]

Nor was the ritual family of the requiem a gender exclusive one. In contrast to the severely limited involvement of women in the funeral, the attendance of women at the requiem was deemed essential, for they were the foundation on which this new family architecture rested. That women stood at the heart of this new, inclusive family construct was repeatedly recognized by contemporaries. The chronicler Monaldi observed how, at the requiem for Niccolò Alberti in 1377, "all the close marital and blood relatives of the lineage," including "all the women who had entered or left the *casa*," gathered to honor him in Santa Croce.[62] Similarly, the requiem held for Messer Vieri de' Medici the day after his burial in September 1395 emphasized the essential incorporation of female kin. Present at the requiem were "a very great number of women, among whom were his daughters and his wife," although, as the anonymous diarist remarked, these women remained "on the other side" of the choir as was customary. Altogether a total of sixty-eight persons "among women and men" were dressed in mourning for Vieri's requiem.[63] The assumed expectation that women were to honor their kin and conjugal bonds in the requiem also underlay Monaldi's sharp criticism of Palla Strozzi's widow, who did not attend his requiem in October 1377.[64] Testamentary projections about one's own obsequies further recognized the desirability of including female kin in the requiem, as did Messer Maffeo Tedaldi's 1377 will which provided mourning clothes for four kinswomen and six kinsmen.[65]

It is important here to emphasize the central place of women in establishing this family definition, particularly because they have been squeezed out of even recent historical discourse about the Florentine family. The debate over the economic versus the social face of the family, over household and lineage, has done little to include women as historical actors. Even in the work of Christiane Klapisch-Zuber, who has done so much to recover the texture of Florentine domestic life, women emerge as displaced and disempowered. By acknowledging that family identities had a base not only in ritual but also in gender, we can clarify our historical vision while addressing subtle forms of empowerment and new arenas of action for women as well as men.

One of the ways kinship was displayed and reinforced at the requiem was by wearing distinctive mourning apparel, which demarcated and claimed the deceased's "family" members. Clothing in Renaissance Florence was a highly complex statement that represented a whole program of social values as well as conspicuous consumption, and mourning clothes were no exception to this scheme.[66] As an essential feature of burial honors, mourning garb accounted for a sizable and often the largest portion of total burial costs.[67] Because mourning apparel was so expensive, family diarists recorded the exact identities of the relations they outfitted, thereby tracing out the kin networks operative at the requiem with some precision.

Family and ecclesiastical accounts confirm that women related to the deceased through a variety of kin connections were a central feature at requiem proceedings. Marco Parenti was attended by his sister, two daughters, son and two young grandsons at his 1497 requiem rite, while Marco's son Piero was mourned in turn by his wife, two sisters, three daughters, two daughters-in-law, and seven sons in 1519; importantly, the household did not purchase clothing for Piero's two sons-in-law.[68] As executors in 1450 for a certain Monna Lulla, the widow of Giulino del Benino, the Badia spent fifteen florins for her sister-in-law's mourning mantle in accordance with her wishes; this money came from her own estate rather than being paid by her brother Bartolomeo.[69] It was clearly necessary for an "honorable burial" to involve women in public as well as in domestic ritual activities.

In particular, the mourning clothes displayed at requiem rites recognized and helped bolster at least one vulnerable area of Florentine family organization: namely, the natal bonds between women that could transcend the often divisive allegiances implied by marriage. Present at women's requiems were not only their marital kin but also their own sisters and mothers. In recording his wife Checha's burial in 1459, Antonio Masi spelled out that those kin who assumed mourning in her honor included her sister, mother, her three daughters-in-law, and her husband's niece, in addition to Checha's nine sons, who ranged in age from fourteen to forty-two. Four women wore mourning at Caterina Parenti's requiem in 1481: her daughters Gostanza and Marietta, her sister Alessandra, and her sister-in-law Selvaggia.[70] Through clothing as well as ritual participation, the requiem honored natal ties in a way that funerals did not.

Within this integrated ritual family of the requiem, mourning clothes strengthened another weak area of domestic organization by combining kinship distinctions with assertions of status. The most obvious distinction among kin was marked by the black clothes of "deep mourning" reserved for such close kin as spouses, children, parents, and siblings and the lesser degree of kinship marked by brown-hued apparel. Even more striking, however, were the status concerns implicated in mourning garb that highlighted the special place of Florentine widows. Like everyday apparel, mourning clothes represented consumption from a particular point of view. Through elaborate cuts of cloth, sumptuous linings, and multiple veils, the outfits worn by Florentine widows laid claims to family status, while at the same time giving widows a central place in the requiem that was sorely lacking in the funeral. In 1380, for example, Valorino Ciurianni spent almost fifty-five florins to dress his father's widow, Lisa Frescobaldi, in a fine outfit that outshone the attire of all other mourners and even the corpse itself. Her garb cost over twice the combined sum Valorino spent to dress himself, a manservant, and his father's corpse.[71] Similarly, at the requiem for Antonio da Panzano in 1423 his widow Martinella Bardi sported an extravagant outfit that consumed twenty-six *braccia* of cloth, over twice the normal amount, in addition to a luscious fur mantle and hood.[72] For widows of the Florentine elite the "widow's weeds" so publicly and prominently displayed at the requiem helped offset their exclusion from the funeral.

Yet membership in the requiem family as signaled by mourning clothes was not simply guaranteed. At times ritual membership demanded that clothing costs be shared among a much wider range of relations than were funeral costs. On the occasion of his wife Checha's requiem in 1459, Antonio Masi dressed his two younger sons Carlo and Piero (ages twenty and fourteen) at his own expense, while his other seven sons paid for their own mourning clothes.[73] This shared burden of expense seems particularly true of the clothing worn by the mothers and sisters of the dead. For example, to honor Barna Ciurianni at his 1380 requiem his mother Pera and his two sisters Margherita and Lena "said they would pay their share" for their mourning garb, thereby reducing Barna's son's expenses for their clothes to a mere seven florins.[74]

Clearly some of the shared venture of mourning clothes stemmed from the strapped financial circumstances of heirs, as the example of Ugolino Michi illustrates. With an estate burdened by the need to repay three dowries, Michi's executors gathered after his death on November 3, 1414, to assess the situation. Michi's mother Giemma, one of the executors, "asked the others what they wished to do about the funeral expenses, and after much discussion, it was agreed that Monna Giemma obligated herself for the funeral expenses up to the sum of 25 florins," while the estate's creditors would bear the necessary cost "to honor Monna Lapa (Michi's widow) in garments and veils," in order that "the burial be made decently as is required." After the burial, however, Lapa promised to return a black gown and the fur mantle to the estate, retaining only the cloth mantle for her use.[75] Moreover, the debts incurred for mourning garb could continue to weave relations between kin long after death, as the following story illustrates. During the fatal illness of Antonio Masi's wife Checha in 1459, Checha's niece asked to borrow from her aunt a new black gown valued at ten florins to mourn her when she died. Checha assented to this request, which was presented indirectly through the girl's mother, Checha's sister. After the requiem and burial, however, Masi had to badger his sister-in-law repeatedly to return the gown, and the contested item eventually grew into a larger financial squabble.[76]

Although the requiem aimed at inclusiveness, the ritual family marked by mourning clothes at the rite was nevertheless a limited one. Brothers wearing mourning in their sisters' honor were still markedly absent at women's requiems, in distinct contrast to the honor sisters paid through their apparel to siblings of both sexes and also in contrast to the recognition brothers gave each other. Moreover, the limitations of *cognatio* were measured by mourning clothes; while the sons-in-law of the deceased may have attended the requiem, they did not don mourning for their wives' fathers unless at their own expense. When honoring his father Parente in 1452, for instance, Marco Parenti subsidized clothing for himself, his wife, mother, and sister Alessandra but not for Alessandra's husband Benedetto Quaratesi, and there is no suggestion in Marco's description of the event that Quaratesi appeared in mourning. This practice held fast for succeeding generations as well. Among the requiem mourners for Piero di Marco Parenti in 1519 were Maddalena Nerli and Maria Rucellai, the wives of his two married sons Marco and Giovanni, all of whom wore mourning, and, although his daughters Caterina and Marietta were also attired in mourning, their husbands Niccolo degli Agli and Lorenzo Dazzi were not.[77] Throughout the fourteenth and fifteenth centuries the Florentine family system was plagued by structural contradictions between *cognatio* and patrilineage that the requiem tried to assuage but could not entirely overcome.

Despite its obvious limitations, however, the requiem rite worked to project visions of the family in new and different directions, creating an expanded sense of what constituted family units. In posing a concept of family reordered along the broad lines of ritual participation, with clothing defining a central core, the requiem moved beyond its functional task of countering the funeral to actively challenge a strictly patrilineal ideology. The requiem posed these new definitions in several ways: first, by defining its operative members as more than a set of households aligned along a patrilineal grid; second, by acknowledging women as makers of family structures; and third, by strengthening natal bonds between women. Moreover, because of Florentine mortality patterns, the ritual family of the requiem was a concept rehearsed over and over again, so that this family construct built on incorporation actually had a basis in daily experience.

In assessing the bonds of kinship represented in death rites, it is thus imperative to consider the plurality of family definitions established by the internal dynamics of ritual. Within the funeral itself the family's economic and social organization both conflicted and meshed with the assorted identities established through ritual participation. On the one hand, funerals and sumptuary strategies document a restricted family organization centered on fractured nuclear units, illuminating the family's economic core as well as the fluidity of wealth with the resulting potential for social mobility. Yet, on the other hand, this fragmentation was offset by an expanded family network, different for men and women, that was active in the cortege itself. These family definitions were in turn balanced and codified by the requiem rite, which introduced new family actors, a sense of cooperation based on shared cost, and its own sense of limitations.

While much of the recent historiographical debate about the Florentine family has centered on the conflict between economic fragmentation and social cooperation, I would argue that it is this very plurality of family definitions, hinging on diverse activities and objectives, that characterizes elite Florentine families both in their structural solidity and structural flaws. The divergent, almost polarized, historical perspectives of the Florentine family have often resulted from isolating one area of family activity from another. Rather than cordoning off family behaviors, what seems essential to understanding fully the complexities of Florentine kinship is an integrative, more synoptic view of family dynamics that includes ritual as well as economic and social identities. For, as contemporaries themselves tell us, the creation of a "ritual family" that excluded, played on, and added to existing bonds of kinship was a process based in part on shared economic burdens, on cooperative social ventures, and most importantly, on the power and process of commonly shared ritual activities that helped assuage the daily frictions of family life and the deeper fissures between family structures.

The need to see kinship and family dynamics in the broadest possible context is nowhere more evident than in the connection between marriage and death, which was a larger version of the internal balancing of family definitions within burial scenarios themselves. While both of these fundamental events in the life cycle were wrapped in ritual security, marriage and death impacted on domestic structures and affective relations in a different yet related way. In legal terms marriage did not bring a father's power over a woman to an end; to obtain the legal status of a separate person required the enabling act of emancipation.[78] Hence marriage did not automatically dissolve the *patria potestas*, and the ties between a married woman and her natal family could be legal as well as affective. Marriage rites paradoxically sustained this connection between a married woman and her natal family to some extent, for a young bride returned to her father's house for a brief period after the marriage celebration.[79]

In funeral rites, however, the ties of a conjugal union largely supplanted those of the woman's natal family. When a wife predeceased her husband, funeral rites publicly sanctioned the primacy of the conjugal household. Although the legal and symbolic links between women and their families of origin were not totally severed in the funeral, they were distinctly subordinated to conjugal demands and their lineal implications; only later, in the requiem, would these older bonds be partially restored. If, in disposing of both daughters and dowries, marriage represented the high point of a father's power, death by contrast disadvantaged fathers, who relinquished control over their married daughters' funerals to newer families.

Death disadvantaged fathers in yet another way, for they had to endure the shame of shabby funerals made for their sons-in-law, as

Luca da Panzano tells us. Luca nicely recorded the honorable burials made for his brother, mother, wife, and son—ceremonies over which he had complete control—but he also recorded with dismay the burial of his son-in-law Jacopo d'Ubertino Risaliti in August 1446.[80] At the time of Jacopo's death, he and his wife Gostanza, Luca's daughter, were residing in Pisa where Jacopo's father was podesta. Following his death on August 5, Jacopo's body was returned to Florence for burial in Santa Croce, which took place the next day with virtually no pomp. As Luca wrote, "he arrived from Pisa in a coffin, and no other obsequies were made for him, as his father Ubertino directed should be done." Though there was little Luca could do about this shameful lack of ceremony, Gostanza herself was quickly reclaimed from the Risaliti house by her brother, uncle, and cousin, along with her dowry of 1,050 florins. While Luca's household and agnates controlled Gostanza's marriage rites and retained legal claims to her dowry and person, their influence over the honor of a conjugal alliance as portrayed in funeral rites was obviously limited.

Like the contrasts established by the funeral and requiem, marriage and death rituals thus sanctioned different aspects of family alliances and organization. Marriage rites symbolically encoded the input of two family groups in the organization and reproduction of yet a new family grouping. Once the genesis of a new family was complete, however, funeral rites framed the primacy of the conjugal union by granting authority to husbands instead of fathers. This is not to say, however, that marriage and death rituals were necessarily at odds with each other. Rather, the rituals of marriage and death collectively described, in a larger and complementary way, the total process of reproducing society. It took both marriage and death to make new families. To isolate family behaviors and priorities in one or another activity is to confine ourselves to only a fragment of a rich historical whole.

What conclusions can we draw about the life of Florentine families from the way they managed death? First, it seems to me that the very diversity of family identities, both within the ritual process and outside it, supported and reinforced a far more complex kinship structure than we have recognized thus far. If historians have disagreed about the nature of that structure, it is in part because kinship in Renaissance Florence drew force from the very suppleness and complexity of its definition, based as it was on different domains of activity and decision making.

As part of a future research agenda, historians need to recognize the complementarity of family behaviors and develop a richer, more sensitive conceptual vocabulary to describe them. The idea of a "ritual family" is a preliminary but hopefully useful start in two directions: first, to signify an actual set of participants, not bound solely by economics or social ventures, but linked as well by common ritual activities; second, to signify the sense that there are, in fact, many facets of family identity that often relate to each other even in their opposition.

The remarkable flexibility of kinship leads us to a second point that bears reminder: in this world where kinship counted, family ties were still markedly fragile. Domestic and lineal structures shifted and reshifted with both marriage and death so that one's definition of kin depended, particularly for women, on the circumstances of the moment. Historians have usually emphasized the power and resilience of kin bonds in the face of trying circumstances, and there is no doubt that kinship stood at the heart of the Florentine social world. But although kinship was indeed a powerful tie, it was nonetheless a fragile and sometimes temporary bond, particularly for cognatic relations. Death constantly reordered family groupings and transformed those very clusters one called kin.

Finally, death rites also disclose the fact that definitions of kinship depended in large part on gender. If death has anything to contribute to the discourse about the Florentine family, it is to highlight how vividly one's gender colored the lenses through which kinship was viewed. Judging from the evidence of death rites, it is not only modern historians who have had divergent visions of the Florentine family, but the mothers and fathers, sons and daughters, husbands and wives of the Florentine past as well. Death rites make clear that the social ideology of the family rested on a larger gender ideology that needs far more exploration. What is striking in using death to illuminate life, then, is how sensitively death rites reveal not only the complex structure of Florentine families but also their ambitions, allegiances, and affections.

Donatello's Tomb of Pope John XXIII

▼

Sarah Blake McHam

Baldassare Coscia died in Florence on December 22, 1419, a broken man. As Pope John XXIII, he had once ruled most of Christendom, but then accused of vile crimes and forced to abdicate the papacy, he had been imprisoned for three years in Germany. On his release to Florence, Coscia was forced to render obeisance to Martin V, whom he must have bitterly resented as his unlawful successor. This humiliation gained the former pope a mere cardinal's hat. Yet the ignominy and suffering of Coscia's last years is belied by the magnificence of his tomb in the baptistry in Florence. This essay will analyze the meanings conveyed by the tomb's site and decoration and suggest the political circumstances that explain the irony that this rejected and humbled man was honored with one of the most imposing tombs ever built in Renaissance Italy.

The tomb of Pope John XXIII in the baptistry of Florence is one of the major monuments of the fifteenth century. Not only is it Donatello's first and only tomb in Florence, but it is the only papal tomb in that city. The structure and decoration of the tomb was unlike those of earlier funerary monuments, and the unequaled prestige of the former pope's tomb made it the model for many later fifteenth- and sixteenth-century tombs, especially in Florence. The tomb was the earliest commission by Donatello to achieve such widespread influence and marks an important turning point in his career as well.

The tomb is one of four located in the baptistry, a site rarely used for funerary monuments (figure 1). This is in contrast to Santa Croce,

1. View of the interior of the baptistry, Florence (photo: author)

for example, where the floor is virtually paved with grave slabs and the walls are ornamented by a regular rhythm of showy tombs. The three other tombs in the baptistry are simple sarcophagi commemorating prominent personages of medieval Florence. These early tombs, as well as the monument to John XXIII, are located alongside the altar, on the west wall of the baptistry. In the fifteenth century the main entrance to the baptistry was from the east through the bronze doors cast by Ghiberti and nicknamed by Michelangelo the "Gates of Paradise." This entrance faces the altar on the opposite wall. Looming above is the forty-foot image of the fearsome Judging Christ, by far the most imposing feature of the encyclopedic Old and New Testament mosaic cycles that ring the dome (figure 2). Beneath this dome the most arresting feature on the walls of the baptistry is the tomb of John XXIII. Twenty-four feet high, it is the tallest structure in the building; indeed, it was the tallest tomb anywhere in Florence at the time it was constructed.[1]

2. View of the dome mosaics, baptistry, Florence (photo: Alinari)

Not only its scale, but its colorful ornament command attention. The tomb is carved from both white and brown marble. The effigy of the former pope is gilded bronze, as are significant details of the rest of the tomb such as the ring that holds up its voluminous canopy and the fringes of the canopy. Moreover, the tomb was originally polychromed,[2] and is now restored to its former splendor.

Many visual and structural connections between the tomb and its setting were cleverly designed to make the tomb seem an integral part of the baptistry. Its canopy, originally painted in a pattern of white, red, and green brocade, matches the magnificence of the white and green inlaid marbles of the baptistry walls, just as its gilded details match the vast gold background of the dome mosaics above it. The tomb is fitted between two of the columns that rim the octagonal perimeter of the baptistry walls. From the cornice supported by these columns hangs the gilded ring holding up the tentlike canopy that drapes over the tomb.

The tomb (figure 3) comprises several vertical sections: a base decorated with seraphim holding garlands and ribbons and a series of niches with the theological virtues, Faith, Charity, and Hope. Above them is a tripartite display of John XXIII's coat-of-arms. The left-hand compartment displays the Coscia family arms, looking more suitable for a can-can dancer than a pope, but, of course, a play on his family name (Coscia), which means thigh.[3] It is surmounted by the papal insignia (figure 4). The central compartment holds the papal arms alone (figure 5), and the right-hand compartment repeats the Coscia family arms topped by a cardinal's insignia. Above this story is a sarcophagus (figure 6) bearing a laconic and ambiguous inscription in Latin. It reads: "John XXIII the former pope [or alternatively, "the late pope"; "quondam" can mean either] died in Florence in the year of Our Lord 1419 on the 11th day before the Kalends of January." By modern reckoning the date would be December 22, 1419. Atop the sarcophagus, the gilded bronze effigy of Coscia dressed as a cardinal is laid out on a bier supported by lions. The portrait of Coscia is compellingly realistic.[4] Overlooking the entire tomb is a marble lunette of a half-length Madonna and Child.

3. Tomb of Pope John XXIII, baptistry, Florence (photo: Alinari)

4. Coscia family arms, detail of tomb of John XXIII (photo: Alinari)

BIOGRAPHY OF JOHN XXIII

Between 1410–15 John was one of three claimants to the papacy. He had been elected pope at the Council of Pisa in 1410, succeeding Alexander V.[5] The council had been convened a year earlier to end the Great Schism that had divided the church into factions in Rome and Avignon, with a different pope in each city. The cardinals gathered at Pisa had extracted promises from the two claimants to the papacy that each would resign if the other did, thus clearing the way, the cardinals hoped, to end the Schism. However, Gregory XII and Benedict XIII, the two claimants, reneged on their promise, and the cardinals, in desperation, held a council in 1409 at which they deposed them both and elected in their stead Alexander V. Not surprisingly, neither Gregory XII nor Benedict XIII accepted the decision of the cardinals, and so, instead of two claimants to the papacy, there were three. When Alexander V died, John XXIII was elected by the Coun-

5. Papal arms, detail of tomb of John XXIII (photo: Alinari)

cil of Pisa and inherited the support of the Pisan cardinals in this three-way contest over papal succession.

John XXIII was backed by Louis of Anjou; Gregory XII by Ladislaus of Durazzo, who then controlled Naples. Louis's armies proved no match for Ladislaus, and John XXIII soon had to withdraw from Rome to Florence. John then tried to negotiate with Ladislaus and, when that failed, turned to Sigismund of Hungary. Sigismund made his support contingent on John's willingness to call another council, this one in Sigismund's territory at Constance. John was forced to agree because he needed Sigismund as an ally to counter Ladislaus.

When Ladislaus unexpectedly died in 1414, John tried to avoid attending the council in Constance, claiming that the restoration to the church of the papal states required his presence in Italy.[6] Sigismund insisted on his attendance, and John went reluctantly to the council.[7] John's presentiments of danger proved valid, and in early 1415 he fled from Constance disguised as a layman. Whether he hoped that his ab-

6. Detail of sarcophagus and effigy, tomb of John XXIII (photo: Alinari)

sence would force the dissolution of the council or whether he feared for his life is unclear. His flight turned out to be a disastrous miscalculation. The council, outraged at John's desertion, ordered his arrest and proceeded to elect Oddone Colonna (Martin V), whose choice did, at last, end the Great Schism. John, meanwhile, was taken prisoner and held in Germany for almost three years. Unable to communicate with his captors, he is said to have passed the long days writing poetry about the fickleness of earthly glory.[8]

Finally, his ransom was negotiated by Giovanni di Bicci de' Medici with the help of Niccolò da Uzzano and transacted through the Medici bank.[9] Giovanni di Bicci was motivated partly by sympathy: Florentines had regarded John XXIII as the true pope and were outraged at what they considered the illegality of his forced deposition.[10]

Moreover, Giovanni di Bicci must have felt he owed it to his old friend. John XXIII had been a long-standing ally of Florence and close associate of the Medici family. Before he had been elected pope,

Baldassare Coscia had served as cardinal legate in Bologna, where his capable rule ensured a much-welcomed measure of stability on Florence's northeastern border.[11] Even if one disbelieves the accusations that Medici money had purchased Coscia's cardinalate in 1402, there is no question he had been a close business associate of Giovanni di Bicci de' Medici since his days in Bologna, if not before.[12] Once he was elected pope, John XXIII consolidated their alliance; he made the head of the Medici bank in Rome depositary general of papal finances. Control of these crucial positions made the Medici bank the dominant firm handling papal finances and was the single most important cause of the family's extraordinary prosperity.[13]

The ransom was, however, just as much spurred by self-interest. John was a valuable political property. The extradition of John XXIII to Florence served the Florentine strategy of provoking Martin V, then resident in Florence because he lacked the strength to march on Rome and reclaim it for the papacy. Although Florentines professed to support Martin, in fact his policies and theirs frequently differed in regard to Italian temporal politics. Florence was a long-standing ally of Braccio da Monteforte, the condottiere who controlled much of Umbria, land that Martin intended to regain as part of the Papal States. Despite the new pope's anger, Florence continued to support Braccio. To Martin's outrage, Florence recognized Joanna of Aragon's "adoption" of Alfonso, whereas the pope wanted them to support the Angevin claim to Naples. Martin countered by maintaining a friendly relationship with Francesco Sforza, against whose armies Florence was fighting for her survival in the 1420s.[14]

All these motives coalesced in the ransoming and return of the former pope to Florence, where he lived out the remaining few months of his life. In 1419, just before his death, he made a public display of his obeisance to Martin V in S. Maria Novella, and Martin in return named him cardinal.[15] John died on December 22, apparently of grief, according to the early sources.[16] They also tell us that, as he lay dying, he ordered a servant to bring the news to Martin V, saying "thou wilt take him the best news he can have." Martin's response confirmed John's cynicism, "Now we are sure of our estate and of the mitre on our head."[17]

When John died, his body was removed to the baptistry and displayed atop the baptismal font under what contemporaries termed an

ornate *pergamo*, that is, a sort of canopy or baldachin.[18] These accounts also describe the elaborate nine-day funeral ceremonies held
in the Duomo, which were paid for by the city of Florence, and attended by the pontifical court and all the ranking officials of the city.[19]
The funeral sermon stressed that Coscia was ready for resurrection
because of his charitable acts and because of his role in bringing peace
and union to the church. The author of the sermon further argued that
Coscia's public burial at the expense of the city was a "sign" of the
symbiotic rapport between the Florentine republic and the papacy.[20]
So many candles burned in Coscia's honor in the baptistry and the
cathedral that it was feared that both buildings would go up in
flames.[21]

Another story repeated by many early chronicles suggests the almost saintly reverence in which the former pope was held. Long after
his death, John XXIII's tomb was opened. Florentine officials were
transfixed by the commanding gaze of his open and luminous eye in
the still-intact body. His mitre was still on his head. Only his signet
ring, which he had used to seal documents while pope, had fallen off
his finger.[22]

Several features of John XXIII's will are of interest to our discussion.[23] Despite the fact that he was Neapolitan, almost all of his charitable bequests were made to Florentine churches and institutions. The
most extraordinary was the gift to the baptistry of the relic of the index finger of John the Baptist. This was supplemented by a generous
sum of money so that a suitably precious reliquary could be commissioned for such a venerated relic.

CONSTRUCTION OF THE TOMB

A large sum was also left for the construction of the former pope's
tomb, but surprisingly John did not specify its intended location. Instead, the four executors of his will, Giovanni di Bicci de' Medici,
Niccolò da Uzzano, Vieri Guadagni, and Bartolomeo Valori, were em-
powered to choose an agreeable site.[24] A little more than two years
after John's death three of the executors appeared before the Calimala
guild to request permission to build the monument in the baptistry.
They confessed that John had told them in secret that he wanted to

be buried there, being too modest to request it in his will. They argued that this should be permitted because of his great devotion to the Baptist, as witnessed by his having selected the name of John when elected pope, and because of his donation of the much valued relic. Palla Strozzi, on behalf of the Calimala guild, stipulated that no chapel could be built in the baptistry because it would spoil its appearance, but that they would allow the construction of a small and inconspicuous tomb. A large tomb was not permitted, according to Strozzi, because the privilege of burial in the baptistry was honor enough in itself.[25]

Work on the tomb began a few years thereafter. The few extant documents yield no indication of how the tomb evolved from the small and inconspicuous monument stipulated by Strozzi into one of the grandest tombs of the fifteenth century. On the one hand, its imposing appearance fits the pattern of the elaborate funeral ceremonies honoring Coscia, which were among the most splendid rites in fifteenth-century Florence.[26] Furthermore, these marks of the city's esteem all accord with her steadfast and sincere support of the papacy of John XXIII. In addition, the construction of such a grand memorial to his deposed predecessor was surely calculated to gall Martin V, with whom Florence had a decidedly ambivalent relationship.

Given the increased jockeying for power among the various factions in Florence in the 1420s, the erection of so lavish a tomb to John XXIII may also reflect a carefully disguised tactic of Medici self-promotion.[27] The fortunes of John XXIII and the Medici family had long been tightly interwoven. Giovanni di Bicci had engineered John XXIII's ransom, extradition to Florence, and acquisition of a cardinalate. He was one of Coscia's executors. He and his son Cosimo took an active role in supervising the tomb's construction. In fact, later sources claim that Cosimo was the commissioner of the tomb, a factual error that may well reveal some truth about the behind-the-scenes role he played in its execution and final appearance.[28] Giovanni di Bicci and his son Cosimo, both consummate politicians, perhaps recognized that in a city like Florence, so fiercely proud of its republican heritage that prominent citizens were never allowed to erect grand monuments to themselves, the construction of an imposing tomb to a highly regarded outsider closely identified with them provided the most effective alternative.[29] In this sense the grandeur of the permanent memorial to John

XXIII suited popular sentiment about the former pope yet also reflected credit and prestige on the Medici family.

The chronology of the construction of the tomb is as unclear as the maneuvers that led to its final appearance. We can surmise that it was under way by 1425 when Cosimo de' Medici, evidently acting for his aged father, and Bartolomeo Valori, requested the the Calimala guild advance 400 florins for the construction of the tomb from the sum deposited with them.[30] The tomb was apparently finished in the late 1420s, probably by mid-1428. Donatello sculpted the tomb in association with Michelozzo. The exact contribution of each is controversial, but there is general agreement that Donatello designed the tomb and sculpted the gilded bronze effigy of Coscia, whereas Michelozzo probably executed most of the rest of the tomb.[31]

RELATIONSHIP OF THE TOMB TO EARLIER MONUMENTS

Although certain features of the tomb of John XXIII can be related to those found on earlier tombs, it is profoundly different from them. For example, the John XXIII tomb moderates the details that suggest the immediacy of a body lying in state that are found on many earlier monuments like Arnolfo di Cambio's tomb of the Cardinal de Braye (figure 7) in the Cathedral of Orvieto. In these tombs the deceased was depicted laid out on a bier with attendants drawing back curtains to reveal the body.[32] On the John XXIII tomb the specific allusion to lying in state is toned down: there are no attendants, and the volumious curtains suggest other associations beyond the grand *pergamo* under which John's body was displayed during the nine days of funeral celebrations.[33] They relate to the Dome of Heaven, a symbolism also found in the tentlike curtains represented in mosaic above them in the cupola.[34] The curtained canopy therefore conveys regal and divine associations, as can be seen by comparison with the similar baldachin over the Virgin on the facade of the Cathedral at Orvieto, sculpted by Maitani in the mid-fourteenth century. Its counterpart can be traced in papal decorations, such as the Stanza di Costantino in the Vatican, where various popes are enthroned under similar baldachins.

Just as the particular details of the funeral ceremony are modified, so too is the imagery that implored the deceased's salvation. In the

7. Arnolfo di Cambio, Cardinal de Braye tomb, Duomo, Orvieto (photo: Alinari)

upper range of earlier tombs like that of the Cardinal de Braye, the deceased was often represented kneeling to the Madonna and Child while being commended by his patron saint.[35] In the John XXIII tomb there is instead only a half-length image of the Madonna and Child.[36] Whereas many earlier tombs like Tino di Camaino's Cardinal Petroni monument (figure 8) of the early fourteenth century were decorated with scenes of Christ's death and resurrection that made an explicit analogy to the hoped-for salvation of the deceased,[37] this tomb has no such imagery.

Earlier tombs generally had inscriptions extolling the accomplishments of their hero and arguing for his redemption because of merit;[38] the inscription on this tomb tersely identifies the deceased and lists his date of death. The brief inscription does, however, imply that John was the true pope; nothing there reminds us that there were two other claimants to the papacy at the same time. The ambiguous wording can even be interpreted as meaning that he was still pope when he died. The years during which John XXIII was pope are not listed. Martin V certainly grasped these connotations. When he saw the tomb of his predecessor, he demanded that the Florentine Signoria change its inscription to "Cardinal Baldassare Coscia of Naples." The early chronicles tell us that the Florentine Signoria replied just as Pilate had when the Jews queried him about Christ, "What is written, is written."[39]

Not only the inscription but the papal coat-of-arms suggest that John XXIII was pope. In addition, the leonine supports for the tomb's bier can be understood as a papal motif, although they carry other meanings as well. The lion imagery suggests both Old Testament and Imperial associations, a combination that made it very appealing to medieval popes. Centuries earlier the motif had been appropriated by the papacy and displayed on objects like the papal throne in Santa Maria in Cosmedin in Rome, dating from 1123.[40] In fact, the only part of the tomb that could have comforted Martin V was the gilded bronze effigy of John XXIII, who is dressed as a cardinal, not as a pope.[41] On the other hand, a full-length portrait in a precious material like gilded bronze certainly conveys the high rank of its subject.[42] There is no precedent for a three-dimensional gilded bronze effigy in earlier Italian tomb sculpture. Its only counterpart is an earlier papal portrait, the six-foot gilt bronze portrait that Boniface VIII commissioned for the balcony of the Palazzo della Briada in Bologna.[43]

8. Tino di Camaino, Cardinal Petroni tomb, Duomo, Siena (photo: Alinari)

Just as the materials, monumentality, and elegance of the tomb bespeak the importance of its subject, so does the choice of Donatello to design and execute it, as he was one of the most highly regarded artists of his time. Remember, John XXIII held only a disputed claim to the papacy and yet his tomb is as grand as almost any preceding papal monument. A comparison of John XXIII's tomb with that of his successor, Martin V, makes clear how remarkable it was. Completed less than two decades after the tomb of John XXIII, the memorial of Martin V is a simple bronze floor slab without any other decoration.[44]

THE TOMB'S SITE IN THE BAPTISTRY

There are many fascinating aspects to the tomb of John XXIII that can be best understood only by a careful examination of the tomb and its context. Its break with earlier tombs that list the merits of the deceased and ask for his salvation has already been noted. The unusually understated inscription of the John XXIII tomb is contradicted, however, by its placement in the baptistry, a site rarely used for tombs. Moreover, there is the tomb's careful coordination to this setting. No earlier tomb became part of its architectural setting to the same extent. The John XXIII monument used the columns of the baptistry to form its side boundaries and the cornice above to support its baldachin.

The way in which the tomb's structure is wedded to the architecture of the baptistry is purposeful. Their tight union imparts to the tomb the venerable associations of its site. The privilege of burial in the baptistry carried potent meaning for fifteenth-century Florentines. The baptistry was the most hallowed location in Florence. It was believed to be the oldest religious structure in the city; it was dedicated to the patron saint of Florence, and all Florentines were baptized there.[45]

The site was equally respected for secular reasons. All through the Renaissance, the baptistry continued to be regarded as a Roman structure, a former Temple of Mars.[46] Borghini's sixteenth-century treatise even depicted the baptistry interior as it was supposed to have looked in Roman times.[47] Its purported Roman foundation made the baptistry the most visible evidence in Florence of the Roman heritage from which the city drew immense prestige.[48] The John XXIII tomb seems to acknowledge the Roman origins of the baptistry: its inscription, which says that John XXIII died eleven days before the Kalends of January, uses the Latin formula for dating, an uncommon practice in Italian tombs of the period.[49]

Furthermore, at this time the baptistry was the exclusive location where Florentines could be baptized, and baptism as a Christian was synonymous with becoming a citizen of the commune. Thus the baptistry was the site where Florentines became part of the secular community as well.[50] Probably because of this, the people of Florence were sometimes nicknamed the "fold of the baptistry."[51] In Florence the political functions of the baptistry were even further developed than in other Italian cities. Government councils regularly met in the baptistry and administered their affairs from the building. Several specific civic functions took place there: notable figures were knighted,[52] criminal pardons were proclaimed, and exiles were readmitted to citizenship.[53] However, the theological associations of baptism must have been even more important in the minds of fifteenth-century Florentines. Burial in a baptistry implies a profound comparison between the death and resurrection of Christ and the death and resurrection of the deceased, because baptism symbolized the future resurrection of man. Unlike the imagery of earlier tombs that expressed the hoped-for salvation of the deceased, burial in a baptistry seems to assume the deceased's redemption.

The symbolism that connects baptism with death, resurrection, and salvation was first elaborated in the New Testament. St. Paul in his Letter to the Romans wrote: "Know ye not, that so many of us as were baptized into Jesus Christ were baptized into His death? Therefore we are buried with him by baptism into death: that like as Christ was raised up from the dead by the glory of the Father, even so should we walk in newness of life."[54] Thus baptism washed away original sin and was a prerequisite to potential salvation. Because the sacrament was specifically interpreted as a parallel to Christ's death and resurrection, baptism traditionally took place on Easter.[55]

The *Symbolum fidei*, the creed recited during the rite of baptism, stresses repeatedly that Christ died, was resurrected, will judge the quick and the dead, and that those he deems worthy will enter Paradise.[56] This fundamental connection is the reason why the dominant decoration of the Florentine baptistry is that of Christ the Judge presiding over the Last Judgment.[57]

The close relationship of the theological concepts of baptism, death, resurrection, and salvation meant that individual graves in the early Christian period were often decorated with the imagery of baptism. On sarcophagi and in catacomb paintings one frequently finds representations of scenes of baptism.[58] It is occasionally even represented on Renaissance tombs, such as the tomb of Giovanni Mocenigo carved by Tullio Lombardo in the early sixteenth century. There we find reliefs not only of the baptism of Christ but the baptism of Ammianus by St. Mark.[59]

The association of baptism with death and resurrection actually influenced the architecture of baptistries. They were generally built on the circular or circle-derived ground plan of mausolea, often specifically that of the Holy Sepulchre, the tomb of Christ.[60] The most obvious example of this imitation is the baptistry in Pisa, which is a centralized, domed structure. In even more explicit imitation its original roof had a truncated conical shape open at the top, an adaptation in stone of the conical wooden dome over Christ's tomb.[61]

The Florentine baptistry followed the model of the Holy Sepulchre also, but in the indirect terms more typical of medieval copies of earlier buildings. The baptistry's ground plan is not just centralized but octagonal to recall that Christ rose from the dead on the eighth day of his Passion.[62] The ground-story supports of the Florentine baptistry alternate between columns and piers as did their counterparts in the tomb of Christ.[63] Similarly, the Florentine baptistry is domed to recall the dome over Christ's tomb and also to suggest the Dome of Heaven.[64] The tent-like motif at the center of the baptistry mosaics is a pictorialization of this Dome of Heaven.[65]

The privilege of being buried in a baptistry thus is not only a burial ad sanctos, that is, near the tomb of a martyr; in symbolic terms it is a burial ad Christum, a burial in the tomb of Christ. It is no surprise that such an honor was coveted, so much so that two different early church councils expressly prohibited burials in baptistries.[66] The Florence baptistry is almost the only example of a baptistry with tombs,[67] and there history reveals a constant tension between individuals wanting burial in the building and their being denied it. The Florence baptistry was evidently built over an early medieval necropolis.[68] Nevertheless, no one was ever allowed burial under the floor of the baptistry, no matter what inducements were offered. According to early his-

9. Bishop Ranieri sarcophagus, baptistry, Florence (photo: Kunsthistorisches Institut, Florence)

tories, a certain Bonifazio Lupi da Parma offered to pay for the mosaic decoration of the walls of the baptistry and to endow in perpetuity the costs of four priests at the baptistry. Despite this generosity he was turned down, we are told, because the commune *"per reverenza del Battesimo"* would not allow tombs or burials inside the building.[69] The best one could hope for was to be close to the building. Florentines "of good family" were entombed around its exterior, apparently in sarcophagi. In the late Dugento, however, even this privilege was revoked. The Florentine government decreed that all these tombs had to be cleared away and moved elsewhere.[70]

In the end only the tombs of several highly regarded former bishops of Florence were allowed to remain in association with the baptistry. The tomb of Ranieri, who died in 1113 after serving as bishop of Florence for forty-two years, is a marble sarcophagus ornamented with only a lengthy inscription lauding his virtues (figure 9).[71] On the left side of the baptistry altar is the sarcophagus of Bishop Velletri who governed the baptistry for twenty-five years and died in 1230. It is a Roman sarcophagus recut for his burial.[72]

These tombs are all simple sarcophagi, very modest in size, in their use of materials, and in their craftsmanship, especially when compared to the tomb of John XXIII. They may not originally have been designed for placement within the baptistry, but were most likely moved indoors when all the other sarcophagi were cleared from the building's exterior. (We know, for example, that the Velletri sarcophagus was originally outside the baptistry.)[73] If that hypothesis is correct, no one had been permitted to construct a tomb within the baptistry before the time of John XXIII. Certainly, when the Calimala guild decided to permit the construction of the tomb of John XXIII, no one had been buried there for almost two hundred years, and no one had ever been allowed to build so large and ornate a tomb anywhere in Florence, let alone in the baptistry.

It should be emphasized again just how unusual was the construction of a tomb within a baptistry. I have been able to find only two corresponding instances of monumental tombs constructed within baptistries, and these both date from the fourteenth century. The first is in Venice, where two fourteenth-century Venetian doges, Giovanni Soranzo[74] and Andrea Dandolo,[75] were commemorated by wall tombs erected in the baptistry of San Marco, the state church. The second example is much more grand and also from northern Italy. In Padua the Carrara dynasty appropriated the city's baptistry and converted it into a family mausoleum. Although the building continued to function as a baptistry, it was fitted with monumental tombs to Francesco I Carrara and his wife, Fina Buzzacarini, and frescoed with an elaborate cycle by Giusto de' Menabuoi.[76]

Not coincidentally, the tombs in Venice and the tombs in Padua commemorate heads of state. It would seem that the profound association between baptism and the coronation of a ruler which developed during the Middle Ages culminated in the fourteenth century with the construction of rulers' tombs in baptistries. The connection between baptism and coronation was seen earlier in the ritual of coronation. Repeatedly throughout the ceremonies of the new king's anointment and coronation, allusions are made to baptism. The new king is born anew as he becomes the embodiment of the state and casts off his previous individual identity, in some cases his mortal identity.[77]

The connection between baptism and coronation is reflected in medieval imagery of the crowned ruler. In the early Middle Ages we can see this conflation in the representation of Old Testament kings. For example, the scene of David being anointed king on the early Byzantine silver plates in the Metropolitan Museum clearly derives from the imagery of baptism.[78] Later medieval scenes of the coronation of a contemporary ruler, such as that from the Warmund Sacramentary, a provincial Italian manuscript of the Ottonian period, allude to the intimate relationship between baptism and coronation. The king's attendant carries two ampullae, one with the chrism of anointment, the other with that of baptism.[79] The relationship between the ritual and visual imagery of coronation and baptism was elaborated throughout the Middle Ages. By the fourteenth century, at least in Italy, it must have seemed acceptable and fitting to entomb rulers in baptistries. Significantly for a pope whose right to head the church was disputed, the association with baptism asserted the validity of his rule: only rulers had ever been allowed to erect tombs in baptistries.

Although the Carrara mausoleum in the baptistry of Padua is probably the most important precedent for the location of the tomb of John XXIII, there was at least one earlier tomb that provided a different type of precedent in its combination of a tomb and Last Judgment imagery.[80] This monument, the Bettino Bardi di Vernio tomb in Santa Croce in Florence of the late Trecento, would have been well known to Donatello and John XXIII's executors (figure 10).

Situating his tomb in the baptistry symbolized John's own salvation because it established an eternal and prominent memorial to the association between the death and resurrection of Christ and that of John XXIII. Furthermore, it placed John's body in eternal and worthy readiness for the Last Judgment represented in the monumental mosaic above him. His funerary monument was positioned next to the sarcophagus of Giovanni Ranieri, the highly respected bishop of Florence, and under the bust of St. Zenobius, her first bishop and a patron of the city,[81] in the ring of saints, martyrs, and other church notables at the base of the cupola. Its placement opposite the main entrance of the baptistry made it one of the first things noticed in the building. It was also constructed as close to the altar as possible, as permitted by the preexisting sarcophagi.

Finally, the location of his tomb on the west wall of the baptistry

10. Bettino Bardi di Vernio tomb, San Silvestro Chapel, Santa Croce (photo: Alinari)

was purposeful because penitents who were to be baptized entered through the west doors, in contrast to very young children or innocents who entered through the east doors. St. Bernard of Clairvaux, who elaborated the distinction most fully, had singled out Mary Magdalene as the exemplary penitent,[82] and later in the fifteenth century Donatello was commissioned to carve a wooden figure of her for the baptistry. If, as seems likely, this figure was placed before the west wall of the interior, the Magdalene was made to correspond visually to the tomb of John XXIII, emphasizing John XXIII's kinship with her as a penitent.[83]

THE TOMB'S INFLUENCE ON LATER FUNERARY MONUMENTS

The tomb of John XXIII, designed to fit the requirements of a unique situation, paradoxically became a prototype for later tombs in several different ways. At least one later tomb, that of Raffaele Fulgosio, a jurist associated with John XXIII, imitated many aspects of his colleague's funerary monument. Features such as bordering the tomb with preexisting architectural elements of its site, the tent baldachin, the bier supported by lions' heads, the two cherubim with the inscription, and finally, the virtues in shell niches at the tomb base, derive from the tomb of John XXIII.[84] No doubt Fulgosio intended that his tomb be recognizably associated with that of the former pope with whom he had been connected in his lifetime.[85]

There was, in addition, a widespread borrowing of the most distinctive features of the tomb, such as its draping tent baldachin. Sometimes it seems to have been appropriated as though to transfer the prestige of John XXIII's tomb to later Florentine heroes. Michelangelo's tomb in Santa Croce, a monument to which virtually the entire artistic community of Florence contributed ideas or decoration, is surrounded by a prominent tent canopy that proclaims its derivation from the papal tomb of 150 years earlier.[86]

A second category of tombs includes those that do not look like the tomb of John XXIII but seem to combine ideas derived from it. These tombs are of particular interest because they depict a Last Judgment scene in the lunette above the deceased and thereby imply that the integration of the tomb of John XXIII with the Last Judgment cycle

in the baptistry was understood. The most important of these is another papal monument, the tomb of Pope Paul II, sculpted between
1464 and 1471 by Mino da Fiesole and Giovanni Dalmata. Its appearance in the fifteenth century must be reconstructed through an illustration from Ciacconius's account of papal history because the tomb
has been moved and is no longer in its original form.[87] The base of
the monument was once ornamented with representations of the three
theological virtues, the same motif one finds on the lower story of the
John XXIII monument. The rarity of the Last Judgment iconography
and its conjunction with the theological virtues suggest that the most
grand, recent papal tomb inspired the monument to Pope Paul II.[88]

By far the most significant impact of the tomb of John XXIII is seen
on a group of prominent fifteenth-century tombs, many of them Florentine, all of which it profoundly influenced in a set pattern. As discussed above, the John XXIII monument had already modified the
traditional sepulchral motifs of hoped-for salvation by omitting all
narrative reliefs, abbreviating the inscription, and replacing the standard lunette image of the deceased kneeling before the Madonna and
Child with a new motif of the isolated half-length Madonna and
Child. The assumption seems to have been that the tomb would be
interpreted within the context of its privileged setting in the baptistry.
These later tombs derive several structural and decorative features
from the John XXIII monument. Examples like that of the Cardinal of
Portugal in San Miniato by Antonio Rossellino (figure 11) or that
erected to Leonardo Bruni in S. Croce by Bernardo Rossellino (figure
12), either used the architecture of the building to frame the tomb, as
the John XXIII monument had done, or built their own simulated
architectural frame. They isolated the upper two-thirds of the design
evolved by Donatello, omitting the lower part. This change completed
the transformation of the multistoried fourteenth-century tomb into
a more coherent, integrated type, a process begun in the John XXIII
tomb.

By omitting the base of the John XXIII monument, the later tombs
removed even the generalized allusion to virtue made by allegorical
personifications. This made the effigy their focal point. Donatello had
already emphasized the effigy far more than in earlier tombs. His
sculpture of John XXIII is compellingly realistic and much more carefully finished than any other part of the tomb. Moreover, it was cast

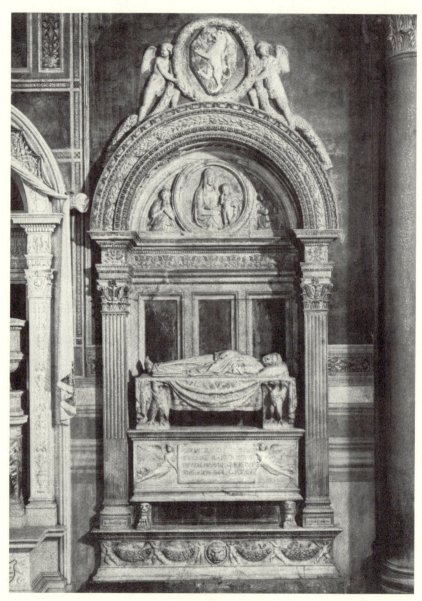

11. Bernardo Rossellino, Leonardo Bruni tomb, Santa Croce (photo: Alinari)

12. Antonio Rossellino, tomb of the Cardinal of Portugal, Santa Miniato
(photo: Alinari)

in bronze and gilded, which made it stand out. The expense of the materials confirms that it was the most important feature of the tomb. However, the John XXIII effigy was placed high above our heads. Later tombs bring the effigy down to the spectator's level, shifting the focus of the tomb to it and, consequently, to the earthly realm.

The Leonardo Bruni tomb also borrows specific motifs from the John XXIII monument: the lunette with the half-length Madonna and Child, the three panel division behind the effigy, emphasized in contrasting marble, the effigy atop a bier on the sarcophagus, the base of angels with garlands. The Cardinal of Portugal tomb appropriates the half-length Madonna and Child lunette and the effigy laid out on a bier on the sarcophagus. Like the John XXIII monument, the Cardinal of Portugal tomb ingeniously connects the tomb to its surrounding architecture, in this case an actual chapel. It even echoes the heavy drapes of the John XXIII tent baldachin in its tied-back curtains.[89]

CONCLUSION

The tomb of John XXIII was erected in the politically tense period just after his forced deposition, when Western Christendom was uneasily reunited under one pope, Martin V, for the first time in more than forty years. The monument eloquently attested to John's position as a true pope and to Florence's steadfast support of his papacy.

No doubt Pope John XXIII's donation to the baptistry of the venerated relic of the finger of John the Baptist eased the way for the extraordinary honor accorded him. At least as important, however, was the fact that John XXIII had been pope. There was considerable prestige attached to John XXIII's selection of Florence as the location for his tomb: it was the first—and only—papal tomb ever constructed in the city.

Moreover, Florence had faithfully backed John XXIII's claim to the papacy for a mixture of pious and pecuniary motives. The former pope had been very popular in the city, whereas Martin V, his successor, was not. Certainly the construction of an imposing tomb to John XXIII in such a venerated site made a clear statement to Martin V about Florentine allegiance to the pope whom Martin had supplanted, a message with pointed implications about Florence's limited and tentative support for Martin.

The construction of the tomb may have also served a carefully camouflaged Medici strategy of self-promotion. John XXIII paid for his own tomb, but his finances and those of the Medici had long been tightly interwoven. There seem to be no documents extant that chronicle the negotiations that must have taken place between the executors of John XXIII and the Calimala guild: we cannot trace precisely how the small and inconspicuous tomb stipulated by the guild was transmuted into the most lavish funerary monument in fifteenth-century Florence. But it seems likely that Giovanni di Bicci de' Medici and his son, Cosimo, played a pivotal role in that transformation. Both are documented as having been involved with the planning and supervision of the tomb's construction, and later sources repeatedly name Cosimo as its commissioner. The Medici may have pushed for a more monumental, lavish tomb for John XXIII, realizing that a grandiose memorial in his honor at least indirectly reflected credit on them. In a sense their involvement in the construction of John XXIII's tomb should be viewed as an early example of the politically astute Medici policy regarding artistic patronage. They understood well that in republican Florence the most effective way to accrue power and prestige to one's own family was through the sponsorship of monuments that bespoke family piety and civic concern, rather than glorified the commissioners.

These messages were primarily conveyed by the choice of site in the baptistry, Florence's most sacrosanct structure, where a tomb had never before been constructed. The unprecedented integration of the tomb with the architecture and decoration of the baptistry meant the concomitant transfer to the tomb of the venerable associations of the baptistry and its mosaic decoration. The former pope's salvation was thereby presented as assured and proclaimed in the permanent testimony of stone.

Ironically, the tomb of John XXIII, designed to fit a very unusual set of circumstances, became the model for a large series of later tombs. These tombs excerpted the structure and decoration of the tomb of John XXIII from its setting in the baptistry, the special context that justified its meaning of assured salvation. This process led to a transformation of the imagery and meaning of Italian tombs.

On Castagno's Nine Famous Men and Women: Sword and Book as the Basis for Public Service

▼

Creighton Gilbert

The fresco cycle by Castagno (figures 1 and 2), from a villa just outside Florence, seems a suitable theme for interdisciplinary discussion about the Quattrocento in that city. Among major works that survive by its major painters, this is the earliest with a secular theme, slightly prior to Uccello's battle series. It has a better claim to be dubbed "humanistic" than much of what is casually so treated, and it immediately suggests itself as a document of literary reputations. Yet there seems not to exist any hypothesis as to what its theme is, or if it even has a theme. Here I shall accept as given the fresco's usual date, very close to 1450, and its usual title, first recorded in 1510 in the only slightly muddled form of: "sibyls and famous Florentine men."[1] A bit more may be said about another observation, that the cycle is a variant on the tradition of the Nine Worthies. It does share its scheme of three groups of three heroes each, its emphasis on a single ethnic identity for each group (but only in two of the three groups), and its military concern (but only in one group). It differs, on the other hand, in that the three military men of Florence—Pippo Spano, Farinata degli Uberti, and Niccolò Acciaiuoli—are complemented not by sets of three other soldiers from other places, but by three nonsoldiers from the same place, Dante, Petrarch, and Boccaccio. The suggestion of the Nine Worthies may have gained more weight than it deserves from our choice of one of the soldiers, Pippo Spano, as our favorite person among the nine. In the very process in which we give the other eight figures less attention than Pippo, we may also conceive of them as pretty much analogous to him but simply less vivid. Yet he is alone in asserting himself with a naked blade and energetic centrifugality of limbs.

However, a true trace of the Nine Worthies model does appear where it might be thought least likely, among the three women, despite their not forming a single ethnic group. When we recall that the Worthies are always made up of pagan, Jewish, and Christian heroes, and then observe here a pagan heroine, Tomyris, and a Jewish heroine, Esther, it may not seem to stretch matters too far to imagine that the planner was assigning Christian status to his third woman, Cumaea (the Cumaean Sibyl), to whom he attached an inscription describing her in full as "the one who prophesied the advent of Christ." The evolution of the Nine Worthies tradition, previously confused, has been admirably ordered by Schroeder in a monograph with a marvelously polyglot title.[2] It turns out that the relatively rare theme of the Nine Women Worthies has two rival strands; one of these, all-classical and all-military, includes Tomyris; in the other, Esther is one of the Jewish women. To be sure, this would at most only signify that our planner found here a handy mine for figures he sought for other reasons.

Another usual assumption, that the system of three threes gives us all the ordering principle we need here, calls for revision. It works for the iconography but not for the design. Salmi surely was right, though he has been often overlooked and occasionally rejected, when he said that the figures also form twos.[3] They turn and address each other in pairs. They are thus a more gentle variant on the formula used, notably, in Donatello's bronze doors in the San Lorenzo sacristy, a work which was seemingly famous at this time, but which had also been criticized by Alberti and others precisely for being too active.[4] Here Pippo turns his head to Farinata, who steps forward toward Pippo. More surprisingly, in annulling the caesura between soldiers and women, Acciaiuoli turns to listen to Cumaea, who addresses him.[5] Esther turns fully toward Tomyris, who swings toward her, while Dante makes a point to Petrarch who replies with a milder point. In every case the right-hand figure seems to step forward toward the left one, who in turn stands and observes. A duple rhythm overlies a triple one. Just as with the Donatello set, an iconographic meaning for this pattern is possible but not required. Certainly the pairs make the figures seem to "speak," as in the topos about painting,[6] and to be more lively through asymmetry and interaction.

Since the figures are nine, the pairs omit the figure furthest to the right, Boccaccio. He alone, however, makes eye contact with us. It would be too fanciful to call the spectator the tenth figure, completing a fifth pair. The arrangement inevitably does, though, recall another literary idea about painting. Alberti, fifteen years before, in writing *Della Pittura*, had proposed that one figure in a picture ought to call our attention to the rest, teach us the story, or invite us in with a gesture of the hand.[7] Among the paintings that illustrate this formula, the most graphic is probably Leonardo's *Virgin of the Rocks*, some thirty-five years after Castagno, where the angel points to the protagonists. A less obvious pioneering version is Fra Angelico's San Marco altarpiece, in process in 1438, just two years after Alberti dedicated *Della Pittura* to Brunelleschi. There, St. Cosmas points out the Virgin while, like Leonardo's angel, he makes eye contact with us. Castagno's fresco should also be linked to another remark by Alberti three paragraphs earlier that the best number of figures for a painting is nine.[8] I have not hit on other paintings of this period with just nine figures, and the point seems not to have been explored. But the San Marco altarpiece, again, might qualify if we count only full-size figures, not the baby or the attendant angels—which is not an improper selectivity. There may well be other cases, but it seems unlikely that others are as ostentatious in their nineness, so to speak, as Castagno.

In addition to these specific Albertian qualities, the fresco matches the book in broader and more fundamental ways. The same part of the book tells us that the first praise for painting is for variety, that is, variety of people, mingling old and young, male and female, with varied poses, gestures, and expressions, hands held up or down, and implications of character.[9] Castagno's picture is indeed a diagram of such variety; to call it an exposition of this point in art theory would be going only a little too far. To be sure, it does not follow Alberti's further inclusion for variety of children, birds, sheep, landscapes, and more, but that is in Alberti a rhetorical extension, as may be seen from the examples he gives of paintings with good variety. The most notable example is Giotto's *Navicella* along with the Meleager sarcophagus; both show varied adult people only, adding in Giotto's case a carpentered framework to hold them, as Castagno does too.

Two objections suggest themselves to this analogy with Alberti. First, Boccaccio does not seem to invite us in with a hand gesture indicating the rest of the people, as Leonardo's angel so vividly does, but he does establish eye contact as the angel does. In addition, with his finger he points to his big book, asking us to focus on it, as Leonardo asks us to focus on the other persons indicated by the angel's finger. This book, a much larger and more emphasized one than either of those held by Petrarch or Dante nearby, corresponds, at the right margin of the cycle, to Pippo Spano's uniquely emphasized sword at the left. What is more, it is the proper vehicle to present Boccaccio telling us about the other people in the fresco, because Boccaccio did just that in his own books. He is famous for writing about Petrarch as his mentor, and for writing a life of Dante. In his book on famous women he wrote about Tomyris and Cumaea,[10] the two seen in full length; he did not discuss Esther, who, I shall argue, is being treated by Castagno as the person here most distant from Boccaccio. He wrote as well about two of the three soldiers. Acciaiuoli, his schoolmate, was later sought by him as a patron; his remarks about him, "a volte elogiative, a volte denigratorie," in the words of a recent scholar,[11] are assembled in the same scholar's essay entitled "Niccolò Acciaiuoli victime de Boccace."[12] Farinata, next beyond Acciaiuoli, appears in Boccaccio's unfinished commentary on the *Inferno*. Its report on him begins: "Before going further, it must be shown who Messer Farinata was,"[13] and then presents a two-hundred-word biography, which seems to be the longest ever written about him. Farinata seems, like Paolo and Francesca, to be famous more as a Dante character than in any other way. Pippo Spano, furthest away from Boccaccio on the wall, of course lived later than he did; I shall suggest that it is germane to the scheme that he is someone whom Boccaccio *could* not have introduced to us.

The larger objection to my analogy between the fresco and Alberti's recommendations for a painting is that this is not a *storia*, the focus of his suggestions. Indeed it is not, but on the other hand the people are not such isolated portrait icons as they seem usually to be considered. When they were cut from their wall in the nineteenth century, glaring fissures remained visible; these were at the center of each framing pilaster separating the single figures and also above them in the inner frame. The result is a flattening effect especially in the architecture and a loss of the link among the figures that the upper frieze provided. A look at the room's end wall, where this cutting did not take place, shows how strongly this upper frieze projects forward, further than the pilasters, and places all the figures in one space. The famous device by which most of the figures' feet and many of their hands extend forward out of their niches moves them not into our space but into this shared space. While this may not make them characters in a *storia*, it does set up what might be called a *profana conversazione*. It follows by about ten years the first *sacre conversazioni*, by Angelico, notably including the San Marco altarpiece, and anticipates such famous secular ones as Signorelli's *Court of Pan* and Raphael's *Parnassus*.

To understand the iconographic reason for the choice of all these figures, and of their poses and gestures, requires looking as far as possible at the whole room. The sixteenth-century report that the room contained a Crucifixion with St. Jerome, although recently cited by Horster without comment, had been shown long before to have been a scribal error; the reference was to a work by Castagno in another building.[14] What we do have is one end wall with three images: Mary with the Child, under a large baldachin, is a half figure over a door and is flanked by full-length figures of Adam and Eve with spade and spindle, as workers after the fall. No proposal seems to exist in the literature as to how these figures might relate iconographically to the nine on the adjacent long wall. I would propose as a clue a famous, but unexpected, text from late Trecento Florence, the *Libro dell'arte* of Cennino Cennini. Although it notoriously devotes almost all its 189 chapters to technical instructions on how to draw and paint, the three introductory chapters are an exception.[15] These at first appear to be routine prayers for help in writing. God, we are reminded, first created man and woman with every virtue, but when Adam and Eve sinned and were expelled from paradise, they had to work. They began with spade and spindle, but eventually men worked at many occupations, involving either mental knowledge or manual labor. One of these is painting, and hence this book. The text has taken us from the creation of the world to the function of the treatise in about six sentences, and from the labor of Adam and Eve in one. After other matters the chapter concludes by invoking heavenly aid, first from Father, Son, and Holy Ghost and last from Luke and other saints. Between these it gives its special emphasis to Mary, explaining in her case why she is appropriately addressed: she is the beloved helper of sinners. Thus the chapter at the end circles back to its initial theme of Adam and Eve becoming sinners. We are given the topos of Mary as a counterpoise to Eve: Eve's sin made us sinners, yet as sinners we get aid from Mary.

The very brief second and third chapters urge us to elect to be painters from a *spirito gentile* rather than to make money and to cultivate such virtues as love, fear, obedience, and perseverance. We should seek a master as early as possible and leave him as late as possible. These remarks, incidentally, help to determine the intended readership of the treatise (a matter usually not addressed). It is for boys who are learning; no outsiders and few masters would have called for it.

Cennini's leap from Adam and Eve working to varied modern professions echoes a general formula of the High Middle Ages,[16] but its specific analogies are in Tuscan works of art. To find them one need only seek sets of images where the presentation of Adam and Eve emphasizes their expulsion and/or work, and then shifts away from the usual Genesis narrative of events to types of labor. No better instance can be offered than the reliefs of the campanile of Florence from 1330. The first two, with the Creation of Adam and Eve, are at once followed, exceptionally, by their portrayal as workers, and then immediately, and even more remarkably, by a large set of representations of skilled trades and professions, including painting. The abruptness of the latter leap is concealed by the fact that the first few professions are personified by such individuals as Noah (inventor of wine) and Jabal (inventor of music) who also appear in Genesis. However, no narrative account of Genesis would show Noah's drunkenness only, without the Flood, nor in any other way proceed as this cycle does. After these figures we continue with other inventors such as Daedalus, taken from different traditions. Still other images are usually labeled today simply as "the art of painting" and the like, but it seems likely enough that the rest too show inventors or chief exemplars; the painter may well be Luke.[17] Passing over the fifteenth-century amendments of the cycle, and moving directly to the upper row of reliefs, we see mental rather than manual work, the seven liberal arts, with the virtues, also corresponding in a general way to Cennini, the planets, and the sacraments. The set of sacraments is interrupted by a Virgin and Child, distinguished from all the other reliefs by larger scale and by being in half-length over a door. The whole program, it will be recalled, was initiated by Giotto, to whom Cennini in the chapter quoted pays homage as his teacher's teacher's teacher. Hence one need not doubt that what he wrote in the late Trecento would record notions common among Florentine artists and guildsmen that had already been reflected in the campanile. Its sculpture and Cennini's book share Adam and Eve working, the leap to modern work, (both manual and theoretical specialties), virtues as an aid for us, and Mary as our advocate.

No other cycle is so rich, but an abbreviated analogue is the civic fountain of Siena, Jacopo della Quercia's Fonte Gaia commissioned in 1409. Again after the story of Adam and Eve—in this case their Creation and Expulsion—history stops. We are shown the virtues, expanded to eight as often in symmetrical layouts; the central area is given to the four cardinal or civil virtues, flanking the Virgin and Child at the very center. At the outer ends are the two full round statues commonly called Rhea Silvia and Acca Laurentia, each shown with two small boys who are usually considered to be Romulus and Remus. Indeed, the then accepted legend that Siena was an early settlement of Roman emigrants is the basis for the identification of these statues in the literature. Yet I must confess to having long been uncomfortable with this arrangement, specifically the identification of one of the women as Acca Laurentia, the foster mother of Romulus and Remus. Rhea Silvia, their mother, is not an implausible name; she received a biography in Boccaccio's book on famous women, and a Roman sarcophagus telling her story was known in Quercia's time, when it was copied in a drawing.[18] Both the biography and the sarcophagus also present various members of her family, and some of these are rather obscure, yet do not include Acca Laurentia. The fact that, if she is indeed presented here, the two boys are shown twice in virtually unchanged situations, is to be sure not something entirely unknown in the iconography of this period, yet it is certainly more usual that each of the images in a set makes a new and different point for us. The explorations of this essay may tentatively allow an alternative hypothesis, to identify the second statue as Eve after the fall with her two boys. This would be the next image after the Expulsion shown elsewhere on the fountain, and the one after it would be Rhea Silvia, with her sons, presented as analogues to Eve and her sons. The figure closely resembles Quercia's figure of Eve after the fall in his cycle at San Petronio in Bologna. Adam is strikingly described by Cennini as 'the chief root and father of us;'[19] a parallel description of Eve would apply to this figure, after whom we would come to Rhea Silvia, mother of all who are Sienese. The one obvious objection to this notion, that the figure has no spindle, might be met by noting either that its existence is preempted by the statics of the marble block, which sets up a close grasp of the two children in her hands, or that it was omitted for the sake of symmetry with Rhea Silvia who has no attribute. I do not insist on this suggestion, but its possibility seems to reinforce the analogy of the Sienese civic program to the Florentine one.

Partial allusions to this schema appear elsewhere. It seems not to have been registered as odd that the Brancacci Chapel in Florence, in 1425–27, does not present the Creation of Adam and Eve but begins with their Fall and Expulsion, thus giving extreme emphasis to Original Sin. From the Expulsion we leap to the New Testament career of Peter, and again the Virgin and Child is the central focus of the altarpiece of the chapel. We understand readily that the major theme, the activity of Peter, was intended to help us move from the sin of Adam and Eve toward salvation, with Mary's assistance. An oddity of the arrangement is that only on the upper tier of the narrative images do we see Adam and Eve, although they are elegantly assigned to the entrance embrasures of the chapel space and so nicely evoke their status as prefatory to our main topic just as in Cennini. The lower embrasure is devoted to some incidents of Peter's life, but these were painted fifty years later than the date of the original plan by Masolino and Masaccio. I would like to think that initially there had been an intent to show more of the prologue of Genesis in these places. If so, we would have seen Adam and Eve as laborers, quite possibly as separate monumental figures on the two sides. They so appear, with spade and spindle, on Ghiberti's doors of paradise, in Castagno as we have seen, and in two splendid drawings by Pollaiuolo. The one of Eve, with two babies, vividly recalls Quercia's "Acca Laurentia." Both drawings perhaps are traces of still another project related to those cited here. I would, however, emphasize that I do not claim to find in them nor in the Brancacci Chapel another case of the same program I find in Cennini and on the campanile and, in a more abstracted way, in the Fonte Gaia. I would only suggest that they may allude to another partly analogous schema.[20]

Let us now return to Castagno's end wall, with the working Adam and Eve at the sides, flanking the half-length Mary over the door (who recalls the one on the campanile). This subset of figures shows us the poles of original sin and of Mary who helps to redeem us; my suggestion is that, intermediate between this beginning and end, the adjacent long wall and the nine famous men and women, contemporary forms of skilled work again exemplify, especially as practiced in Florence. Certainly the most obvious models for professional writers would be Dante, Petrarch, and Boccaccio, and the three soldiers were considered good models too, as I shall discuss later. The presentation might seem to match Cennini's binary division into manual and theoretical work. The right hands of all three soldiers, grasping their weapons, project decisively forward of their niches and distinguish them from the three writers and the women. Yet this approach seems less attractive if it restricts the offered careers to only two, in contrast to the full range seen on the campanile or the generalization that may be implied on the fountain. The six men, however, are certainly not meant to guide us only to their specialties. Inspecting them in greater detail, we can again start with Pippo Spano, with his military stance, naked sword, and an inscription that calls him conqueror of the Turks.[21] Next to him, Farinata is considerably milder in pose, his sword is sheathed and the unhooking of his breastplate gives central emphasis to his cloth tunic. His inscription, calling him liberator of his country, is also less directly military, as would have been obvious to those who knew him best through Dante, for he saved Florence not by fighting but by giving speech. The third figure, Acciaiuoli, has not even a sheathed sword but a baton, hides his armor even more, and is correctly labeled an administrator.

This gradual dilution of military and physical emphasis gains further interest when the right-hand group of writers is seen to show an analogous pattern. At the far right Boccaccio points to his big book, holding it in both hands with his body uniquely motionless. He alone of the nine figures has neither a foot nor hand projecting out of his niche; the only hint of projection comes from the overlap of his wide sleeve. Next to him, Petrarch holds a smaller book, and we only see part of it, tucked under his arm. He does not point to it, but gestures as a speaker, with the fingertips of his other hand overlapping his frame. Dante shifts still farther in the same direction. A book is again under his arm, but it is open; instead of part of a book we see part of a page, or one might prefer to say part of half a book. His speaking hand projects further than Petrarch's, and a foot also projects, picking up the motif of the soldiers. These literary figures get a little more active as they near the military side, just as the soldiers get less active the closer they come to the writers.

This might be read in a linear way, as a steady lessening of force and motion from left to right, from pure emphatic sword to pure emphatic book. However, what negates that idea is the presence of the three middle figures, the women. It seems not to have been registered that the two women in full length are tied to the duality of military and literary, since one holds a book and the other wears armor. Cumaea's main motifs are the closed book under her arm and the speaking gesture of her other hand; she shares these attributes with Petrarch, the middle writer, and him alone, and both turn to address our left. Tomyris, whose main motifs are a vertical weapon resting on the ground and her other arm akimbo, shares this pair of attributes with Farinata, the middle soldier, and him alone, and they also turn to address our left. Indeed, these four figures are the only figures who do so. Tomyris and Farinata are also the only full-length figures labeled as liberators of their country.

This pairing extends the sets of exemplars with swords and books to women. This was not easy to arrange. Only one writer is found, for instance, among the 104 women in Boccaccio's biographies, and she, Sappho, is presented as unhappy. Cumaea, however, was famous for *having* books, and Boccaccio's account of her focuses on them. Quite a few women generals were available, for instance among the classical set of nine women worthies, but most of them, the Amazons, also had negative images. So for the intention indicated, to introduce (with approval) female analogues of the military and literary men, the choices could hardly have been otherwise.

The inclusion of the women in the bipolar series negates the possibility of reading all nine from left to right from pure sword to pure book, for the interesting reason that the places of the women are reversed, Cumaea with her book next to the male generals and armed Tomyris next to the male writers. To read the set as a unified design, as we presumably should, we then would incline to try the one other usual scheme, a symmetrical focus on the center. Moving in from either end, we shift from the emphatic poles to a moderate center, where the soldier has evolved into an administrator and the author has evolved into a speaker, evidently still using sword or book but shifting from such use in itself to making it a means to an end. This moderation is certainly indicated in the women near the center, especially if we have been thinking of career models for soldiers and writers. Cumaea, as noted, did not write at all, but only read from the inspired book given her. Tomyris, Boccaccio's biography tells us, during most of her life never practiced the trade of arms, but only took it up when widowed, needing to save her country and her son.[22] (Her armor is almost hidden under her dress.) Instead of being good instances of writer and general, they are respectively prophetess through the instrumentality of the book and liberatress through the sword, all the more to be admired. They move further from writing and fighting careers than the innermost soldier and writer, who still retained those professions even if they used them for added functions.

The reversal of the women suggests that, as the military or bookish emphasis is diluted and turned into a means for an end near the center, each encounters the other. However, when the poets get less emphatically bookish they do not tend to become soldiers, nor is Acciaiuoli when less physically military any more bookish; indeed he was known to have been *senza lettere*.[23] The central emphasis builds on both extremes to something higher: Acciaiuoli, his label tells us, moved into governing, and Dante proceeded from being a poet to being a theologian. The central figure, Esther, was notably involved both in governmental administration and in the context of religious faith, but had no direct involvement with sword or book as a basis for her achievements.

The notion that sword and book provided bases for right living was a notorious Renaissance topos. A famous token of it is Raphael's small painting called the *Dream of Scipio*. Avoiding the specialized debates about its sources and symbolism, I shall cite what seems to be agreed, that the allegorical lady offering both sword and book to the sleeping armed youth is advising him to use both and that we should approve.[24] The other lady offering flowers is often called "contemplative life," and it seems acceptable that sword and book are both parts of active life. This is not a contrast of active sword and contemplative book. J. B. Trapp has neatly described the topos: "The Renaissance formulation of a finished gentleman, whose education was in arms and arts . . . was powerful. The motto *ex utroque Caesar* is a variant of the ancient *sapientia et fortitudo*, most frequently represented by the figure of a Roman emperor with a book in one hand and a sword in the other."[25] What all this says is that the good goal to which both sword and book lead is total education and then right living—most obviously for a ruler but by extension for others. To be sure, the best known citations of this topos are in the sixteenth century, as from Raphael or the passage in the *Cortegiano* debating whether letters or arms should dominate education[26] or the discussion by the Panofskys of an image of Francis I.[27] Earlier cases are, however, abundant. A recent study has drawn attention to the remark by King Alfonso of Naples that letters and arms are equally important, as recorded in 1456 in the commentary of the future Pope Pius II on a work by the humanist Panormita; one could hardly ask for thicker Quattrocento name-dropping.[28] Woodward's classic survey of Renaissance theories of education brings us at once to the widely used text of 1404 by Pier Paolo Vergerio; he tells a ruler: "You had the choice of training in arms or letters, and either would lead to fame and honor. But to your great credit you chose to be proficient in both."[29] In 1440 the future Pius II wrote *De Liberorum Educatione* for the boy king of Bohemia and declared that mind and body must be developed side by side; military training and arts and letters are specifically cited.[30] After Guarino's famous school, this was to be the model for nineteenth-century Rugby, the sound mind in a sound body. If I bear down here, it is because the standard idea has not been seen or apparently even hinted in relation to Castegno's frescoes or other images of their time. Here again the fault may lie in the linear readings from the admired Pippo onward, which perhaps have carried the tacit feeling that the literary portraits were dull.

In Florence itself a notable educational text is Matteo Palmieri's *Della Vita Civile* (1430s). Only when read, as in the case of Cennini, does it emerge as being focused on education for youth. Book one notes the desirability of training both in arms and in *esercizi dell'animo*, though not as a central point.[31] More interestingly, books two and three emphasize the virtues, specifically the four civil or cardinal ones. Three are discussed in book two, and book three is given entirely to justice, emphasizing its function in civil life of providing for the *salute pubblica*, both *dentro della città e fuori*. Just actions operate in peace and war, disputation and force, in the government of republics.[32] The many examples given are mainly classical, but include Farinata, whose *magnifica voce* restored the republic and *salva fece al fiorentino popolo*;[33] the phrase is congruent with our inscription and is explicitly the good outcome of the recommended education.

Palmieri's preface is still more directly of interest. He apologizes, in the usual way, for writing the book, by saying he could find nothing on the subject. He goes on to say that the best sources he could find, *autori più atti a poter dare sufficiente notizia da poter giovare la vita ai virtuosi*, begin with Dante, worthier than all others not only as poet but as orator and as theologian. Next, Petrarch is perhaps *in poche parti inferiore*, and a good deal below him is Boccaccio.[34] This ranking of the three men as poets is commonplace, but here they are ranked instead as teachers of the civil life, in the same order of quality, with Dante moving up to be an orator. When I add that Palmieri in the 1440s wrote a life of Acciaiuoli—the only one between the brief notice in Filippo Villani's Trecento group biography and the nineteenth century[35]—I should probably add at once that I do not propose Palmieri as the programmer of our frescoes. As in most similar analogies, it must be remembered that these similarities would be shared by the small number of Florentines of the same generation interested in such issues; the programmer could have been another friend, who either took or gave Palmieri's ideas. It is relevant that the points quoted are not the focus or structure of his book but appear scattered through it. In 1426 the Florentine political leader Rinaldo degli Albizzi wrote a friend that he was sending his young son to stay with Pippo Spano, evidently as a kind of page. He remarked that Pippo was comparable for magnificence with Acciaiuoli, who thus was apparently considered the ideal.[36] Here too we are being offered models for education, by precept and example, by book and sword and what rests on their foundations, to bring up Florentines to govern the city.

Taking these nine figures as models for our modern labors, it thus seems confirmed that here as elsewhere Adam and Eve on the end wall are starting points for our work in manual and theoretical learning, and Mary is the final helper. Before considering Mary, however, we should turn to Esther, the central figure among the nine. Perhaps because she alone is only a half figure, she has gotten little attention. She shares the status as a ruler of Tomyris and Acciaiuoli, and like them is labeled as having liberated her people. Furthest removed in the series from the poles of simple sword and book, she instead presents the highest, most mediated achievement in what might be called civil service. She does not show training or skill with sword or book, or even the second level of what can be accomplished with such tools, but a third level of public accomplishment, the most that can be achieved.

As we know, her way of saving her people was by a courageous appeal to the great king Ahasuerus. The appeal itself is the focus of a painting by Filippino Lippi (Comte de Vogué, Paris), a central element in a cycle of six paintings by him of the story of Esther; the rest are in public collections and much more famous. This is the one major image other than Castagno's in Quattrocento Florence that makes Esther a key figure. It was this action of intervening with the king for mercy that made Esther a type of the Virgin Mary; Mary, assumed into heaven and made queen, was able in the same way to be the advocate of us sinners. The notion was a commonplace. We may see it illustrated around 1470 in the block book *Biblia Pauperum*, where the Assumption of the Virgin is flanked by the appeal of Esther. Earlier, St. Bernard, writing on the Assumption, had hailed Mary as *quasi altera Esther, adducta ad cubiculum Assueri;* his words were echoed in thirteenth-century Italy by the Franciscan St. Bonaventura, when he wrote that Esther is the Virgin *quae ducata est in cubiculum regis in assumptione;* both texts continued to be quoted in later commentaries on the Book of Esther.[37] The same link was set up visually by Filippino when he designed his Esther scene using the standard formula for scenes of the Assumption. He probably took it from an altarpiece by his father, but another example by Botticini was commissioned by none other than Matteo Palmieri for a family chapel, perhaps the only painting he ever owned.[38] When we view the central figure of our nine as a type of Mary, the group seems all the more a *profana conversazione.*

Esther as central half-length alludes to the half-length Mary on the center of the short wall. With Mary the sequence ends, it seems, as in Cennini. The huge baldachin over her, a curtain drawn aside, recalls the aspect of Mary as opening the veil closed by the sin of Adam and Eve. As all this implies, I consider that the Esther was in half-length

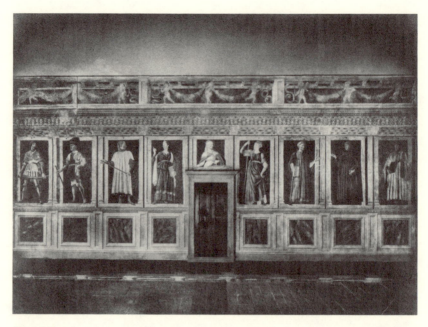

Figure 1

Figure 2

originally, though the literature often seems to indicate that she has been cut down from an original full-length. That view does not take into account the related half-length Mary or the finding by Salmi that the door of the room under Esther is of Quattrocento date, with a moulding of that period on its exterior side.[39] The notion of the cutting arose, I would guess, not only from the standard linear reading, but from seeing the frescoes in the vacuum of the museum. As this further implies, I consider the inscriptions to be original too, including the one under Esther. Dario Covi kindly informs me that he is of the same view.

We left Palmieri after his third book. His fourth and last has a surprisingly different kind of tie to our fresco. It urges citizens to be magnificent, as Albizzi had said was true of Pippo Spano and especially of Acciaiuoli. In particular they are urged to produce villas and other splendid buildings, as Castagno's patron did in this case. Palmieri concludes by assuring salvation to those who have lived as he asks.[40] However, I would repeat that I do not insist upon any precise parallel between the frescoes and any of the texts cited; they vary, in part no doubt because they deal with the education of diverse people.

Castagno differs markedly from his contemporaries by including women among the exemplars for civil life. When we discard the linear reading, we cannot even say that his women get only half as much attention as his men. The women, at the center, get all the highest promotions. Flanking Queen Esther, one woman has a book to foretell the incarnation of Mary's son, and the other's fame focused on being bereaved of her own only son; each may be thought to allude to Mary's role in Christ's birth and death. Only at the sides of the "triptych" do men represent the early stages of the recommended training.

A curriculum for study by women was recommended by Leonardo Bruni, which Woodward describes as "on its moral and intellectual side, identical with that of a man, with perhaps a little less stress on rhetoric and more on religion."[41] Castagno's scheme seems to fit this, both in its inclusion of women and in the specific details that the religious figures are women and that the rhetorician is the male Dante.

But a different reason for the inclusion of women here is suggested by analogies on a level quite separate from those with educational texts. Castagno's cycle is one of only three secular fresco programs in

Florentine Quattrocento villas by leading artists. The second, by Pollaiuolo, suggests no analogy, but the third has a suggestive likeness to
ours. This is Botticelli's set of 1486 from the Villa Lemmi.[42] As all
agree, one section shows a young man of the owner's family meeting
the seven liberal arts, who are under the control of the civil virtue
Prudence. Thus the theme is to recommend an education, if with a
different curriculum; neither Castagno's nor Botticelli's iconography,
then, seems so isolated as they have appeared. The other fresco from
the room shows the young man's bride, meeting the Three Graces introduced by Venus. This indicates her education for life, and it certainly is a more limited one than the kind that Bruni called for. The
wife's education being by the graces will recall that Raphael's image
of the young knight being educated in arts and letters belongs to a
pair of small paintings of which the other presents the graces. The
analogy with Botticelli's pair of frescoes, of which one also shows a
young man's education through allegorical figures, and the other a
young woman's by the graces, would seem to permit the hypothesis
that this second panel by Raphael shows that same theme, offering a
relaxed solution to the traditionally intricate question of Raphael's
subjects.

Of other analogues in painting from the same general context, one
of unusual interest is first evoked through the paradoxical status of
Castagno's Esther, who on the one hand is at the center of the set and
has the highest rank, yet is the only figure limited to a half-length and
thus is given the least attention. The paradox is evidently to be resolved through the fact that in the long walls of grand rooms of this
kind doors are commonly centered; hence, a centered (and thus important) image may tend to be in half-length (as above a door).

This brings up a remarkable set of panels painted around 1490 for
a grand house in Siena; there are eight separate panels, scattered
among seven museums and brought to light over a long period.[43]
They are standing figures except one, which is half-length. The figures
are Judith, Artemisia, Claudia Quinta, Sulpicia, Alexander the Great,
Eunostos of Tanagra, Scipio, and Tiberius Gracchus the elder, firmly
identified either by inscriptions or small scenes in the background.
The half-length figure is Judith (by exception identified by an attribute); this panel is commonly thought to have been cut, though the
pictorial design is complete. What is striking is that she is the only

one in the set taken from the Bible in a group otherwise from secular sources, just as Castagno's half-length Esther is; their similarity goes even further, as they are two Old Testament heroines. When we look at the others to see if the analogy to Castagno extends to them, we find that they are two Roman men (one general and one civilian), two Greek men (again one general and one civilian), two Roman women (one married and one a virgin), and just one Greek woman (married). These patterns have not been noted in the literature and suggest that the set would have been rounded out if it also included a Greek virgin. If so, its analogy to Castagno's would extend to the number nine, which has been remarked on as the normal number of sets of heroes,[44] as well as to a similar emphasis on ethnic clusters and to the not so usual near equality of female and male heroes within one set. That ethnic grouping played an articulate role in producing this set of panels seems implicit in the fact that all the surviving Greeks in it are by the same artist, the Griselda Master, while Judith and the Romans were divided among five different painters (the Griselda Master did one, as did Matteo di Giovanni, Francesco di Giorgio, Neroccio, and Orioli).

The literature has concentrated on attributions but has not noted the correlation with the nationality of the figures. There is an obvious available candidate to have been the Greek virgin; this is Hippo, who appears in Siena at the same date as a standing figure in another set of three panels, which has been cited as the nearest analogue to our set.[45] The set of eight has generally been tacitly treated as complete, but with no obvious reason other than that it presents four women and four men.[46]

Tatrai has argued, interestingly, that its theme was to be a model of behavior for bride and bridegroom.[47] This reasonable idea was based on the inscriptions, which specify the particular virtue of each figure, and the small background scenes which show how the hero exemplified the virtue. It turns out that each of the equivalent Greek and Roman figures shows much the same virtue not found in others of the set. Both generals were noted for restraint in dealing with women who were their prisoners,[48] and both male civilians met death as the result of the honor they gave to women. The Roman wife had appeared in a classical text simply as the person acclaimed as an ideal wife; there probably was no other story so neatly suitable to show admirable virtue in the category of wives. But the Greek wife is close;

she devoted herself entirely to giving her husband the greatest of tombs. If Hippo was the Greek virgin, she and the Roman virgin both were the heroines of stories focusing on rivers. It is an odd motif and would work well visually, yet leave doubt that Hippo was the figure represented.

What was the layout? The pairings of one Greek and one Roman might suggest that such pairs were side by side, and so probably all the males were on one side of the central Judith and the females on the other. This would conform with the segregation of sexes that Mode called typical of such sets.[49] However, Judith would then generate an asymmetry of the sexes, and the ethnic groups would be played down. Another arrangement would remove those difficulties if each analogous pair was distributed symmetrically, one figure on each side of Judith, giving one side to Greeks and one to Romans. Segregation of sexes would be retained if, as seems plausible, Judith was immediately flanked by the pair most like her, the two wives (since she was one), then as we move outward by the other two women, then by the civilian men, and finally by the generals. This would produce the same sort of reading from the outer remote poles to the culminating center that we saw in Castagno. From men who were generous to women, we would move in to men whose honor for women led them to die, then to women themselves, and finally to Judith, whose action—one possible only for a woman—acquired political value in saving her country, like Esther's. Only at this point do we seem to see a full analogue to Castagno, the rest of the figures being models primarily for personal virtue. The fact that the analogy is less in the particular message than in the figural design may argue for the especially close likenesses in the latter aspect here proposed.

Notes

▼

DEATH IN HISTORY: THE FUNCTION AND MEANING
OF DEATH IN FLORENTINE HISTORIOGRAPHY
OF THE FIFTEENTH AND SIXTEENTH CENTURIES
ALBERTO TENENTI

1 Lelio Arbib, ed., *Istorie della città di Firenze* (Florence, 1838–41), vol. 1, bk. 2, p. 83.

2 *Commentarj dei fatti occorsi dentro la città di Firenze dall 'anno 1215 al 1537*, 2 vols. (Trieste, 1859), I, 126–27.

3 "Cum natura res omnes initia habent imbeciliora, cum aetate accrescunt simul atque ad postremum senescentibus, quae aucta tandem fuerint, dilabuntur." In *De historia florentinorum* (Rome, 1677), bk. 3, p. 76.

4 "Di tutte le cose nostre avviene il medesimo che di noi stessi; i quali, dopo il nostro nascere al mondo, ancora che ei si consumi sempre il migliore, andiamo in un certo modo e crescendo e augumentando sino al mezzo della età nostra; ed appresso apertissimamente già logorandoci e sminuendo, ci risolviamo poi finalmente in polvere e vento" (For all our possessions the same thing happens as for ourselves, who, after our birth into the world, assuming that the best of us will survive, we go on growing and flourishing until the middle of our lifespan; and after that, already plainly wearing out and fading away, we finally disperse in dust and wind). Aurelio Gotti, ed., *Della istoria d'Europa* (Florence, 1888), bk. 3, p. 153.

5 Ibid. Such considerations enable the historian to give meaning to the fortunes of the Carolingians and especially to explain the ruin of their house with the colorless reign and death of Charles the Simple.

6 Ibid., bk. 5, p. 284.

7 Cf. Guido di Pino, ed., *Istorie fiorentine* (Milan, 1944), bk. 3, chap. 12, p. 63.

8 "Io sognavo che io fuggivo dinanzi a una moltitudine di villani e che, quanto più li fuggivo, da tanti più mi trovavo circondato e ferito; e di uno dirupato

scoglio mi pareva cadere per l'acqua voltolarmi come cosa morta" (I dreamed that I was running away from a mob of peasants and the more I ran from them the more I found myself surrounded and wounded. It also seemed that I was falling from a precipitous rock and wallowing in water like a dead body). Ibid., 64.

9 Ibid., 66.

10 Cf. Franco Gaeta, ed., *Historie fiorentine* (Milan, 1962), bk. 7, chap. 34, p. 505.

11 Guicciardini was undoubtedly among them. He writes, for example, on Pier Soderini, gonfalonier for life: "Il gonfaloniere o persuadendosi, contro alla sua naturale timidità, che gli inimici disperati della vittoria dovessino da se stessi partirsi o temendo de' Medici in qualunque modo ritornassino in Firenze, o conducendolo il fato a essere cagione della ruina propria e delle calamità della sua patria." (The gonfalonier was either persuading himself, against his natural shyness, that the desperate enemies of victory would leave by themselves or was fearing that the Medici would return to Florence by any means. Also it might have been that fate itself was directing him to be the cause of his own ruin and of the misfortune of his country.) In Costantino Panigada, ed., *Storia d'Italia* (Bari, 1967), vol. 3, bk. 11, chap. 4, pp. 229–30.

12 This is the case, for example, of Benedetto Varchi who declares: "Tutte le cose che quaggiù si fanno dagli uomini sono prima da Dio ottimo grandissimo disposte e ordinate su in cielo" (All things men do down here are first disposed and ordered in heaven by God, the perfect and the greatest). He had previously written that "il che di certo veniva fatto, se i consigli e le forze degli uomini contra gli ordinamenti e disposizioni delle stelle alcuna cosa potessero, o più tosto, se l'ineffabile avarizia e lussuria con tutte l'altre nefande sceleratezze, e specialmente della corte di Roma, la tarda ma grave ira di nostro signore Dio a giustissima indignazione e vendetta eccitato e commosso non avessono" (this [the resistance of Frundsperg] surely was being made if the judgment and power of men could have done anything against the plan and the dispositions of the stars, or rather, if unspeakable avarice and lust, together with all other nefarious crimes, especially those of the Roman court, had not yet stirred and moved the late but solemn wrath of God, our Lord, to the most rightful anger and vengeance). In Lelio Arbib, ed., *Storia fiorentina* (Florence, 1828–41), vol. 2, bk. 11, p. 268, and vol. 1, bk. 2, pp. 100–101.

13 Ibid., vol. 3, bk. 15, p. 240. Still more clearly Bernardo Segni declares on the subject: "Se il fato suo fuor d'ogni ragione nollo conduceva a quella sorte, Lorenzo avrebbe tentata invano quell'impresa" (If his own fate [Alessandro's] had not led him beyond any comprehension to that destiny, Lorenzaccio [the murderer] would have attempted that venture in vain). In *Storie fiorentine* (Milan, 1806), vol. 2, bk. 8, p. 129.

14 Giovanni Battista Adriani, *Istoria de' suoi tempi* (Prato, 1822), vol. 1, bk. 2, chap. 1, p. 102.

15 Let us quote, for example, what Nerli writes: "Avrebbono i Medici con tale
occasione potuto più facilmente assicurarsi nello stato e meglio l'avrebbono
potuto stabilire, ma altri migliori modi messe loro innanzi la fortuna ed
altrimenti dispose Iddio ottimo e grandissimo per esaltazione e grandezza
della casa loro" (With this opportunity the Medici could have more easily
assured their position in the state and better established their power in it,
but fortune put before them other greater means and God the highest and
the greatest disposed otherwise for the glorification and greatness of their
house). *Commentarj . . .*, I:197, p. 123. For the union between Fortune and
the heavens, see ibid., p. 286. II:239–40.

16 *Storia d'Italia*, vol. 3, bk. 12, chap. 9, p. 337. Cf. for similar reflections regarding the murders of Oliverotto and Vitellozzo perpetrated by Valentino
on December 31, 1502, ibid., vol. 2, bk. 5, chap. 11, p. 58.

17 *Storia fiorentina*, vol. 3, bk. 15, p. 240.

18 Ildefonso di San Luigi, ed., *Istorie* (Florence, 1785), vol. 3, p. 95.

19 Ibid., 175.

20 *Istorie fiorentine*, bk. 2, chap. 30, p. 183.

21 *Storia d'Italia*, vol. 3, bk. 11, chap. 7, pp. 248–49.

22 "Per la qual morte ne seguì tanti rivolgimenti di paesi, tanto scandalo tra
gli uomini, tanto disfacimento del regno che ancora ne sentiranno quelli che
nasceranno prossimani alla fine del secolo" (From whose death [Duke Louis
d'Orléans' in 1407] followed such upheavals in towns, such scandal among
men, such undoing of the kingdom that those who will be born from now
until the end of the century will feel it). *Istorie fiorentine*, bk. 7, chap. 19,
p. 218.

23 *Storia d'Italia*, vol. 2, bk. 5, chap. 6, p. 31. This comment follows the news
of Agnostino Barbarigo's death and of Leonardo Loredan's election.

24 *La historia universale de' suoi tempi* (version of the *Historiarum florentini
populi libri duodecim*) (Venice, 1561), bk. 2, fol. 38.

25 *Istorie*, vol. 2, p. 68. Machiavelli writes on the subject: "E come dalla sua
morte ne dovesse nascere grandissime rovine ne mostrò il cielo molti eviden-
tissimi segni; intra i quali, l'altissima sommità del tempio di Santa Reparata
fu da uno fulmine con tanta furia percossa che gran parte di quel pinnacolo
rovinò, con stupore e maraviglia di ciascuno" (Heaven showed very clear
signs that the greatest ruin would ensue from his death; among them, the
highest summit of the temple of Santa Reparata was hit by lightning with
such fury that to everybody's astonishment and surprise a good portion of
the pinnacle collapsed). *Istorie fiorentine*, bk. 8, chap. 36, pp. 576–77.

26 *Storie fiorentine*, vol. 1, bk. 4, p. 251; cf. J. Nardi in *Istorie della città di
Firenze*, vol. 2, bk. 8, pp. 196–97.

27 *Storia fiorentina*, vol. 3, bk. 15, p. 278.

28 *Storie fiorentine*, vol. 2, bk. 8, p. 160.

29 "Quando in Montepulciano sua patria venne la nuova della sua creazione, i
Priori di quel luogo messono l'armi sua al palazzo, ebbono di lui un cattivo
augurio perchè subito rovinarono e rimesse un'altra volta seguitarono di

cadere in terra. Le campane ancora comandate che sonassono a festa, suo-
narono a morto per dappocaggine ed ignoranza di chi le tirava e per fato
che dimostrava il suo esito. Il giorno trenta d'aprile l'armi sue che erano
state poste al palazzo, combattute dai venti si rivoltarono e coprirono l'arme
rimboccandole al muro per segno della sua morte, che seguì in quella notte
a sei ore." (When in his native Montepulciano the news came of his investi-
ture, the priors of that place put his armor in the palace. It was an ill omen
for him because immediately it fell, and when it was put back up it kept
falling on the ground. Moreover, the bells, which were supposed to ring
cheerfully, tolled instead thanks to the ineptitude and ignorance of the one
who was pulling them and to fate, who revealed his end. On April 30 his
arms, which were kept in the palace, hit by the winds, turned over and
covering his escutcheon pushed it up against the wall as a sign of his death,
which followed that night at six.) Ibid., vol. 3, bk. 15, p. 129.

30 *Istorie della citta' di Firenze*, vol. 1, bk. 5, pp. 457–58.

31 *Commentarj*, bk. 12, p. II:241.

32 Let us quote on the subject a meaningful passage by Adriani on the relationship between Charles V and Francis I in 1544: "Ma la fortuna, che sempre
era stata amica di Cesare, trovò la via onde egli con suo onore si potesse da
tale obbligo sciorre; perchè, . . . createsi alcune infirmità pestilenziali e
fatto gran progressi in molte provincie, avvenne che il misero giovane duca
d'Orléans gravemente se ne infermò e in pochi giorni morì con dolore infinito
del re suo padre che in un punto medesimo si vedeva privato del figliuolo
proprio . . . e della speranza della pace e della grandezza di casa sua." (But
fortune, which was always Caesar's friend, found a way for him to rescind
such an obligation with honor; because, . . . since some pestilential diseases
had greatly spread in many provinces, it happened that the wretched young
duke of Orleans fell gravely ill and died in a few days to the boundless grief
of the king, his father, who at once saw himself deprived of his own son . . .
and of the hope for peace and greatness for his house.) *Istoria de' suoi
tempi*, vol. 2, bk. 5, chap. 2, p. 178.

33 *Della istoria d'Europa*, bk. 6, p. 360.

34 Cf. *Istorie*, vol. 2, p. 185: "Non volendo la divina giustitia sopportargli più, gli
a fatti rimanera presi nel laccio giustamente" (Divine justice being unwill-
ing to tolerate them anymore, made them rightly fall into a trap). On the same
carnage Guicciardini finds quite rightly "che e' morisse per tradimento chi
poco innanzi aveva per tradimento ammazzato crudelissimamente" (that the
one who a little earlier had mercilessly murdered treasonously should die
by treason). In *Storia d'Italia*, vol. 2, bk. 5, chap. 11, p. 59. Cf. also J. Nardi
in *Istorie della città di Firenze*, vol. 1, bk. 4, p. 259.

35 *Istorie fiorentine*, bk. 3, chap. 20, p. 253.

36 Ibid., bk. 7, chap. 34, p. 507.

37 "Ma non fuggì, per ciò, nè poi il giudicio divino nè allora l'infamia e odio
giusto degli uomini, ripieni per questa elezione di spavento e di orrore, per
essere stata celebrata con arti sì brutte" (But he [the newly elected pope] did

not escape for this reason either divine judgment or the shame and rightful hate of men, who were full of fright and horror for this election because it had been celebrated with such base artifices). *Storia d'Italia*, vol. 1, bk. 1, chap. 2, pp. 6–7.

38 Ibid., vol. 2, bk. 6, chap. 4, p. 97.

39 Ibid., 98.

40 For example, here is how Varchi describes the death of Chiappino Vitelli in 1529: "Ma Iddio, il quale (como dice il proverbio dè volgari) non paga il sabato, riserbò il suo gastigo e la meritata pena al signor Chiappino Vitelli e permisse che fosse—dopo avere egli ucciso la marchesa sua moglie come impudica del nipote proprio e adultera—in una stalla d'un'osteria nella quale tutto tremante s'era fatto nascondere e coprire di letame, miserabilmente, ma non già immeritamente dal fratello della moglie con più colpi ammazzato." (But God, who [as the vernacular saying goes] does not pay on the Sabbath, reserved his punishment and merited suffering for Lord Chiappino Vitelli. He allowed him to be miserably, but not undeservedly, killed by his wife's brother with many blows in the stable of the tavern in which he tremblingly had had himself hidden and covered with dung, after he had killed the marquise, his wife, because she was wanton with her own nephew and an adulteress.) Cf. *Storia fiorentina*, vol. 2, bk. 10, pp. 253–54.

41 *Istoria de' suoi tempi*, vol. 1, bk. 2, chap. 1, p. 109: "cosa miserabile pensando all'instabilità dell'umana fortuna, ma ne' governi degli Stati necessaria e dalle leggi non solamente comportata ma comandata" (a wretched thing if one thinks of the instability of human fortune, but necessary in the governments of states and not only tolerated, but ordered by laws).

42 "Miseria troppo grande, stimando la felicità poco innanzi di lui e la buona fortuna. . . . Ma io non so, se gli è fatale di quella casa, la quale per numero d'uomini e per ricchezze e per grandezza d'animo è tra le principali di Firenze, presumere sempre nello stato più che a cittadino non si conviene e col travaglio della patria cercando inalzarsi, più in basso cadere. . . . Avvengachè di sua propria sventura se ne possa eziando dar parte alla giustizia divina la quale lui, come alcuni altri cittadini sempre inquieti e turbatori del buono e onorato stato della lor città, . . . a cotal miseria condusse." (Too great a misery, were one to compare it with earlier happiness and good fortune. . . . But I do not know whether it is inevitable for that house, which for the number of men, for wealth and spiritual greatness is among the chief ones in Florence, always to rely on the state more than is convenient for a citizen and to try to use the toil of the country to prosper only to fall down lower. . . . It happened that divine justice also contributed to his own misfortune by leading him to such misery—as it did for some other citizens who, like him, were always restless and disturbed the good and honored state of their city.) Ibid., chap. 3, pp. 156–57.

GIOVANNI CAROLI (1460–1480)

DEATH, MEMORY AND TRANSFORMATION

SALVATORE I. CAMPOREALE

For helping me draft this study in English, I wish to warmly thank professors Christine Smith, Melissa M. Bullard, David Quint, and Maurizio Gavioli, as well as the friends and colleagues at the Harvard University Center for Italian Renaissance Studies, Villa I Tatti, Florence.

1   This study continues the work of previous essays with appendixes of unedited texts; cf. S. I. Camporeale, "Giovanni Caroli e la 'Vitae fratrum S. M. Novellae'. Umanesimo e crisi religiosa (1460–1480)," *Memorie Domenicane*, n.s. 12 (1981), 141–267 (appendix, 236–267); idem, "Giovanni Caroli. Dal 'Liber dierum' alle 'Vitae fratrum'," *Memorie Domenicane*, n.s. 16 (1985), 199–233 (appendix 218–33); idem, "Humanism and the Religious Crisis of the late Quattrocento: Giovani Caroli O.P., and the 'Liber dierum lucensium'," to be published in *Christianity and the Renaissance: Image and Religious Imagination in the Quattrocento*, ed. Timothy Verdon and John Henderson (London and New York, forthcoming, 1988). Henceforth we will cite the first two essays above as: *G. Caroli* (1981) and *G. Caroli* (1985). The seminal study on Caroli's life and works (both edited and unedited) still remains S. Orlandi, *Necrologio di Santa Maria Novella: 1235–1504, Testo e commento biografici* (Florence, 1955), 1:203–5, 2:353–80. For further studies, see: G. Pomaro, "Censimento dei Manoscritti della Biblioteca di S. M. Novella. Parte I: Origini e Trecento," *Memorie Domenicane*, n.s. 11 (1980), 325–470; idem, "Censimento dei manoscritti della Biblioteca di S. M. Novella. Parte II: Sec. XV–XVI," *Memorie Domenicane*, n.s. 13 (1983), 203–353; and A. F. Verde, *Lo Studio Fiorentino: 1473–1503. Ricerche e Documenti*, vol. 4 (Florence, 1985), 1288–91 and 1348–61.

2   The autograph of the *Liber dierum lucensium*, originally in the convent of Santa Maria Novella, is now in the Biblioteca Nazionale of Florence, *Conv. Soppr., C.8.279*, 1–56v. The incomplete autograph of the *Vite nonnullorum fratrum beate Marie Novelle* is to be found in the manuscript of the Biblioteca Laurenziana in Florence, *Plut. 89, inf. 21*. Two of the seven Laurentian biographies that comprise the complete work are lacking in the *Vitae fratrum: Vita Angeli Acciaioli* and the *Vita Johannis Dominici*. The two biographies, missing in the Laurentian manuscript, are found in *Vat. Lat., 8808* of the fifteenth century (*Vita Angeli Acciaioli*), 95 ff., and in *Vat. Lat., 6329* of the sixteenth century (*Vita Johannis Dominici*) 280 ff. For the manuscript tradition and the editorial chronology of the *Liber dierum* and of the *Vitae fratrum* see *G. Caroli* (1981), 148 ff. and 161 ff:; Pomaro, *Censimento II*, 30 ff., 239 ff., 309 ff.

3   Cf. R. Creytens, "La déposition de Maître Martial Auribelli O.P. par Pie (1462)," *Archivum Fratrum Praedicatorum* 45 (1975): 147–200; and Enea Silvio Piccolomini (Pio II), *I Commentari*, ed. L. Totaro (Milano, 1984), 659, 1941–45.

4   *Liber dierum*, lv.

5   The text of the third part of the *Liber dierum* is found in G. Caroli (1985), 217–33. Forthcoming in *Memoire Domenicane* will be the text of the prologue and of the first and second parts of the *Liber dierum*.

6   G. Caroli (1985), 221.

7   Ibid., 224.

8   Ibid., 219.

9   G. Caroli (1981), 169–78; in the appendix (236–67) of the *Vitae fratrum* are found: the *epistola dedicatoria al Landino*, the *laudatio domus*, and the *praefationes* to the individual (seven) biographies that comprise Caroli's entire work.

10   Ibid., 189, 191–97.

11   Ibid., 193.

12   For a study of the concept of death in the fifteenth century, see the rich volume by R. L. Guidi, *Aspetti religiosi nella letteratura del' 400*, vol. 5; *La morte nell'età umanistica* (Vicenza, 1983).

13   *Liber dierum*, lv.

14   Ibid.

15   Cf. J. Hillman, *Re-visioning Psychology* (New York, 1977), 128 ff. and n. 9, 205–28; idem, *Suicide and the Soul* (Dallas, 1983), 41 ff., 56–76, 147–49.

16   G. Caroli (1981), 190 ff., 198 ff.

17   Ibid., 191.

18   See Verde, *Lo Studio*.

THE HEALTH STATUS OF FLORENTINES
IN THE FIFTEENTH CENTURY
ANN G. CARMICHAEL

I am especially grateful to Elizabeth B. Carmichael for her help with the modern medical aspects of this paper and to the National Endowment for the Humanities for support of my project on "Morbidity and Mortality in Early Modern Milan," no. RH20835-87.

1   David Herlihy and Christiane Klapisch-Zuber, *Les Toscans et leurs familles: Une étude du catasto florentin de 1427* (Paris, 1978), 443–68; Ann G. Carmichael, *Plague and the Poor in Renaissance Florence* (New York, 1986); Lorenzo del Panta, *Le epidemie nella storia demografica italiana (secoli XIV–XIX)* (Turin, 1980); and Massimo Livi Bacci, *La Société italienne devant les crises de mortalité* (Florence, 1978). And in general see Michael W. Flinn, *The European Demographic system, 1500–1830* (Baltimore, 1981), 47–64.

2   For a discussion of flight from Florence during plagues see Maria Serena Mazzi, "La peste a Firenze nel Quattrocento," in R. Comba, G. Piccini, G. Pinto, eds., *Strutture familiari epidemie e migrazioni nell'Italia medievale* (Naples, 1984), 91–115.

3   See Claudine Herzlich and Janine Pierret, *Illness and Self in Society*, trans. Elborg Forster (Baltimore, 1987).

4 On the general history of tuberculosis see Lester S. King, *Medical Thinking: A Historical Preface* (Princeton, 1982); and René and Jean Dubos, *The White Plague: Tuberculosis, Man and Society*, foreword by David Mechanic, introductory essay by Barbara G. Rosenkrantz (reprint, New Brunswick, N.J., 1987 [1952]), 10.

5 Andrea Corsini, *Malattie e morte di Lorenzo de' Medici, Duca d'Urbino: Studio critico di medicina storia* (Florence, 1913).

6 The account of Bartolomeo Cerretani, reprinted by Corsini, *Malattie e morte*, 221–22, claims that Maddalena died with the "mal franzese," infected by Lorenzo. On the new disease of syphilis there is an abundant literature. Two recent articles review much of it: Anna Foa, "Il nuovo e il vecchio: l'insorgere della sifilide (1494–1530)," *Quaderni storici* 19 (1984): 11–34; and Francisco Guerra, "The Dispute Over Syphilis: Europe versus America," *Clio Medica* 13 (1978): 39–61.

7 Corsini, *Malatie e morte*, 6–65, summarizes these clinical cases.

8 Yvonne Maguire, *The Women of the Medici* (London, 1927), passim; and Janet Ross, *Lives of the Early Medici, As Told in Their Correspondence* (Boston, 1911), 112–15.

9 Corsini, *Malattie e morte*, 66–139.

10 Ibid., 141–42.

11 Ibid., 200. "Circa certe doglie che alle volte li vegano alle gunture et nelle stinchi, dubitano [i medici] che non siano di spetie di mal francoso" shows that the physicians considered syphilis.

12 Ibid., 209: "Questi medici attendano a far tutti quelli rimedii che posano per maturare questo catarro della ex.a del duca et fargielo sputare et prohibire che dal capo non ne cada più, et questa nocte passata S. Ex.a per havere quasi continuo sputato si è poco riposati" (April 26, and 208–9: "el male della Ex.a del duca ogni hora si dimostra di più importantia et più pericoloso rispecto a questo catarro che è nel pecto, el quale ogni hor a più difficilmente S. Ex.a expurga" (April 28).

13 See Dubos and Dubos, *White Plague.* One of the best clinical descriptions of the variety of ways tuberculosis can contribute to heavy infant and childhood mortality and morbidity is by William Osler, "Tuberculosis," in Louis Starr, ed., *An American Text Book of the Diseases of Children*, 2d ed. (Philadelphia, 1898), 270–302.

14 Ibid., 209–10.

15 On the history of gout, see W. S. C. Copeman, *A Short History of the Gout and the Rheumatic Diseases* (Berkeley, 1964). On gout among the Medici, see George F. Young, *The Medici* (New York, 1930), Copeman's source. Although his bibliography cites the study of Antonio Costa and Giorgio Weber, "Le alterazione morbose del sistema scheletrico in Cosimo dei Medici il Vecchio, in Piero il Gottoso, in Lorenzo il Magnifico, in Giuliano Duca de Nemours," *Archivio "De' Vecchi"* 23 (1955): 1–69, Copeman clearly did not read the article. Costa and Weber systematically defeat the diagnosis of gout among the Medici in favor of a possible diagnosis of the exceptionally rare

syringomyelia in Lorenzo and Giuliano and chronic rheumatoid arthritis in Piero and Cosimo. In the Milanese sample there were twenty-eight deaths from gout, all but three over age sixty at death.

16   Costa and Weber, "Le alterazioni morbose."

17   Ross, Lives of the Medici, 51, 55, 62, 77.

18   Ross, Lives of the Medici, passim; Maguire, Women of the Medici, 60–126. Gout was a very popular diagnosis in the Renaissance; see Thomas G. Benedek and Gerald P. Rodnan, "Petrarch on Medicine and the Gout," Bulletin of the History of Medicine 37 (1963): 397–416.

19   Costa and Weber, "Le alterazioni morbose," found destruction of the thoracic vertebrae in all four Medici victims and large joint destruction particularly severe in Piero il Gottoso. The spinal lesions are consistent with characteristic tuberculous bone changes; see, for example, Vilhelm Møller-Christensen, "Leprosy and Tuberculosis," in Gerald D. Hart, ed., Disease in Ancient Man (Toronto, 1983), 133; Dan Morse, "Tuberculosis," in Diseases in Antiquity, ed. D. R. Brothwell and A. T. Sandison (Urbana, Ill., 1967), 249–71, who discusses the difficulties diagnosing tuberculosis from bone alone.

20   See Ross, Lives of the Medici, 69–70; and Maguire, Women of the Medici, 68–69. Later this year (1463) Giovanni de' Medici (Piero's brother) died. See Juliana Hill Cotton, "Benedetto Reguardati of Nursia (1398–1469)," Medical History 13 (1969): 176, 184; and Gonario Deffenu, Benedetto Reguardati: Medico e diplomatico di Francesco Sforza (Milan, 1955), 152, giving the text by Benedetto's letter to Sforza.

21   See Maguire, Women of the Medici, 83–84; Ross, Lives of the Medici, 111–12. Lucrezia was attended by Benedetto Reguardati, a physician to the Medici family even though he was employed by Francesco Sforza of Milan. Benedetto described her complaints as involving a tumor of the left breast, pains in the upper abdomen, and "sciatica" on the right side. See Cotton, "Benedetto Reguardati," 185.

22   Ross, Lives of the Medici, 179; Maguire, Women of the Medici, 101–9, who says the bugs were as big as "capers," not capons. Neither source provides the original text.

23   Clarice began to suffer from catarrh as early as September 1478, late in pregnancy: see Maguire, Women of the Medici, 158–60, 233–34. Lorenzo and Clarice's daughter, Lucrezia, was the only one of more than seven children to live to old age, troubled only by a little "catarrh" in her seventies (ibid., 176); and see 173–95 for descriptions of the fates of the younger Medici. Maguire claims that Lorenzo, duke of Urbino, died of "consumption, possibly by infection from his uncle Giuliano," even though he may have been previously infected with syphilis.

24   Among the case studies where a diagnosis of tuberculosis might clarify the surviving clinical details are those of Henry VIII of England and Erasmus of Rotterdam. In both examples uncommon medical problems have been thought to account for the chronic sufferings of these two men. See N. R. Barrett, "King Henry the Eighth," Annals of the Royal College of Surgeons of En-

gland 52 (1973): 216–33, who attributes Henry's leg ulcers to amyloid disease secondary to chronic infection and suggests Henry VIII was dropsical rather than obese in his last years. Other suggestions include syphilis, in J. F. D. Shrewsbury, "Henry VIII: a Medical Study," *Journal of the History of Medicine and Allied Sciences* 7 (1952): 141–85, severe varicose veins, or scurvy. See also A. S. MacNalty, *Henry VIII: A Difficult Patient* (London, 1952). And see Hyacinthe Brabant, "Erasme, ses maladies et ses médecins," in Jean-Claude Margolin, ed., *Colloquia Erasmiana Turonensia* (Toronto, 1972), 2: 539–68; Brabant presents as well the evidence for syphilitic infection in the case of Erasmus. Erasmus lived into his seventies. C. D. O'Malley, "Some Incidents in the Medical History of Desiderius Erasmus," in P. Smit and R. J. Ch. Van ter Laager, eds., *Essays in Biohistory and other Contributions* (Utrecht, 1970), 153–62, discusses Erasmus's gout, as does Thomas Benedek, "The Gout of Desiderius Erasmus and Willibald Pirckheimer: Medical Autobiography and Its Literary Reflections," *Bulletin of the History of Medicine* 57 (1983): 526–44. One of the best extended descriptions of tuberculosis, undiagnosed, through a life course is that by Marjorie Nicolson and George S. Rousseau, *"This long Disease, My Life:" Alexander Pope and the Sciences* (Princeton, 1968).

25 Antonio Costa and Giorgio Weber, "L'inizio dell'anatomia patologica nel Quattrocento fiorentino, sui testi di Antonio Benivieni, Bernardo Torni, Leonardo da Vinci," *Archivio "De' Vecchi"* 39 (1963): 429–878; and C. D. O'Malley and J. B. deC. M. Saunders, *Leonardo da Vinci on the Human Body* (New York, 1952), 17–26.

26 Antonio Benivieni, *De Abditis Nonnullis ac Mirandis Morborum et Sanationum Causis*, trans. Charles Singer and Exmond R. Long (Springfield, Ill., 1954); Ralph H. Major, "Antonio di Pagolo Benivieni," *Bulletin of the Institute of the History of Medicine* 3 (1935): 739–55; and Enrico Coturri, "L'inizio di una 'Practica' Lasciata incompiuta e ancora inedita di Antonio Benivieni," *Episteme* 8 (1974): 3–25. As Coturri describes, Singer and Long did not include, nor translate, the additional eleven cases published in the nineteenth century by Puccinotti, *Storia della medicina*, 2, 2 vols. in 3 (Livorno, 1850–59), pt. 1; ccxxxiii and 232–55. Puccinotti located the original Benivieni manuscript; Costa and Weber," Anatomia patologica," provides the full text and translation, plus an Italian translation.

27 Benivieni, *De Abditis*, case 79, pp. 157–59 (Singer translation).

28 Ibid., xxxviii–xxxix. Singer had here the advice of pathologist-historian Esmond R. Long.

29 Ibid., 159.

30 Ibid., 93–94 (case 43).

31 See Coturri, "L'inizio di una 'Practica,' " 5–6.

32 Benivieni, *De Abditis*, xliv and 93 (case 42).

33 Leonard Wilson makes the same argument about Addison's Disease, a destruction of the suprarenal gland that can be caused by tuberculosis. Wilson argues that Addison was able to identify cases of this very rare endocrino-

logical disturbance because he lived during a time of high tuberculosis prevalence and worked in a hospital where complications of the disease were
often seen. See "Internal Secretions in Disease: The Historical Relations of
Clinical Medicine and Scientific Physiology," *Journal of the History of Medicine and Allied Sciences* 39 (1984): 263–302.

34 Katherine Park's *Doctors and Medicine in Early Renaissance Florence*
(Princeton, 1985) is especially rich in details of medical practice in Florence;
still useful is Dean Lockwood, *Ugo Benzi: Medieval Philosopher and Physician: 1376–1439* (Chicago, 1951), and Francesco Puccinotti, *Storia della medicina*, 2, pt. 1, 232–55.

35 Carmichael, *Plague and the Poor*.

36 Bruno Casini, *Il catasto di Pisa del 1428–29* (Pisa, 1964). Morbidity is not a
direct determinant of birth, marriage, and burial rates and so has received
little attention from historical demographers.

37 Antonio di Giovanni, "Malatti e malattie di altri tempi," *Scientia Veterum*,
no. 58 (Pisa, 1964).

38 B. S. Rose, "Gout in the Maoris," *Seminars in Arthritis and Rheumatism* 5
(1975): 121–45.

39 Mirko D. Grmek, *On Aging and Old Age: Basic Problems and Historic
Aspects of Gerontology and Geriatrics* (The Hague, 1958), 50–69.

40 See Dante E. Zanetti, "La morte a Milano nei secoli XVI–XVIII: Appunti per
una ricerca," *Rivista storica italiana* 88 (1976): 803—51; Emilio Motta, "Morti
in Milano dal 1452 al 1552," *Archivio storico lombardo* 18 (1891): 241–86;
and most recently Giuliana Albini, *Guerra, fame, peste: Crisi di mortalità e
sistema sanitario nella Lombardia tardomedioevale* (Bologna, (1982). For
comparative studies of Italian death registers see Carlo M. Cipolla, "I
libri dei morti," in idem, ed., *Le fonti della demografia storica in Italia*,
1 vol. in 2 (Rome, 1974), 1, pt. 2, 851–952. Milan's population at this period
was about 60,000, growing slightly, a city about 25 percent larger than
Florence.

41 Archivio di stato, Milano, Fondo popolazione, parte antiqua, Necrologi,
cartellae 73–75, discussed in detail by Albini, *Guerra, fame, peste*, 127–38.

42 On the association of dropsy, rheumatic fever, and scarlet fever (streptococcal infections) see Lawrence A. May, ed., *Classic Studies of Infectious
Diseases* (Oceanside, New York, 1977), 38–51; and Copeman, *Short History
of the Gout*, 126–39. Before antibiotics rheumatic fever, caused by strepto-
coccus bacilli, had its peak incidence among six- to ten-year-old children.
Many recovered to die of dropsy or infection during their thirties and forties.

43 Dubos and Dubos, *White Plague*, 10.

44 Thomas E. Cone, *History of American Pediatrics* (Boston, 1979), 174–75; and
Arthur L. Bloomfield, *A Bibliography of Internal Medicine: Communicable
Diseases* (Chicago, 1958), 133–62.

45 See Roger Des Prez, "Tuberculosis," in James B. Wyngaarden and Lloyd H.
Smith, eds., *Cecil Textbook of Medicine*, 16th ed. (Philadelphia, 1982), 1538–
54. Cell-mediated immunity, which is largely responsible for suppressing

tuberculosis infection, decreases as well with pregnancy. Thus high levels of tuberculosis prevalence insures increased morbidity and mortality for women during the childbearing years. See Eugene D. Weinberg, "Pregnancy-associated immune suppression: Risks and mechanisms," *Microbial Pathogenesis* 3 (1987): 393–97.

46 See the excellent study of I. S. Loudon, "Leg Ulcers in the Eighteenth and Early Nineteenth Centuries," *Journal of the Royal College of General Practitioners* 31 (1981): 263–73, and 32 (1982): 301–309.

47 For a description of twentieth-century morbidity patterns in the United States see James F. Fries, "Aging, Natural Death, and the Compression of Morbidity," *New England Journal of Medicine*, July 17, 1980: 130–35, here, p. 132. And see James C. Riley, "Disease without Death: New Sources for a History of Sickness," *Journal of Interdisciplinary History* 17 (1987): 537–63; idem, *Sickness, Recovery, and Death* (London, forthcoming, 1989).

PETRARCHAN FIGURATIONS OF DEATH IN
LORENZO DE' MEDICI'S SONNETS AND *Comento*
WILLIAM J. KENNEDY

1 For examples see the anthology edited by Antonio Lanza, *Lirici toscani del Quattrocento* (Rome: Bulzoni, 1973).

2 For efforts to define political power and privilege in terms of literary learning and talent see Franco Gaeta, *Letteratura italiana: Il letterato e le istituzioni* (Turin: Einaudi, 1982), 237 ff.

3 See Bruno Maier, "Il Realismo letterario di Lorenzo il Magnifico," in Lorenzo de' Medici, *Opere scelte*, ed. Bruno Maier (Novara, 1969), 1–49. See also Cecilia M. Ady, *Lorenzo dei Medici and Renaissance Italy* (London, 1955), 128–42; J. R. Hale, *Florence and the Medici* (London, 1977), 53–59; and Judith Hook, *Lorenzo de' Medici: An Historical Biography* (London, 1984), 145–49.

4 For contemporary estimation see Paolo Orvieto, *Lorenzo de' Medici* (Florence, 1976), 37–53.

5 Quotations from *The Stanze of Angelo Poliziano*, trans. David Quint (Amherst, 1979). For the laurel as political symbol, see Janet Cox-Rearick, *Dynasty and Destiny in Medici Art* (Princeton, 1984), 15–31.

6 For the political background see Nicolai Rubinstein, *The Government of Florence Under the Medici, 1434 to 1494* (Oxford, 1966), 195–228.

7 Quotations from Francesco Petrarca, *Rime*, ed. Ferdinando Neri (Milan, 1951); *Petrarch's Lyric Poems*, trans. Robert M. Durling (Cambridge, Mass., 1976).

8 Lorenzo de' Medici, *Opere*, ed. Attilio Simioni, 2 vols. (Bari, 1913–14), 15; all subsequent quotations refer to this edition.

9 See André Rochon, *La Jeunesse de Laurent de Médicis* (Paris, 1963), 246–48.

10 See Rochon, 144–64.

11   *Prosatori Latini del Quattrocento*, ed. Eugenio Garin (Milan, 1952), 796; the following quotation also refers to this edition.

12   Quotations from *Le Opere di Dante*, ed. Michele Barbi et al. (Florence, 1960); and *La Vita Nuova of Dante Alighieri*, trans. Mark Musa (Bloomington: Indiana University Press, 1962).

13   For Petrarch's responses to private losses through death see Renée Neu Watkins, "Petrarch and the Black Death: From Fear to Monuments," *Studies in the Renaissance* 19 (1972): 196–223.

14   The most ambitious attempt at dating Lorenzo's poetry is Mario Martelli, *Studi Laurenziani* (Florence, 1965). On pages 64–108 Martelli studies the tribute to Lorenzo in Poliziano's *La Nutricia* (1486) and ingeniously links the order of the imagery in lines 752–62 to the supposed order of nineteen sonnets composed in 1473–74 but set in a version of the *Comento* in 1486. For a criticism of the rigidity of this scheme see Tiziano Zanato, *Saggio sul "Comento" di Lorenzo De' Medici* (Florence, 1979), 285–321.

15   The poetry of the *Vita nuova* was first printed in *Sonetti e Canzoni di diuersi antichi autori toscani* (Florence, 1527); the first printed edition that included the prose was *Vita nuova di Dante Alighieri con xv canzoni del medesimo e la vita di esso Dante scritta da Giovanni Boccaccio* (Florence, 1576); see Michele Barbi, *Della Fortuna di Dante nel secolo XVI* (Florence, 1890).

16   For the mode of Lorenzo's commentary see Zanato, 198–238, and Sara Sturm, *Lorenzo de' Medici* (New York, 1974), 63–76.

17   For Landino see Craig Kallendorf, "Cristoforo Landino's *Aeneid* and the Humanist Critical Tradition," *Renaissance Quarterly* 36 (1983): 519–46; and Mario Di Cesare, "Cristoforo Landino: The Virgilian Commentator and Critic as Hero," in *The Early Renaissance, Acta*, vol. 9 (1982), ed. Anthony L. Pellegrini (Binghamton, 1985), 19–32. For Poliziano see Vittore Branca, *Poliziano e l'umanesimo della parola* (Turin, 1983), 1–36; and Anthony Grafton, "On the Scholarship of Politian and Its Context," *Journal of the Warburg and Courtauld Institutes* 40 (1977): 152–88. For an overview see Anthony Grafton, "Renaissance Readers and Ancient Texts: Comments on Some Commentaries," *Renaissance Quarterly* 38 (1985): 615–49.

18   Quotations from *Opere*, 3–8. For the attribution to Poliziano, see Mario Santoro, "Poliziano o il Magnifico," *Giornale italiano di filologia* 1 (1948): 139–49; but see also Sara Sturm, "The Case for Lorenzo's Authorship of the *Epistola*," *Renaissance and Reformation* 8 (1971): 69–78.

19   Cristoforo Landino, *Scritti critici e teorici*, ed. Roberto Cardini, 2 vols. (Rome, 1974), 1:40. For dates see Arthur Field, "Cristoforo Landino's First Lectures on Dante," *Renaissance Quarterly* 39 (1986): 16–48, esp. 31–32. For the political motive, see Mario Santoro, "Cristoforo Landino e il Volgare," *Giornale storico della letteratura italiana* 131 (1954): 501–47. For the view that political forces did not prevail, see Cecil Grayson, "Lorenzo, Machiavelli, and the Italian Language," *Italian Renaissance Studies*, ed. Ernest Fraser Jacob (London, 1960), 410–32.

20 John Shearman, *Raphael's Cartoons in the Collection of Her Majesty the Queen and the Tapestries for the Sistine Chapel* (London, 1972), 16–17, 50, 77–80. See also Cox-Rearick, 39–40, 248.

21 References to Ficino's Latin translations of Plato are to Plato, *Opere*, ed. R. B. Hirtschig, 2 vols. (Paris, 1891).

22 Marsilio Ficino, *Opere* (Basel, 1561), 1330; the following quotation refers to this edition.

23 Creighton E. Gilbert, *Italian Art 1400–1500: Sources and Documents* (Englewood Cliffs, N.J., 1980), 128.

24 Angelo Poliziano, *Opere*, ed. Ida Maier, 3 vols. (Turin, 1970–71).

25 Mario Fubini, "Nota sulla prosa di Lorenzo" in *Studi sulla letteratura del Rinascimento* (Florence, 1947), 126–37.

CONTINUITY AND CHANGE IN THE IDEALS OF HUMANISM:
THE EVIDENCE FROM FLORENTINE FUNERAL ORATORY
JOHN MC MANAMON S.J.

1 Cecil Grayson, "Il *Canis* di Leon Battista Alberti," in *Umanesimo e Rinascimento a Firenze e Venezia: Miscellanea di studi in onore di Vittore Branca III*, 2 vols., Piblioteca dell'*Archivum Romanicum* 180 (Florence, 1983), 1:204: "Vale igitur, mi canis, atque esto, quantum in me sit, prout tua expetit virtus, immortalis." See further Grayson, 1:193–95; Paul-Henri Michel, *Un idéal humain au XVe siècle: La pénsee de L. B. Alberti (1404–1472)* (Paris, 1930; reprint, Geneva, 1971), 229–55; Eugenio Garin, "Leon Battista Alberti e il mondo dei morti," *Giornale critico della filosofia italiana*, 4th ser., 4 (1973): 178–89; and Emilio Mattioli, *Luciano e l'umanesimo* (Naples, 1980), 74–100. For information on funeral oratory during the Italian Renaissance, see McManamon, *Funeral Oratory and the Cultural Ideals of Italian Humanism* (Chapel Hill, N.C., 1988).

2 Grayson, "Canis," 196; and Jacqueline de Romilly, *Magic and Rhetoric in Ancient Greece* (Cambridge, Mass., 1975).

3 Plutarch *Pericles* 1.1–2.4; A. E. Wardman, "Plutarch's Methods in the *Lives*," *The Classical Quarterly*, n.s. 21 (1971): 254–61; D. A. Russell, *Plutarch* (London, 1972); Vito R. Giustiniani, "Sulle traduzioni latine delle *Vite* di Plutarco nel Quattrocento," *Rinascimento*, n.s. 1 (1961): 3–62; Gianvito Resta, *Le epitomi di Plutarco nel Quattrocento*, Miscellanea erudita 5 (Padua, 1962); Roberto Weiss, *Medieval and Humanist Greek: Collected Essays*, Medioevo e umanesimo 8 (Padua, 1977), 204–77; Ronald Witt, "Salutati and Plutarch," in *Essays Presented to Myron P. Gilmore*, ed. Sergio Bertelli and Gloria Ramakus, 2 vols. (Florence, 1978), 1:335–46; and Edmund Fryde, "The Beginnings of Italian Humanist Historiography: The *New Cicero* of Leonardo Bruni," *English Historical Review* 95 (1980): 533–52.

4 Grayson, "Canis," 197–200.

5 Ibid., 200: "Tametsi quis fortitudinem anteponat pietati, fidei, religioni, quas omnes virtutes esse iustitie partes commemorant? Non ingrediar eam di-

sputationem eorum qui dicunt apud quem una sit virtus, eundem omnes alias habere virtutes. Quid an non iustitia sit nos ut hostes et amici simul diligant? Fortitudone ut, cum timeant, oderint? Fortes in castris intra armorum tumultus versantur in rapinis, in cede, si recte interpretamur, consenescunt militando; qua in re una maxime fortitudini locus est. Iusti in laribus patriis et domesticis cum penatibus et caris civibus quietem tranquillitatemque colunt. Animi audacia et viribus pacem et otium fortasse queritat miles. Per equitatem autem ac leges otio et pace cives fruimur." Leonardo Bruni had rated "fortitudo" the preeminent virtue in his eulogy for Nanni Strozzi (1428). See, for example, Bruni on Strozzi (1428), p. 5: "Ea siquidem virtus [i.e., fortitudo] una est quae homines magis illlustrat quam ulla virtutum caeterarum. Itaque res bellicae pacis artibus sine controversia praeferuntur," and p. 7: "Est enim fortitudo splendidissima virtus, ac nescio an supereminentissima virtutum caeterarum, plena spiritus, plena vigoris, plena justissimae animositatis, mascula profecto quaedam atque invicta."

6 Grayson, "Canis," 201–2; Leonardo Giustiniani, "Funebris oratio . . . pro Carlo Zeno," *Rerum italicarum scriptores* (hereinafter RIS), n.s. 19/6:142; Cicero *Tusc.* I.2.4; and Quintilian I.10.19.

7 Vinzenz Buchheit, *Untersuchungen zur Theorie des Genos Epideiktikon von Gorgias bis Aristoteles* (Munich, 1960); Wilhelm Kierdorf, *Laudatio Funebris: Interpretationen und Untersuchungen zur Entwicklung der römischen Leichenrede*, Beiträge zur klassischen Philologie 106 (Meisenheim am Glan, 1980); K. R. Walters, " 'We Fought Alone at Marathon': Historical Falsification in the Attic Funeral Oration," *Rheinisches Museum für Philologie* 124 (1981): 204–11; and D. A. Russell and N. G. Wilson, "Epideictic Practice and Theory," *Menander Rhetor* (Oxford, 1981), 11–34.

8 Bruni, "Laudatio [ca. 1403–4]," 258–62; Bruni on Nanni Strozzi (1428), 3–5, citing Sallust *Cat.* 7.2; Hans Baron, *The Crisis of the Early Italian Renaissance*, rev. ed. (Princeton, N.J., 1966), 47–78, 199–224, 412–39; idem, *From Petrarch to Leonardo Bruni: Studies in Humanistic and Political Literature* (Chicago and London, 1968), 102–23, 151–71; Cesare Vasoli, "Considerazioni sulla *Laudatio urbis Florentinae* di Leonardo Bruni," *Studi sulla cultura del Rinascimento* (Manduria, 1968), 48–68; Hermann Goldbrunner, "Leonardo Brunis Kommentar zu seiner Übersetzung der pseudo-aristotelischen Ökonomik: Ein humanistischer Kommentar," in *Der kommentar in der Renaissance*, ed. August Buck (Boppard, 1975), 99–118; and Quentin Skinner, *The Foundations of Modern Political Thought I: The Renaissance* (Cambridge, 1978), 69–112.

9 Salutati made his remarks in a letter to Peregrino Zambeccari in 1398. See *Epistolario di Coluccio Salutati*, ed. Francesco Novati, 4 vols. (Rome, 1891–1911), 3:285–308. The English translation quoted here is that by Ronald Witt in *The Earthly Republic: Italian Humanists on Government and Society*, ed. Benjamin Kohl and Ronald Witt (Philadelphia, 1978), 95.

10 Bruni on Nanni Strozzi (1428), 4–7; Skinner, 75–77.

11 Bruni, "Laudatio [ca. 1403–4]," 251–58; Bruni on Nanni Strozzi (1428), 7.

12 Bruni, "Laudatio [ca. 1403–4]," 243–44; Bruni on Nanni Strozzi (1428), 3. Subsequent orators continued to join the values of *libertas* and *imperium*. See, for example, Antonio Pacini on Lorenzo di Giovanni de' Medici (1440), fol. 1r–v ("Hinc enim tot nobilissimi viri Fabritii, Metelli, Fabii, Scipiones, Marcelli, Cesares, Emilii emanarunt, qui non modo quod suis virtutibus atque animi magnitudine summam patrie libertatem con-/parassent, verum etiam latissimum agrum amplissimumque imperium clarissimis triumphis per orbem terrarum vendicavere"), fols. 3v–4 (regarding the war against Lucca); Giannozzo Manetti on Giannozzo Pandolfini (1456), fol. 20v ("primo libertatem vestram custodire et vos deinde in antiquata privilegiorum nostrorum dignitate facilius conservare ac denique imperium vestrum adaugere ac longe lateque amplificare valeatis"); and Cristoforo Landino on Donato Acciaiuoli (1478), fol. 12 ("Quamobrem nemo ignorat Donatum Acciaolum et in ea patria natum que non solum florentissimis opibus libera semper fuerit, sed plerisque olim liberis civitatibus summa cum dignitate imperitet"). The imperialist strain found reinforcement in Cicero's account of the dream of Scipio (*Rep.* VI.13.13) where God rewarded those who preserved, aided, and *enlarged* the state.

13 Cicero *Brut.* 12.45. See, for example, Matteo Palmieri, *Vita Civile*, ed. Gino Belloni, Istituto Nazionale di Studi sul Rinascimento, Studi e testi 7 (Florence, 1982), 44–45: "Il perchè riconosca da Dio chi ha ingegno l'essere nato in questi tempi, i quali più fioriscono d'excellenti arti / d'ingegno, che altri tempi sieno stati già sono mille anni passati, solo che e' piacesse a chi tutto governa per gratia dare lunga et tranquillissima pace all'umile nostra Italia."

14 Marcello Adriani on Giuliano de' Medici, duke of Nemours (1516), fols. 72v–73.

15 Bruni, "Rerum suo tempore gestarum commentarius [AA. 1378–1440]," RIS n.s. 19/3:445–46; and Giannozzo Manetti on Leonardo Bruni (1444), 95–96. Hans Baron, "The Year of Leonardo Bruni's Birth and Methods for Determining the Ages of Humanists Born in the Trecento," *Speculum* 52 (1977): 595–96.

16 Anonymous (Donato Acciaiuoli?) on Ioannes Hunyadi (1456), fols. 83v (where Hungary is described as the walls of the Christian republic), 84r–v (where the efforts of Roman heroes to defend the state or extend its rule for personal glory are contrasted to Hunyadi's efforts to defend the common liberty of Christians in Christ's name) and 84v–85 (where the Turks are compared to ancient barbarians like the Goths and Vandals).

17 Werner Jaeger, *Paideia: The Ideals of Greek Culture*, trans. Gilbert Highet, 3 vols. (Oxford, 1939–44), 3:46–155; and Lucia Gualdo Rosa, "Le traduzioni latine dell'*A Nicocle* di Isocrate nel Quattrocento," in *Acta Conventus Neo-Latini Lovaniensis*, ed. J. Issewijn and E. Ke ler (Leuven/Louvain, 1973), 275–303. Ead., *La fede nella "Vaideia": Aspetti della fortuna europea di Isocrate nei secoli XV e XVI*, Studi storici, fasc. 140–42 (Rome, 1984), 27–28.

18 Brooks Otis, *Virgil: A Study in Civilized Poetry* (Oxford, 1963), 313–17; Alamanno Rinuccini, "Forma decreti faciendi vel rogationis promulgandae in

honorem Cosmi Medicis," *Lettere ed orazioni*, ed. Vito R. Giustiniani, Nuova collezione di testi umanistici inediti o rari 9 (Florence, 1953), 125; and Donato Acciaiuoli on Cosimo de' Medici (1465), 261. Cf. also Giannozzo Manetti on Giannozzo Pandolfini (1456), fols. 11v–15v.

19 Seneca *De clem.* I.14.2; Antonio Pacini on Lorenzo di Giovanni de' Medici (1440), fols. 3v–5; and Alison Brown, "The Humanist Portrait of Cosimo de' Medici, Pater Patriae," *Journal of the Warburg and Courtauld Institutes* 24 (1961): 186–221.

20 Cristoforo Landino on Donato Acciaiuoli (1478), fols. 13r–v ("Missus est et in Pistorienses, genus hominum ex natura ferocius quam opportet et diversarum partium studiis vehementer accensum, et tamen cum prudentia ac diligentia sua, tum auctoritate quae propter rerum (recte: Ricc. MS 626) administratarum famam non mediocris illi erat et tumultuantes ad concordiam reduxit et antiquas simultates vehementer / mitigavit"), fol. 13v ("Erat vera religio, semper paci, semper concordiae favebat"), 13v–14v (for his courage on diplomatic missions and for the ecphrasis of Giuliano's murder), fols. 17v–18 (where Florence itself states its gratitude to Donato); Eugenio Garin, "Donato Acciaiuoli cittadino fiorentino," *Medioevo e Rinascimento* (Bari, 1954), 211–87; Roberto Cardini, "Alle origini della filosofia landiniana: La *Praefatio in Tusculanis*," *Rinascimento*, n.s. 10 (1970): 119–26; Margery A. Ganz, "Donato Acciaiuoli and the Medici: A Strategy for Survival in '400 Florence," *Rinascimento*, n.s. 22 (1982): 33–73. The theme of the "factious Pistoians" also appears in Giannozzo Manetti on Giannozzo Pandolfini (1456), fol. 11v; Benedetto Colucci on Antonio Partini (1455–1456), 70–72; and Antonio da Montecatini on Niccolò Forteguerri (Pistoia, 1473), fol. 141v. Further portraits of humanists as upright public servants are supplied by Poggio on Niccolò Niccoli (1437), 274–75; and Alamanno Rinuccini on Matteo Palmieri (1475), 83–84.

21 Sharon Therese Strocchia, "Burials in Renaissance Florence, 1350–1500," Ph.D. diss., University of California, Berkeley, 1981; and Domenico Moreni, *Pompe funebri celebrate nella . . . basilica di San Lorenzo dal secolo XIII a tutto il regno Mediceo* (Florence, 1827). Orators who underline the new situation created by the election of Giovanni de' Medici as pope include Marcello Adriani on Giuliano de' Medici, duke of Nemours (1516), fols. 76–78; and Francesco Cattani on Lorenzo de' Medici, duke of Urbino (1519), fol. 366v. Cf. also Rosemary Devonshire Jones, "Lorenzo de' Medici, Duca d'Urbino, 'Signore' of Florence?" in *Studies on Machiavelli*, ed. Myron P. Gilmore, Biblioteca storica Sansoni 50 (Florence, 1972): 297–315.

22 For Cosimo see Marcello Adriani on Giuliano de' Medici, duke of Nemours (1516), fols. 73v–74v, esp. fol. 74 ("Laudandum in eo illud etiam quod in Medice gentis laudibus dictum alias a nobis est, naturam illi et continuum fuisse studium ex bello pacem et in infida pace rennovato iterum bello tutius et certius id bonum vobis reddere"); Battista Casali on Giuliano de' Medici, duke of Nemours (Rome, 1516), fols. 63–64v; and Francesco Cattani on Lorenzo de' Medici, duke of Urbino (1519), fols. 362v–63. For Lorenzo see

Marcello Adriani on Giuliano de' Medici, duke of Nemours (1516), fols. 75v–76 ("uno illo cive / vestro incolumi a tantis bellorum cladibus que secute postea sunt incolumem et vestram et aliorum tota Italia rem futuram"); Battista Casali on Giuliano de' Medici, duke of Nemours (Rome, 1516), fols. 64v–66, esp. fol. 65v ("Ex illo expertus quantum esset in pace boni ad pacem spectare, pacem velle, bellum odisse"); Francesco Cattani on Lorenzo de' Medici, duke of Urbino (1519), fol. 363; and Nicolai Rubinstein, "Lorenzo de' Medici: The Formation of His Statecraft," *Proceedings of the British Academy* 63 (1977): 71–94. For the tradition of praise of this sort, see Brown, "Humanist Portrait." Battista Casali, in his eulogy for Giuliano, duke of Nemours (Rome, 1516), fol. 67r–v, described how the Medici duke governed according to the law and acted more like a citizen among citizens than a prince (*princeps*).

23 Cicero *De orat.* III.14.55; Quintilian I.Pr.9; George Kennedy, *The Art of Rhetoric in the Roman World 300 B.C.–A.D. 300* (Princeton, N.J., 1972), 57, 100–101; Bruni, "Oratio in hypocritas," Florence, Bibl. Nazionale, MS Magl. 8:1311, fols. 45–48v; Heinz Willi Wittschier, *Giannozzo Manetti: Das Corpus der Orationes,* Studi italiani 10 (Cologne and Graz, 1968): 183–85; and Donald Wilcox, "Matteo Palmieri and the *De captivitate Pisarum liber,"* in *Renaissance Studies in Honor of Hans Baron,* ed. Anthony Molho and John Tedeschi (De Kalb, Ill., 1971), 275–76.

24 Bruni, "Laudatio [ca. 1403–4]," 235–40, esp. 238: "Sed hec tanta admiratio, hic tantus stupor, tam diu apud homines est quam diu hanc pulcerrimam urbem non aspexerunt neque viderunt eius magnificentiam. Ceterum ubi illam intuiti sunt, omnis talis evanescit abitque admiratio"; and anonymous on Baldassare Cossa (1420), fol. 53r–v.

25 Girolamo Aliotti on Bartolomeo Zabarella (1445), 315; "Sui quoque in vos atque in urbem vestram amoris praecipui testimonio sunt ii sumptus magnifici quos in aedibus ipsis pontificiis vel ornandis vel resarciendis profudit." Cf. also Antonio Pacini on Lorenzo di Giovanni de' Medici (1440), fols. 5v–6; Poggio on Lorenzo di Giovanni de' Medici (1440), 281–82, 285; Giannozzo Manetti on Giannozzo Pandolfini (1456), fol. 2; and Marcello Adriani on Giuliano de' Medici, duke of Nemours (1516), fols. 72–73.

26 Bruni, "Commentarius," RIS, n.s. 19/3: 428; Giannozzo Manetti on Leonardo Bruni (1444), 92; anonymous on Leonardo Bruni (1444), 150; and Eugenio Garin, "Ritratto di Leonardo Bruni Aretino," *Atti e memorie della Accademia Petrarca di lettere, arti e scienze,* n.s. 40 (1970–72): 1–17.

27 Anonymous (Donato Acciaiuoli?) on Ioannes Hunyadi (1456), fol. 83: "utque posteri imaginem fortissimi viri ante oculos habeant quem amare, quem imitari, quem sibi ducem in omni vita agenda constituere possint"; and Charles Trinkaus, "The Question of Truth in Renaissance Rhetoric and Anthropology," in *Renaissance Eloquence: Studies in the Theory and Practice of Renaissance Rhetoric,* ed. James J. Murphy (Berkeley, Los Angeles, London, 1983), 207–20.

28 See, for example, Poggio's description of the home of Niccolò Niccoli (1437),

276: "Templum quoddam virtutis et decoris existimabatur domus illa et tanquam habitaculum honestatis, in qua accendebantur omnes ad virtutem et bonarum artium disciplinas. Hic librorum ingens numerus, tum Latinorum tum Graecorum. Hic signa et tabulae, hic veterum imagines, hic nummismata usque a priori illa aetate qua aes primum cudi et moneta obsignari est coepta conspiciebantur. Hinc varia illustrium virorum exempla hunc ad virtutum incitamenta proferebantur. Aderat semper quod et oblectaret oculos, et animum solaretur."

29   Bruni, "Commentarius RIS, n.s. 19/3:431–32; Giannozzo Manetti on Leonardo Bruni (1444), 93–94; anonymous on Leonardo Bruni (1444), 151; Poggio on Leonardo Bruni (1444), 119; and Edwin Ramage, "Velleius Paterculus 2.126.2–3 and the Panegyric Tradition," *Classical Antiquity* 1 (1982): 266–71.

30   Leonardo Bruni, "Prologus in Basilii Epistolam," *Humanistisch-Philosophische Schriften*, ed. Hans Baron (Berlin and Leipzig, 1928), 99–100; Wittschier, *Giannozzo Manetti*, 74–77; and Ronald G. Witt, *Hercules at the Crossroads: The Life, Works, and Thought of Coluccio Salutati*, Duke Monographs in Medieval and Renaissance Studies 6 (Durham, N.C., 1983), 395–413.

31   Poggio on Niccolò Niccoli (1437), 272: "Quae [litterae Graecae] quantum utilitatis nostris hominibus attulerint, tum ad eloquentiam tum ad plurimarum rerum scientiam quis ignorat? Videntur prisca illa tempora quibus eloquentia cum sapientia coniuncta vigebat esse hoc saeculo renovata"; Giannozzo Manetti on Leonardo Bruni (1444), 101; anonymous on Leonardo Bruni (1444), 151–52; Poggio on Leonardo Bruni (1444), 123; and Jerrold E. Seigel, *Rhetoric and Philosophy in Renaissance Humanism: The Union of Eloquence and Wisdom, Petrarch to Valla* (Princeton, N.J., 1968), 99–136. Manetti, 102–3, claimed that Bruni revived the golden age of Latin letters by comparing Bruni to Livy and Cicero. Bruni himself, in his eulogy for Nanni Strozzi (1428), 4, assigned special credit to Florence for the "renaissance of good letters."

32   Poggio on Niccolò Niccoli (1437), 271–72, 276–77.

33   George Kennedy, *The Art of Persuasion in Greece* (Princeton, N.J., 1963), 23, 30–32, 96–99; Poggio on Lorenzo di Giovanni de' Medici (1440), 284–85; and Alfonso De Petris, "L'*Adversus Judeos et Gentes* di Giannozzo Manetti," *Rinascimento*, n.s. 16 (1976): 204–5.

34   Cicero *Fin.* III.6.21; Leonardo Bruni, "Prologus in Phaedonem Platonis," *Humanistisch-Philosophische Schriften*, ed. Baron, 4; and Leonardo Bruni on Otto Cavalcanti (Viterbo, 1405), 144. In the "Laudatio [ca. 1403–4]," 233, 258–59, Bruni used the same term (*convenientia*) to describe the ideal concord among Florence's citizens.

35   Matteo Palmieri on Carlo Marsuppini (1453), fol. 69r–v, esp. fol. 69r: "Omnem enim doctrinam divinarum et humanarum artium uno quodam societatis vinculo continebat"; Cristoforo Landino on Donato Acciaiuoli (1478), fols. 15v–16; Garin, "Donato Acciaiuoli," 236–41; Paul Oskar Kristeller, "Francesco da Diacceto and Florentine Platonism in the Sixteenth Century,"

Studies in Renaissance Thought and Letters (Rome, 1956), 287–336; and idem, "The Unity of Truth," *Renaissance Thought and Its Sources*, ed. Michael Mooney (New York, 1979), 196–210. Palmieri himself was buried with a copy of his eclectic and controversial poem, *Città di vita*. Alamanno Rinuccini on Matteo Palmieri (1475), 82–83; Gino Belloni Peressutti, "Palmieri, Matteo (1406–1475): Matteo Palmieri e la trattatistica civile nel Quattrocento," *Dizionario critico della letteratura italiana*, 3 vols. (Turin, 1973), 2:751–52; Richard J. Palermino, "Palmieri's *Città di vita*: More Evidence of Renaissance Platonism," *Bibliothèque d'Humanisme et Renaissance* 44 (1982): 601–4.

36 See the letters in praise of Salutati by Poggio and Pier Paolo Vergerio in *Epistolario di Coluccio Salutati*, ed. Francesco Novati, 4:471–73, 479; Giannozzo Manetti on Leonardo Bruni (1444), 97, 104; Poggio on Leonardo Bruni (1444), 108, 109 (referring to Manuel Chrysoloras), 114 (referring to Carlo Marsuppini); Matteo Palmieri on Carlo Marsuppini (1453), fol. 69r–v; Seigel, *Rhetoric and Philosophy*; and Hanna Gray, "Renaissance Humanism: The Pursuit of Eloquence," *Journal of the History of Ideas* 24 (1963): 497–514.

37 Giannozzo Manetti on Leonardo Bruni (1444), 105–14, citing Cicero *De orat.* I.16.70, III.7.27. Petrarch wrote the comment about Vaucluse in the margin of a codex of Pliny, which he acquired at Mantua in 1350. The manuscript is now in Paris, Bibl. Nationale, MS Par. lat. 6802. See Armando Petrucci, *La scrittura di Francesco Petrarca*, Studi e testi 248 (Vatican City: Bibl. Apostolica Vaticana, 1967), 48–49, 127; J. B. Trapp, "The Owl's Ivy and the Poet's Bays: An Enquiry into Poetic Garlands," *Journal of the Warburg and Courtauld Institutes* 21 (1958): 227–55; idem, "The Poet Laureate: Rome, *Renovatio* and *Translatio Imperii*," in *Rome in the Renaissance: The City and the Myth*, ed. P. A. Ramsey, Medieval and Renaissance Texts and Studies 18 (Binghamton, N.Y., 1982), 93–130; O. B. Hardison, Jr., "The Orator and the Poet: The Dilemma of Humanist Literature," *The Journal of Medieval and Renaissance Studies* 1 (1971): 33–44; and Riccardo Fubini, "Osservazioni sugli *Historiarum florentini populi libri XII* di Leonardo Bruni," in *Studi di storia medievale e moderna per Ernesto Sestan*, 2 vols. (Florence, 1980), 1:435–41.

38 Alamanno Rinuccini on Matteo Palmieri (1475), 80–81: "Cum enim duplex foelicitatis genus a philosophis propositum duplicem vivendi rationem nobis ostendat, et earum una in communibus vitae civilis actionibus versetur, altera procul ab omni actione remota, altissimarum rerum / adipiscendae cognitioni duntaxat intenta sit, prudentissimus vir, medium quendam inter utranque viam modum sequutus, magnam statim ab initio futurae virtutis concitavit expectationem, quam subsequuta mox vita longe superavit." Vito R. Giustiniani, *Alamanno Rinuccini 1426–1499: Materialien und Forschungen zur Geschichte des florentinischen Humanismus* (Cologne and Graz, 1965), 228; Poggio on Leonardo Bruni (1444), 121, 125–26; Matteo Palmieri on Carlo Marsuppini (1453), fol. 69; and Cristoforo Landino on Donato Acciaiuoli (1478), fol. 15v.

39 Aristotle *Rhet.* II.12.3; Cicero *Off.* I.34.122, *Sen.* 11.36; and Poggio on Niccolò Niccoli (1437), 270 ("Nicolaus vero cum ad idem exercitium a patre vocaretur, ipse autem honestioris mercaturae genus quaerendo, videlicet virtutis curam sibi proposuisset, ad linguae Latinae cognitionem se transtulit"), 271 ("Ad eam [virtutem] capescendam sentiebat maxime esse accommodata studia litterarum, quae sola verum virtutis iter demonstrare et vitia compescere existimantur. Cum autem variae essent discendi facultates, quibus homines pro animi affectione applicare ingenium solent, humanitatis studia sibi delegit, velut ea quibus boni viri effici maxime consueverunt et minime rerum cupidi"). Leonardo Bruni on Nanni Strozzi (1428), 4; Poggio on Lorenzo di Giovanni de' Medici (1440), 280–81; and Vito R. Giustiniani, "Homo, Humanus, and the Meanings of 'Humanism,'" *Journal of the History of Ideas* 46 (1985): 167–95.

40 Giannozzo Manetti on Leonardo Bruni (1444), 100; Paul Oskar Kristeller, "Humanism and Scholasticism in the Italian Renaissance," *Renaissance Thought and Its Sources*, 98; anonymous on Leonardo Bruni (1444), 152–53; David Robey, "Humanism and Education in the Early Quattrocento: The *De ingenuis moribus* of P. P. Vergerio," *Bibliothèque d'Humanisme et Renaissance* 42 (1980): 43–44, 47; McManamon, "Innovation in Early Humanist Rhetoric: The Oratory of Pier Paolo Vergerio the Elder," *Rinascimento*, n.s. 22 (1982): 6; and Antonio Pacini on Lorenzo di Giovanni de' Medici (1440), fol. 13. Cf. also Poggio on Niccolò Niccoli (1437), 273–74.

41 Poggio on Niccolò Niccoli (1437), 271 (for Luigi Marsigli); Giannozzo Manetti on Leonardo Bruni (1444), 93; Poggio on Leonardo Bruni (1444), 119 (for Manuel Chrysoloras); and Andrea Alamanno on Giovanni di Cosimo de' Medici (1463), fol. 87 (for Carlo Marsuppini). I express my gratitude to the National Endowment for the Humanities and to Villa I Tatti in Florence for funding the research on which this paper is based and to Alison Brown, Maurizio Bettini, and Ned Mattimoe, S.J., for suggesting ways to improve it.

The Art of Dying Well AND POPULAR PIETY
IN THE PREACHING AND THOUGHT
OF GIROLAMO SAVONAROLA
DONALD WEINSTEIN

I am grateful for the help of Alan E. Bernstein, Heiko A. Oberman, Beverly J. Parker, and Richard H. Rouse in the preparation of this essay.

1 Alberto Tenenti, *Il senso della morte e l'amore della vita nel Rinascimento (Francia e Italia)* (Torino, 1957). Indispensable also is Tenenti's *La vie et la mort à travers l'art* (Paris, 1951).

2 For a list of editions see Girolamo Savonarola, *Prediche sopra Ruth e Michea*, ed. Vincenzo Romano, 2 vols. (Rome, 1962), 2:488. For two slightly different versions of the text see ibid., 362–97 and 446–74. My references will be to the first of these. On the illustrations of Savonarola's writings the funda-

mental work is Gustave Gruyer, *Les illustrations des écrits de Jérôme Savonarole publiés en Italie au XVe et au XVIe siècle et les paroles de Savonarole sur l'art* (Paris, 1879).

3 For the history and a general critique of the two-tiered model, Peter Brown, *The Cult of the Saints: Its Rise and Function in Latin Christianity* (Chicago, 1981), 12–22.

4 For an excellent survey of the literature and the issues as well as some prescriptions of its own, see John Van Engen, "The Christian Middle Ages as an Historiographical Problem," *American Historical Review* 91 (1986): 519–52.

5 Brown, 18. A variant of the two-tiered paradigm may be seen in Richard C. Trexler's *Public Life in Renaissance Florence* (New York, 1980). In defining religion as common behavior, over against the intellectualist prejudice that it is common belief (xviii), Trexler stands the familiar model on its head, without, however, integrating the two tiers of practices and ideas.

6 Tenenti, *Il senso della morte*, esp. 112–14.

7 See, for example, "Bisogna dire la istoria [of Ruth and Boaz] a queste donne e anche a questi omini che non leggono." *Prediche sopra Ruth e Michea*, 2:362. This suggests either that Savonarola assumed that the women and some of the men in his audience could not read or that some of the women and some of the men could not.

8 Savonarola invariably uses male nouns and pronouns when speaking of humanity collectively, and most of his examples of behavior and thought are male; for example, "Ma e bene cosa difficile a indurre l'omo a questa cogitazione del morire." *Prediche sopra Ruth e Michea*, 2:362. I have tried to avoid repeating this usage wherever I can without changing his meaning or distorting his intention.

9 Savonarola here refers to an earlier sermon in which he advised the three pictures (Ibid., 372). I have been unable to find such a sermon.

10 Like Savonarola, I follow here the Vulgate numbering of the Psalms.

11 Ibid., 392. As noted, Savonarola had said earlier that love of eternal life and fear of damnation were the two stimuli to a good life (Ibid. 374–75).

12 On the medieval use of the metaphor of life as a chess game with the Devil, the stake being the human soul, see H. J. R. Murray, *A History of Chess* (Oxford, 1932), 475 n. 56.

13 In a sermon of February 23, 1306, in Florence, the Dominican Fra Giordano da Pisa referred to the invention of eyeglasses less than twenty years earlier by a man to whom he himself had talked. This passage has been used to date the invention shortly after 1286, probably in Pisa. Edward Rosen, "The Invention of Eyeglasses," *Journal of the History of Medicine and the Allied Sciences* (1956), 13–45, 183–218. I have enlisted the help of Professor R. H. Rouse in looking for earlier uses of the metaphor of death spectacles in preaching, but so far neither he nor I have found any.

14 For the text of Poliziano's account in his letter to Jacopo Antiquario (May

18, 1492), see *Prosatori Latini del Quattrocento*, ed. Eugenio Garin (Milano, 1952), 886–901.

15 Girolamo Savonarola, *Triumphus Crucis*, ed. Mario Ferrara (Rome, 1961), 62.

16 For a review of this question as well as a careful statement of the argument for regarding Savonarola as a forerunner of Evangelical Catholicism, see Paolo Simoncelli, *Evangelismo italiano del Cinquecento* (Rome, 1979), chap. 1. For a detailed argument that Savonarola's Meditations on Psalms 30 and 50 influenced Martin Luther in the development of his doctrine of justification by faith alone, see Josef Nolte, "Evangelicae doctrinae purum exemplum: Savonarolas Gefängnismeditationen im Hinblick auf Luthers Theologische Anfänge," *Kontinuität und Umbruch*, ed. J. Nolte et al. (Stuttgart, 1978), 59–72.

17 "Sed vita christiana ad hoc potissimum tendit, ut, posthabitis creaturis omnibus tam spiritualibus quam corporeis, per contemplationem et amorem se totam in Deum transfundat et fiat unus spiritus cum deo." It is interesting to compare this with Savonarola's own more qualified rendering into Italian: "la vita cristiana tutta consista in alienarsi, non solamente dalle cose temporale, ma *etiam* da ogni amore proprio e accostarsi per amore e contemplazione a Dio, per assimigliarsi in tutto a lui e diventare, quanto e possibile, una medesima cosa con esso lui." *Triumphus Crucis*, lib. 2, cap. 3. (Savonarola's translation is here published following the Latin text.)

18 "Expositio in Psalmum Miserere Mei, Deus," *Operette spirituali*, 2:227.

19 "Expositio Orationis Dominicae" in Girolamo Savonarola *Operette Spirituali*, ed. Mario Ferrara, 2 vols. (Rome, 1976), 1:228.

20 Girolamo Savonarola, *Prediche sopra i Salmi*, ed. Vincenzo Romano, 2 vols. (Rome, 1974), 1:128.

21 Strictly speaking, Savonarola did not here use the term *laici*, but *seculari* (and elsewhere, *secolari*). His distinction was between those who pursued the *vita attiva* and those who followed the *vita contemplativa*; so that secular priests might be included in the first of the two categories; but the context and his references to avarice and ambition strongly suggests that here, as elsewhere, it is the laity he had in mind. "Trattato in defensione e commendazione dell' orazione mentale," in *Operette spirituali* 1:176–78.

22 "Vel certe diversae viae, diversae sunt vitae: per aliam namque incedunt clerici, per aliam monachi, per aliam mendicantes; aliam tenent matrimonio coniuncti, aliam in viduitate degentes et continentes, aliam virgines; aliam sequuntur principes, aliam doctores, aliam mercatores: denique diversi status hominum per diversas vias ad patriam caelestem proficiscuntur. Docebo itaque iniquos vias tuas unumquemque iuxta conditionem et captum suum; et impii ad te convertentur, quia praedicabo eis non me ipsum sed Christum crucifixum." *Operette spirituali*, 2:224–25.

23 The account has been published twice: by F. Polidori, "Narrazione del caso di Pietro Paolo Boscoli e di Agostino Capponi (1513)," *Archivio storico*

italiano, 1 (1842): 275–309; and by R. Bacchelli, *La morte di Pietro Paolo Boscoli* (Florence, 1943). I have consulted both.

24   For the death of Savonarola, see especially *La vita del Beato Ieronimo Savonarola,* ed. Piero Ginori Conti (Florence, 1937), chap. 45.

25   Samuel Y. Edgerton, Jr., *Pictures and Punishment: Art and Criminal Prosecution during the Florentine Renaissance* (Ithaca, 1985), chap. 5. Boscoli's death is discussed briefly, 183–84.

26   Two important readings of Luca della Robbia's account of Boscoli's death are: Delio Cantimori, "Il caso del Boscoli e la vita del Rinascimento," *Giornale critico della filosofia italiana* 4 (1927): 241–55; Trexler, *Public Life in Renaissance Florence.* My own interpretation is closer to Cantimori's in emphasizing the religious rather than the political nature of Boscoli's agony. While Boscoli's counselors tried to persuade him to give up thinking of himself as a martyr to liberty, the context shows clearly that they did so because they feared such thoughts diverted him from dying as a Christian, that is, as a confessed sinner, not because they wanted him to accept the state's right to put him to death, as Trexler maintains. (Cf. Savonarola's reprimand to Fra Silvestro Maruffi, one of the two friars condemned to die with him, because Silvestro wanted to proclaim their innocence: *Vita anonima,* 178–79.) Trexler does not mention the final passage in which Fra Cipriano and Luca condone Boscoli's attempted tyrannicide on the authority of St. Thomas.

A RENAISSANCE ARTIST IN THE SERVICE
OF A SINGING CONFRATERNITY
CYRILLA BARR

Research for this essay was supported in part by a grant from the National Endowment for the Humanities. I wish to thank also Gino Corti for assistance with problems of transcription and Professor John Henderson, Cambridge University, for permission to quote from his unpublished work.

All references to occurrences prior to March 25 have been altered to reflect modern dating. References to archival and library sources from Florence are cited according to the following abbreviations:

ASF   Archivio di Stato, Florence

CRS   Compagnie Religiose Soppresse

BNCF   Biblioteca Nazionale Centrale, Florence

BRF   Biblioteca Riccardiana, Florence

Documents referring to the Company of St. Agnes are from the Archivio di Stato, Compagnie Religiose Soppresse, Compagnia di Santa Maria delle Laudi, detta di Sant'Agnese. They are given below, and all subsequent entries will be referred to by number only.

CRS 4, Registro, Libro di Partiti, A, 1483–1509

CRS 24, Fogli diversi, Entrata e Uscita, 1440–47

CRS 98, Entrata e Uscita segnata B, 1424–41

CRS 99, Entrata e Uscita segnata D, 1447–1519
CRS 100, Entrata e Uscita dei sindaci, 1466–81
CRS 114, Debitore e Creditore, 1447–65
CRS 115, Libro Campione A, 1377–1510
CRS 125, Entrata e Uscita, 1471–1512
CRS 126, Entrata e Uscita della Festa di Sant'Agnese, 1514–33
CRS 145, Debitore e Creditore, 1417–29

1   Martin Wackernagel, *The World of the Florentine Renaissance Artist*, trans. Alison Luchs (Princeton, N.J., 1981), 18.

2   The singing of *laude* played an important part in the devotions of the *disciplinati* as well, but the flagellant companies of Florence never employed professional musicians as did the *laudesi*.

3   Devotion to both St. Agnes and the mystery of Christ's ascension are evident very early in the history of the company. Among the treasures of the church was a relic claimed to be the foot of Saint Agnes given to the Carmelites by the bishop of Florence, Giovanni de' Mangiadori, and kept in a reliquary beneath the altar in the chapel of the *laudesi*. See Giuseppe Richa, *Notizie historiche delle chiese fiorentine* (Florence, 1762), 10:16–17.

4   The company's records appear to have been overlooked for some time, undoubtedly because they were not initially entered in the inventory of the Compagnie Religiose Soppresse but came into the archive under the heading of the Bigallo.

5   Concerning the gradual secularization of the activities see Gilles G. Meersseman, *Ordo Fraternitatis Confraternite e pietà dei laici nel medioevo* (Rome, 1977), 2:997–98; and John Henderson, "Piety and Charity in Late Medieval Florence: Religious Confraternities from the Middle of the Thirteenth to the Late Fifteenth Century," (Ph.D. diss., University of London, 1983), 28–29.

6   Henderson, 55.

7   On the use of the rood screen as stage see Marcia B. Hall, "The *Tramezzo* in Santa Croce, Florence, Reconstructed," *Art Bulletin* 56 (1974): 340. See also the description of the Ascension play of 1439 as recorded by the Russian bishop, Abraham of Suzdal, quoted in Alessandro d'Ancona, *Origini del teatro italiano*, 2d ed. (Turin, 1891), 251; and Cesare Molinari, *Spettacoli fiorentini del quattrocento* (Venice, 1969), 47.

8   Henderson, 55, table 2.1.

9   Henderson, 64, table 2.4. Documents granting the subsidies are found in ASF Provv. Reg. 126, 195v–196v, August 28, 1435, "pro augenda devotione e civitatis atque continuo student circa novas inventiones faciendi pro maiori veneratione solemnitatis eiusdem"; and Provv. Reg. 136, 212v–213r, "a honore di Dio e a magnificentia di questa città"; Provv. Reg. 156, 255v–256r, 1465. The subsidy for 1455 appears to be missing, but the document from 1465 refers to one granted ten years earlier.

10 Eve Borsook, *The Companion Guide to Florence* (London, 1979), 302. Borsook believes the building nestled beside the east flank of the church to be the oratory of the company.

11 See, for example, the studies of Frank D'Accone, "Alcune note sulle compagnie fiorentine dei laudesi durante il quattrocento," *Rivista italiana di musicologia* 10 (1975): 86–114; idem, "Le Compagnie dei laudesi in Firenze durante l'ars nova," *L'ars nova in Italia del trecento* 3 (1970): 253–82; and idem, "Music and Musicians at the Florentine Monastery of Santa Trinità, 1360–1363," in *Memorie e contributi alla musica dal medioevo al età moderna offerti a Federico Ghisi nel settantesimo compleanno, 1900–1971* (Bologna, 1971), 131–51.

12 Neri's hand is seen prominently in CRS 100, 114, 115.

13 See Bruno Santi, ed., *Neri di Bicci, Le Recordanze, 10 Marzo 1435–24 Aprile 1475* (Pisa, 1976).

14 CRS 99, 3r. Elected July 1, 1448, for four months.

15 CRS 99, 20r. January 1, 1454, "Nieri del Brinci [sic] dipintore."

16 CRS 115, 1r–66v.

17 CRS 115, 163v. "Io Neri di Bicci di Lorenzo Bicci, dipintore, chome sindacho e prochuratore della Chompagnia di S. Maria e S. Agnesa che si rauna nella chiesa di Santa Maria del Charmino di Firenze, farò qui rochordo e inventario, ogi questo dì 17 di Genaio 1466, di tute le maserizie e chose si trova questo presente dì la detta chonpagnia ne' luogho e fuori de' luogho, e a quello che dette maserizie ànno a servire."

18 See Appendix A for the titles.

19 CRS 115, 163v–164r, part 1, Maserizie da sopelire e morti, and part 2, Maserizie e fornimenti de' legio da dire le laude.

20 Henderson, 113.

21 See *Libro degli ordinamenti de la Compagnia di Santa Maria del Carmino scritte nel 1280*, ed. Giulio Piccini (Bologna, 1867), 19.

22 CRS 115, 163v. "Una choltre grande, di baldachino ros[s]o chon Giesù bianchi e altre opere, sopanata di panno lino rosso, suvi uno drapellone di tafettà nel quale è dipinto uno Christo quando va in cielo. Chon 4 nappe di chermusi e d'oro, chon botoni a dette nape, le quali s'apichano a detta choltre quando s'adopra.

Una choltre verghata, di tafettà azuro, verghe g[i]alle, da tenere in chasa, suvi el segnio della chonpagnia.

Uno ghuanc[i]ale a uso di detta choltre, di medesimo drapo, pieno di piuma overo penna fine, chon 4 nape verdi.

Uno ghuanc[i]ale ispogliato, pieno di penna fine, da tenere nella bara sotto el chapo a' morti. (Gloss: Venderonsi perch'erano ghuasti a entrata di chapo sindacho, Segnata A, a c. 18)."

23 CRS 115, 163v, "Un paio di torchi grandi da portare e achonpagniare e morti."

24 The large number of *lauda* manuscripts which contain the text only has led some observers to believe that the *laude* were only recited. See Vincent Moleta, "The Illuminated Laudari Mgl[1] and Mgl[2]," *Scriptorium* 32 (1978): 29, 36.

25 CRS 115, 164r. "Uno legio a chariuola, dapiè chon uno armario cholla topa e chiave, dove e laldieri tenghono chandele e chose che bisognia."

26   CRS 115, 164r, "Un paio di feri, e quali s'apichano a detto legio quando si
dichono le laude, in su' quali s'apichano le chandele, e adopransi e dì feriale.
Uno paio di feri grandi, a uso di detto legio e quali s'adoprano e dì festivi,
lavorati di fero richamente di più pezi e 3 fughuse di legniame di rilievo,
c[i]oè Nostra Donna in cima di detti feri, e due ang[i]oletti dallato."

27   CRS 115, 164r, "Una tovaglia da detto legio di tafettà nero, sopanata di panno
lino nero, franc[i]ata di g[i]allo e freg[i]ata di freg[i]uzi di biancho. . . .
Un'ata tovaglia di panno lino nero, per detto legio, adoprasi e dì de' morti,
frang[i]ata dattorno di frange."

28   CRS 115, 164r, "Una tovaglia di tafettà biancho, sopanata di panno lino
biancho, frang[i]ata di frange di più cholori, suvi dua segni della chompagnia.
Una tovaglia per detto legio, di tafetta chang[i]ante, verghata e frang[i]ata
di verdi, cho' segni della chonpagnia, di pano lino rosso sopannata. Una
tovaglia richamata di seta e verghata, cho' storie, una di Nostra Donna
e una dell'Ascensione di Christo, sopanata di panno lino. Chon una chas-
[s]etta lungha, in che istà detta tovaglia."

29   CRS 115, 164r, "Una choreg[i]a di seta ros[s]a e verde, chon uno pendente di
cristallo leghato in otone, che ss'adopra a detto legio per lle solenità."

30   CRS 115, 164r, "Uno libro grande choverto d'assi, choperte di chuoio chom-
passi d'otone e bullette grosse, richiamente fatto, suvi iscritto molte laude
cho' molti begli mini, istoriato, di charta pechora. U' libro choverte d'assi e
di chuoio, di charta pechora, suvi molte laude antiche, dipintovi suso in cro-
cifiso e più altri mini. Adoperasi ogni dì. Uno libro di laude, choverto d'assi,
charta pechora, miniato di mini grandi a penello e a penna. Uno libro di
laude choverto d'assi chon bullette, charte di pechora, iscritovi suso molte
laude zolfate e fighurate basso. Uno libro di charta pecora, choverto d'asse,
imbulletato, iscritovi suso laude."

31   See Agostino Ziino, "Laudi e miniature fiorentine del primo trecento," *Studi
musicale* 7 (1978): 40–83.

32   CRS 115, 164r, "Uno libro charta banbagina choverto d'assi chon bullette in
sul quale è iscritto e vangeli in rima.
Uno libretto choverto d'assi, imbulletato, in sul quale è iscritto la pasione
di Christo in rima."

33   CRS 4, 52v. Payment made to Niccolò Mascalzoni, "tinoristo . . . la qua-
resima passata cantò insieme chon uno che lui tolse in adiuto, la passione
in pergamo come è di consueto . . . per havere cantato decta passione et
per sua faticha gli stantiarono L. una e s. dieci, cioè, L. una per lui et s.
dieci al compagno che gli aiutò."

34   For example MS 20 of the Archivio Capitolari, Assisi, which describes the
disciplinati devozione in detail, and BRF MS 2566, the Statutes of the Compagnia di San Zenobi dell'Assunta in Florence, 7v.

35   For example, BRF MS 391, Statutes of the Laudesi of Orsanmichele, 6v: "ssi
debbia fare luminaria la sera alla lauda con candelotti accesi in mano dinanzi
alla ymagine de la Vergina Maria." Also, BNCF MS Banco rari 336 (già Pala-
tino 1172), the Statutes of the Company of San Gilio, 11r: "Anche ordiniamo

che ciascuno de la compagnia quando vede la sera acciese le candele nela chiesa di San Gilio a cantare le laude, debbia intrare nela detto chiesa et in cantando et respondando debbia ubidire i suo' capitani."

36 Discussed in Ugo Procacci, "L'incendio della chiesa del Carmine del 1771," *Rivista d'Arte* 14 (1932): 151.

37 CRS 115, 164v. "Una risedenza di legname chon chas[s]a a spagliere, dove seghono e nostri chapitano quando sono nella chonpagnia. Una ispaliera in detta chonpagnia chon sei chasse, cholle toppe e chiavi, al servigio di più maserizie di detta compagnia. Uno descho in detta chonpagnia el quale istà inanzi a' chapitani, dove si rachoglie el partito, chon uno armario in detto descho, e 2 bosoli da richore e partiti, e una taferia. Uno chalamaio di tera invetriato, verde, el quale s'adopra per gli bisogni de' luogho di detto chonpagnia."

38 CRS 115, 164v. "Uno libro di charta pechora, choverte d'asi chovertato di chuoio verde, inchatenato alla risedenza de' chonsiglieri, in sul quale è iscritto tuti e leghati e obrighi e entrata e uscita alla nostra chonpagnia."

39 CRS 115, 164v. "Una tavola d'altare a tre cholmi: nel mezo una meza Nostra Donna, e da llato 4 istorie de Sa' Giovanni Batista e altri Santi. Istà sopra la risedenza de' chapitani."

40 CRS 115, 164v. "14 fighure di legniame, c[i]oè 12 apostoli e una Nostra Donna, tute ginochioni e dipinte, e quali si pohgnono in sul descho G[i]ovedì Santo; e uno Domene dio."

41 CRS 114, 153 right side. "Albizo di Dino, familglio dela Chompagnia d'Santa Angniesa de' dare adì 17 d'aprile 1465 . . . per suo faticha vene[r]di Santo, quando pose gli Apostoli al descho, L. 1, s. 1."

42 See Cyrilla Barr, "Lauda Singing and the Tradition of the *disciplinati mandato*: A Reconstruction of Two Texts of the Office of Tenebrae," *L'ars nova italiana del trecento* 4 (1978): 21–44.

43 See Rab Hatfield, "The Compagnia de' Magi," *Journal of the Warburg and Courtauld Institutes* 33 (1970): 109.

44 CRS 115, 165r. "Una istella cho' razo di legname grande chon questi fornimenti che qui apresso diremo, c[i]oè: 24 agnioli di charta inpastata, grandi e dipinti richamente da ogni parte d'oro fine e di fini cholore; e quali s'apichano a' razi di detta istella.

23 Serafini da uno lato, e dal'altro Cherubini, e quali s'apichano a' razi di detta istella.

22 nugholette pichole, nelle quali è dipinto uno Christo quando va in cielo, così sempricemente

22 segni della chonpagnia, dipinti in chonpasi; e quali s'apichano a' razi di detta istella."

45 CRS 115, 165r. "Una chanpanetta pichola al servigio di detta chapella quando si lieva el Signiore e quando entra a messa

4 paia di torchi d'asti e altrimenti fatti, sansa cera, d'acendere alla messa quando si lieva el Signiore."

46   There is evidence that the *laudesi* at San Zenobi were actually incorporating their activities into the celebration of the mass. See Henderson, 49–50.

47   For a complete discussion of the portions of the Inventory that relate to the Ascension play as described by Abraham of Suzdal see Cyrilla Barr, "Music and Spectacle in Confraternity Drama of Fifteenth-Century Florence: The Reconstruction of a Theatrical Event," in *Christianity and the Renaissance* (Syracuse, N.Y., in press).

48   CRS 115, 165v. "1 chastello di legniame, dipinto, per gli bisogni della festa
"1 monte in sulle volte a uso e bisogno di detta festa
"1 pezo di panno lino el quale fa monte dove iscendono gli agnoli di paradiso in sulle volte."

49   CRS 115, 167r. "Una nughola di rilievo, razata, a uso di mandorla razata intorno e nel mezo uno agnello di rilievo, chon dua palme e uno ghanbo di giglio in mezo, cholorita e messa d'azuro e razi di stagno dorato."

50   CRS 100, 89v. April 28, 1467. "A Simone intagliatore che fu discepolo di Donatello lire una chontanti perchè a fe' di rilievo uno agnello e altre chose sulla nuova nugholetta abiàno fatta fare per sopra la porta della chiesa."

51   Transcription contained in Appendix A.

52   There are frequent references to Piero del Massaio for the purchase of materials and especially for services rendered. For example, CRS 114, 84r, entry for 1453. "Piero del Massaio dipintore de' avere per insino a questo dì, XI di Novembre, lire sette e s. sei e d. 8 per ispese fatte nella nuova nughola fatta per la festa della Ascensione nell'anno 1453 chome apare in più partite in un quadernucc[i]o tunuto per Lionardo di Ghualtieri, isceglitore, titolate Richordanze, segnato nughola, c. 3 L. VII, s. VI, d. VIII."

53   For example, note 52 above. Also, CRS 115, 31 left side. "E deono dare per insino adì primo d'Aghosto 1467 che fini el mio sindichato fatto per uno anno, lire ventitre s. 17, d. 8, de' quali n'ò dati a Ghuelfo nostro laudiere per dire le laude quest' anno 1466–67 finito adì primo d'aghosto, lire 12, s. 7, d. 8, chome nè in questo a suo chonto, a c. 14."

54   See D'Accone cited in note 12 above.

55   CRS 98, 81r. "A' piferi dele parte [Guelfa?] insino adì XXV di Magio, lire oto soldi cinque, sono per sonare ala festa del As[c]ensione, L. viii, s. v." Fol. 91r: "A Parissi di Giovanni e chonpagni, nostri piferi, per lla festa, lire sette, s. dieci, pli, portò Parissi detta, L. 7, s. 10." Fol. 95v: "Al Vinci pifero, per parte di sonare per la festa, lire due, L.2." Fol. 96r: "Al Vinci pifero e a' chompagni per sonare, lire sette, s. dieci, L. 7, s. 10."

56   For example, CRS 114, 70r. "Ispese dela chonpagnia deono dare . . . adì 12 d'Aprile 1450 lire tre, s. sei piccioli, date a Frate Giovanni di Lorenzo da Prato . . . sono per suo salario dele lalde chantò di Qhuaresima."

57   CRS 115, 34 left side. "Ghuelfo di Bartolomeo barbiere, famiglio della nostra chonpagnia e chantatore delle lalde, de' avere per prezo e sua mercé, quando arà sodisfatto allo infrascritto obrigho, lire venti in uno anno, el quale anno inchominiciò insino dì primo di Novembre 1466 e de' finire a

detto dì 1467. El quale obrigho fia questo, c[i]oè, che'l detto Ghuelfo in detto anno deba chon sollecitudine ogni dì di festa chomandata venire a dire le laude nella chiesa del Charmino di Firenze, nelle 23 e 24 ore, e aparechiare el legio e chosì isparechiare. E quando manchase deba esergli ischonto del suo salare s. 5 per ogni volta manchase. E oltre al dire le laude, deba ogni dì e ora fusi richiesto o dal proposto de' nostri chapitani o da' sindachi, che dovesi andare a raunare e chapitani o altri ufici o uomini della nostra chonpagnia, chon sollecitudine andare a fare quanto di sopra è detto. E in chaso no'llo facesse o manchase per suo difetto o nigrigenza, per ogni dì se gli deba torre s. 5 del suo salaro, così del dire le laude chome de' raunare e chapitani e di questo n'abia a stare alla choscienza de' sindachi che pe' gli tenpi saranno. El detto salaro deba al detto Ghuelfo pagliare el sindacho di detta chonpagnia, overo chamarlingho, ogni due mesi." Similar prescriptions apply to two other singers who sang with him. See fol. 35 right side.

58 CRS 4, 36v. "Et adì decto [December 25] a Giovambatista di Currado, laudiere, L. una e s. quattro, sono per tucto quello resta havere di suo servito pe' sei mesi proximi passati che finiscono per tucto el presente mese di dicembre 1490. Et la cagiano fu perchè stette alcun mesi che lui non ci cantò perchè serviva a Santa Croce e non potea essere et là et qui a un tempo medesimo."

59 CRS 4, 52v: "essendogli migl[i]oratogli la boce assai e cantar meglio."

60 By 1455 the *laudesi* of San Piero Martire, for example, were paid thirty *soldi* per month for singing on feast days only, while those who sang for daily exercises received forty *soldi* per month. Between 1431 and 1433 the Company of San Zenobi was paying thirty-five *soldi* per month for daily singing and singers of Orsanmichele received as much as two *lire* for the same services.

61 CRS 100, 143v.

62 CRS 100, 144r, May 22, 1478. "A'Ndrea di Cristofano chazaiuolo, nostro tinore alle laude," and "A Bartolomeo di Lorenzo, nostro tinore."

63 For example, CRS 114, 112 right side. "E de' avere adì [omission] dicembre 1457 lire tre, s. tre piccioli, pagliò per noi a Giuliano di Domenicho chalzaiolo, sono per paia tre di chalze diede per noi a 3 fanc[i]uli e quali disono le lalde ala nostra chapela di Santa Agniesa." Later evidence is found in CRS 4, 1506, 116v. "Item detto dì [October 2] e prefati chapitani insieme chon tutti loro officiali atteso che egl' è cosa laudabile di fare dire le laude il dì delle feste comandate, chome antiquamente si faceva, ma che dette laude far dire non si possano sanza qualche spesa. Et atteso che e fanciulli della compagnia di Sancto Alberto quelle chantono volentieri, ma non ànno tenori, et inteso che Lorenzo d'Antonio di Lucha, famigl[i]o di detta compagnia, è idoneo a tenere el tenore, et lui à certi compagni atti et idonei acciò, et etiam atti a insegnare laude a detti fanciulli."

64 CRS 115, 99 right, 1490.

65 See Pierre Louis Ducharte, *The Italian Comedy* (New York, 1966), 73.

66 CRS 100, 95v., entry no. 82, May 5, 1467. "A Ghualberto detto Pesce e a suo chonpagnia, sonatori de' suoni grosi del paradiso lire tre chontanti . . .

per prezo e loro merzé a sonare e detti suoni grossi quando si farà la festa."

67 Ibid.

68 Translated from Alessandro d'Ancona, *Origini del teatro italiano* 1:251–52.

69 Even after the expulsion of the Medici in 1494 the plays continued to be a part of such special occasions as the visit of Margaret of Austria in 1533, the marriage of Joan of Austria to Francesco de' Medici in 1565, and the marriage of Virginia de' Medici to Cesare d'Este in 1586. During the time of Lorenzo il Magnifico the plays were an important part of the elaborate festivities for the visit of Duke Galleazo Maria Sforza to Florence in 1471.

70 ASF, Camera del Commune, *Notaio di Camera Campione*, no. 3, *Provvisioni*, 1436–39, through no. 21, *Uscita Generale, Campione*, 1498–1516, are rich in references to the employment of instrumentalists. The most frequent are shawms (*pifferi*), trombones (*tromboni*), trumpets (*trombe*), a bagpipe-type instrument (the *cennamella*), and castanets (*nacherini*).

71 See especially CRS 4, 50r (1492) through 59v (1493), and CRS 115, 99 right (1490) through 170 right (1511).

72 Described in Serafino Razzi's Life of Savonarola, BFR MS 2012, quoted in Giuseppe Conti, *Fatti e aneddoti di storia fiorentina*, (Florence, 1902), 292. Various *laude* attributed to Savonarola are found in Razzi's *Libro primo delle laude* of 1563.

73 CRS 115, 112 left.

74 CRS 115 in particular records numerous vigil services with *lauda* singing in the last decade of the century. See especially 112 left and right. Vigils for the Orlandini and Ardingheli are frequent.

75 CRS 4, 95r–v, April 24, 1503. "E prefati chapitani . . . deliberorono che a laude et honore dell'onnipotente Idio e del nostro Redemptore Giesù Christo et della gloriosa Madre S. Maria et di S. Agnesa nostra advocata, et a chonsolatione del popolo fiorentino et degli uomini di nostra compagnia, che si facci la festa dell'Ascensione del nostro Signore Christo Giesù, et dipoi quella della gloriosa Madre Maria, e che s'elegha chapitani e fes-taioli . . . con questo . . . che non si possa spendere danaio alchuno di quelli della compagnia in detta festa."

76 CRS 126, 113r. "Addì primo di giennaio (1514) Richordo questo dì sopradetto chome noi abbiamo alloghato a fare lo edifizio del cielo del charmino, chon che si cielebra la nostra festività della Ascensione, a Amadio di Alberto, legniaiulo, in questo modo, cioè, che detto Amadio abbia a mettere la per-sona sua e l'opere di quelli gharzoni che avesse di bisogno, e rifare tutto detto edifizio dal piano del cielo in giù tutto quello mazzo e nughole, se-chondo uno modello fatto per detto Amaddio e poi dipinto nel muro dello spogliatoio della Chompagnia del Crocifisso del Charmine. E noi per detto efetto gli abbiamo a dare tutti e legnami, ferramenti e ogni altra chosa apartenente per fare detto edifizio. El quale chondotto lo arà, gli abbiano a pagliare per suo magisterio ducati quatro d'oro . . . questo di XI di Marzo abbiamo alloghato a fare al sopradetto Amadio uno modo di tirare per in cielo, per tirare tutto el mazzo del 'dificio."

77 CRS 126, 112r. "Addi 9 di Luglio (1514) Richordo questo dì sopradetto chome essendo raghunati e nostri signori capitani di S. Agniese cho' loro chonsiglieri, fu chonsiderato essere chose oportuna di dovessi fare la festa della Ascensione di nostro Signore, la quale si chostuma fare per lli huomini di nostra chonpagnia. E perchè gli edifizi oportuni a quella erono tutti ghuasti e in disordine, per loro partito deliberorono di eleggiere quatro huomini di nostra chompagnia chon autorità di potere porre a tutti gli huomini di nostra Chompagnia una inposta, perchè in detto chaso non si può tocchare danari della entrata di nostra chonpagnia ma bisogna eschino delle borse degl'uomini . . . chome tutto chiaramente apare per chontratto roghato ser Baldassare Bondoni, notaio di detta chonpagnia."

DEATH RITES AND THE RITUAL FAMILY

IN RENAISSANCE FLORENCE

SHARON T. STROCCHIA

The research for this essay was carried out during my fellowship at the Harvard University Center for Italian Renaissance Studies (Villa I Tatti), Florence. I wish to thank the staffs of the Villa and the Archivio di Stato, Florence, for their kind assistance; the National Endowment for the Humanities, which supported the project; and the University of South Carolina for an extended research leave.

1   Leon Battista Alberti, *The Family in Renaissance Florence*, trans. René Neu Watkins (Columbia, S.C., 1969), 149.

2   The following works have helped shape my thinking about Florentine strategies of honor: Gene Brucker, *Florentine Politics and Society, 1343–1378* (Princeton, 1962), and *The Civic World of Early Renaissance Florence* (Princeton, 1977); Richard Goldthwaite, *Private Wealth in Renaissance Florence* (Princeton, 1968), and *The Building of Renaissance Florence* (Baltimore and London, 1980); Dale Kent, *The Rise of the Medici* (Oxford, 1978); F. W. Kent, *Household and Lineage in Renaissance Florence* (Princeton, 1977); Julius Kirshner, *Pursuing Honor While Avoiding Sin: The Monte delle Doti of Florence*, Quaderni di "Studi Senesi," 41 (1978); Thomas Kuehn, "Honor and Conflict in a Florentine Family," *Ricerche Storiche* 10 (1980): 287–310; and Richard Trexler, *Public Life in Renaissance Florence* (New York, 1980).

3   Among the many useful works developing cultural perceptions of honor in the Mediterranean, two deserve specific mention: J. K. Campbell, *Honour, Family, and Patronage* (Oxford, 1964), J. G. Peristiany, ed., *Honour and Shame* (Chicago, 1966). Colette Beaune, "Mourir noblement à la fin du Moyen Age," in *La Mort au Moyen Age* (Strasbourg, 1977), 125–43, examines the forms and functions of honorable burials in late medieval France.

4   Unless otherwise noted, all archival material is housed in the Archivio di Stato, Florence. Carte Strozziane (hereinafter Cart. Strozz.), ser. 2, 17, Ricordi of Manno and Giovanni Petrucci, 1440–50, 24r. "[F]ugli fato grande onore chome richiedeva lo stato nostro."

5   Conventi Religiosi Soppressi (hereinafter Conv. Sopp.), 89 (S. Trinità), 46, Memoirs and expenses, 1416–23, 37r. "A di primo daprile mercholedi . . . deliberato avevano i prelati dellordine insieme chon la famiglia degianfigliazi per loro chonsolatione e honore che lonoranza del corpo si facesse in questa chiesa e monistero di sancta trinita."

6   Cart. Strozz., ser. 2, 17 bis, Ricordi of Marco and Piero Parenti, 1447–1519, 86r. "Fecili publica honoranza secondo che il grado suo e mio meritava."

7   Giuliano's funeral is described by Giovanni Cambi, *Istorie*, in *Delizie degli eruditi toscani*, ed. P. Ildefonso di San Luigi, 24 vols. (Florence, 1770–89), 21:278–79; and Bartolomeo Masi, *Ricordanze di Bartolomeo Masi dal 1478 al 1526* (Florence, 1906), 195–99.

8   Accounts of Ginori aims and successes are documented by Kent, *Household and Lineage*, and less critically by P. Ginori-Conti, *La Basilica di S. Lorenzo di Firenze e la famiglia Ginori* (Florence, 1940). Isabelle Hyman, *Fifteenth Century Florentine Studies* (Ph.D. diss., New York University, 1968), 83–84, notes Ginori help in realizing the Medici palace.

9   This information is culled from Provveditori e Massai del Commune, Campioni d'entrate e uscite, 1–8. The account book for 1389 is missing, and that of 1392 is incomplete. Between 1384 and 1392 the commune sold at least 233 licenses permitting Florentines to surpass the legal limits on funeral display. Of this group there were at least six minor guildsmen identified by occupation who either bought licenses or were so honored, including the mercer Marco di Tommaso, who bought a permit for his wife dated June 3, 1385 (Campioni, 2, 23v), the heirs of Francesco d'Agnolo, a *pezzaio*, dated April 22, 1388 (Campioni, 5, 291v), and the heirs of the keymaker Rinieri di Jacopo, dated September 15, 1390 (Campioni, 6, 310r). Niccolo Bartolucci, described as a knifemaker, obtained a permit to honor Messer Giovanni Gherardini, March 27, 1385 (Campioni, 2, 15r); the shoemaker Simone di Michele bought a license for Monna Betta di Bertino, August 31, 1387 (Campioni, 4, 307v); and the coppersmith Piero di Pero obtained one for Bernardo di Lipi, August 6, 1390 (Campioni, 6, 310r). In addition, the heirs of a certain "Jacopo, called Bianco," also bought a sumptuary permit for his funeral, dated June 10, 1388 (Campioni, 5, 291v), but no information about his trade was given.

10 On escalating dowry prices, Julius Kirshner and Anthony Molho, "The Dowry Fund and the Marriage Market in Early Quattrocento Florence," *Journal of Modern History* 50 (1978): 403–38, and their forthcoming work on the *monte delle doti* records.

11 Philip Jones, "Florentine Families and Florentine Diaries in the Fourteenth Century," *Papers of the British School at Rome* 24 (n.s. 11) (1956): 183–205.

12 See the useful reading of family systems using *ricordanze* developed by Christiane Klapisch-Zuber in *Women, Family, and Ritual in Renaissance Italy*, trans. Lydia G. Cochrane (Chicago, 1985).

13 Peter Brown, *The Cult of the Saints* (Chicago, 1980), 24–26.

14 A. N. Galpern, for example, maintains that "Catholicism at the end of the

Middle Ages was in large part a cult of the living in the service of the dead." See his "The Legacy of Late Medieval Religion in Sixteenth Century Champagne," in *The Pursuit of Holiness in Late Medieval and Renaissance Religion*, ed. C. Trinkaus (Leiden, 1974), 141–76.

15 Christiane Klapisch-Zuber, "Kin, Friends, and Neighbors: The Urban Territory of a Merchant Family in 1400," in her *Women*, 68–93; D. V. and F. W. Kent, *Neighbours and Neighbourhoods in Renaissance Florence* (Locust Valley, N.Y., 1982). See also Diane Owen Hughes, "Kinsmen and Neighbors in Medieval Genoa," in *The Medieval City*, ed. Harry Miskimin (New Haven, 1977), 95–111.

16 The introduction by David Nicholas, *The Domestic Life of a Medieval City: Women, Children, and the Family in Fourteenth-Century Ghent* (Lincoln, Nebr., and London, 1985), reviews the conflicting evidence for various models of European family structures. Both Philippe Ariès, *Centuries of Childhood* (New York, 1965), and Lawrence Stone, *The Family, Sex and Marriage in England, 1500–1800* (New York, 1977), argue that affective bonds between family members are a modern creation. More recently David Herlihy, *Medieval Households* (Cambridge, Mass., 1985), in plumbing the documented evidence available to judge the affective family, has rejected the evaluations of Aries and Stone. The two polar views on the Florentine family are usually taken to be Kent, *Household*, and Goldthwaite, *Private Wealth*, as noted by Anthony Molho, "Visions of the Florentine Family in the Renaissance," *Journal of Modern History* 50 (1978): 304–11. For Florentine family demographics, D. Herlihy and C. Klapisch-Zuber, *Les Toscans et leurs familles* (Paris, 1978), and Herlihy, *Medieval Households*, esp. 144–56. On cultural perceptions and legal prerogatives, Nino Tamassia, *La famiglia italiana nei secoli decimoquinto e decimosesto* (Milan, 1910), and Manlio Bellomo, *Ricerche sui rapporti patrimoniali tra coniugi* (Milan, 1961). The bibliography on Venetian family structures, which pose interesting comparisons with those of Florence, can best be approached through Stanley Chojnacki, "Kinship Ties and Young Patricians in Fifteenth-Century Venice," *Renaissance Quarterly* 38 (1985): 240–70. For Genoa, Diane Owen Hughes, "Urban Growth and Family Structure in Medieval Genoa," *Past and Present* 66 (1975): 3–28, and "Domestic Ideals and Social Behavior: Evidence from Medieval Genoa," in *The Family in History*, ed. Charles Rosenberg (Philadelphia, 1975), 115–43.

17 See the reservations about historical ethnology expressed by David Herlihy in his foreword to Klapisch-Zuber, *Women*, vii–xi.

18 Trexler, *Public Life*; Edward Muir makes a similar point for Venice in his *Civic Ritual in Renaissance Venice* (Princeton, 1981).

19 Ronald F. E. Weissman, *Ritual Brotherhood in Renaissance Florence* (New York, 1982), esp. chap. 1.

20 Leon Battista Alberti, *I Libri della famiglia*, ed. Ruggiero Romano and Alberto Tenenti (Torino, 1969). Jack Goody, *The Development of the Family and Marriage in Europe* (London and New York, 1983), argues for the

continuance in medieval Europe of several types of kindred organized to achieve specific functions. Richard Goldthwaite, "Organizzazione economica e struttura famigliare," in *Atti del III Convegno di studi sulla storia dei ceti dirigenti in Toscana* (Florence, 1981), 1–13 (offprint pages), notes the diverse ties that gave the "family" its structure.

21 On the symbolics of processions, Clifford Geertz, "Centers, Kings, and Charisma: Reflections on the Symbolics of Power," in *Culture and Its Creators*, eds. J. Ben-David and T. N. Clarke (Chicago, 1977), 150–71.

22 On the development of the requiem, Mario Righetti, *Manuale di storia liturgica*, 3d ed., 4 vols, (Milan, 1969), 3:470 passim; H.-R. Philippeau, "Introduction à l'étude des rites funéraires et de la liturgie des morts," *La Maison-Dieu* 1 (1945): 37–63; J. Jungmann, *Missa Solemnia*, 2 vols. (Torino, 1953); and T. Maertens and L. Heuschen, *Doctrine et pastorale de la liturgie de la mort* (Bruges, 1957). For specific aspects of the requiem liturgy, see the issue devoted to "Les funerailles chrétiennes," *La Maison-Dieu* 44 (1955).

23 Biblioteca Nazionale di Firenze (hereinafter abbreviated as BNF.), Conventi Soppressi, C. 4, 895, Ricordanze of Pagolo di Matteo Petriboni, 1419–59, 184r.

24 Quoted in Benjamin G. Kohl and Ronald G. Witt, *The Earthly Republic: Italian Humanists on Government and Society* (Philadelphia, 1978), 78. San Bernardino's admonitions are given by Herlihy and Klapisch-Zuber, 612.

25 *Cronica fiorentina di Jacopo Salviati*, in *Delizie*, 18:193.

26 L. Frati, *La vita privata a Bologna* (Bologna, 1928), 50–53. Another neighboring example comes from the 1377 statutes of Ascoli Piceno, located in the eastern Marches. According to their preamble, these statutes were modeled on the 1325 Florentine statutes of the Capitano del Popolo. Rubric 67 states that "che ad nisciuna domna, che plagnesse over corruptasse, sia licito excire over stare nante casa de lu morto innante che se porte a la ecclesia ad sepellire; et allora, quando lu morto se trahe de casa et da poi che li homini vando a la ecclesia ad seppellire, se alicuna domna corruptando excesse fora de casa, sia punita in cinquanta soldi." *Statuti di Ascoli Piceno dell'anno MCCCLXXVII*, ed. L. Zdekauer and P. Sella (Rome, 1910), 129.

27 These Roman statutes and sumptuary legislation, approved by Pope Paul II in 1471, are printed in the preface to Marc Antonio Altieri, *Li nuptiali*, ed. E. Narducci (Rome, 1873), 48.

28 Archivio di Stato, Mantua. Archivio Gonzaga, 1621. My thanks to Evelyn Welch of the Warburg Institute for making her transcription of this letter available to me.

29 B. Cecchetti, "Funerali e sepolture dei Veneziani antichi," *Archivio Veneto*, 1st ser., 34 (1887): 284 n. 1.

30 Herlihy and Klapisch-Zuber, *Les Toscans*; Kent, *Household*; and Herlihy, *Medieval Households*, 138–56, document the demographics and variety of Florentine household arrangements.

31 Herlihy, *Medieval Households*, 82–92.

32 BNF, Conv. Sopp., C. 4., 895, 124r and 125v.

33 Paolo Cammarosano, "Les structures familiales dans les villes de l'Italie

communale XIIe–XIVe siècles," in *Famille et Parenté dans l'Occident médiéval. Collection de l'Ecole Française de Rome* 30 (1977): 181–94.

34 Accounts of Giuliano de' Medici's funeral appear in Masi, 195–99, and Cambi, 92–95.

35 A brief description of the *bele onoranze* made for Filippo Strozzi, May 17, 1491, appears in "Ricordanze tratte da un libro originale di Tribaldo d' Rossi," in *Delizie* 23:257.

36 Herlihy and Klapisch-Zuber, *Les Toscans*, appendix 5, tables 1 and 2.

37 For the Dugento and early Trecento, R. Davidsohn, *Storia di Firenze*, trans. G. B. Klein, 7 vols. (Florence, 1965), 7:707–18, documents the separation of men and women in front of the house before the procession began and the final place in the cortege occupied by kinswomen, whose presence becomes far less visible after mid-century. An anonymous chronicler of Pavia writing around 1330 suggests new restrictions of women's ceremonial participation in that city's funeral processions: "Postremo sequuntur mulieres, ex quibus propinquiores defuncto a duobus viris hinc inde sustenantur, et ita procedunt ad Ecclesiam cum luminaribus, et sonitu campanarum. Laici vero intrantes Ecclesiam recedunt, remanentibus cum funere in Ecclesia, et usque ad sepulcrum prosequentibus solis Clericis, Sacerdotibus, et mulieribus. Nunc audivi ab hujusmodi processionibus foeminas interdictas." These remarks of the "Anonymous Ticinensis" are given in his *Commentarius de laudibus Papiae*, published by L. A. Muratori in *Rerum Italicarum Scriptores* (Milan, 1727), 11, at col. 25.

38 Klapisch-Zuber, *Women*, 117–31. *Commentarius de laudibus Papiae*, ed. R. Maocchi and F. Quentavalla, in *Rerum Italicarum Scriptores* (Città di Castello, 1903–6), 11.

39 Alberti's comments from his *Libri della famiglia* are translated by Thomas Kuehn, *Emancipation in Late Medieval Florence* (New Brunswick, N.J., 1982), 57. Kuehn discusses social norms and idealized relations between fathers and sons (pages 55–71) and analyzes one conflictual relationship in his article "Honor and Conflict." Richard C. Trexler offers a highly interpretive view of one set of father/son relations in "In Search of Father: The Experience of Abandonment in the Recollections of Giovanni di Pagolo Morelli," *History of Childhood Quarterly* 3 (1975): 225–51.

40 Manoscritti, 89, Ricordi of Antonio di Ser Tommaso di Ser Francesco Masi, 1455–59, 14r, entry dated 1456: "E vendemo per la morte di nostro padre tute nostre masserizie e pani di nostro padre e nostra madre a bartolo rigatiere stimo circha Fl. 300 si vendesino. E stimo si spendesi nel mortoro in panni Fl. 100 e veli e nellonoranza Fl. 40." The same entry states that Ser Tommaso died in 1405 ("quando Ser Tommaso morì che fu lano 1405").

41 Cart. Strozz, 3, 132, 60, Letter of Palla to Simone di Filippo Strozzi, Venice, March 28, 1422. Some of Nofri's funeral expenses (he died on April 3, 1418) are documented in Conv. Sopp., 89 (S. Trinità), 10, entries and debits, 1405–23, 31v.

42 For the Bonvanni, Catasto, 824 part 2, 552r. Elaine Rosenthal kindly gave me

this reference. The most comprehensive listing of Ser Luca Federighi's funeral expenses is by his son Ser Antonio: Catasto, 42: 8r–11v, with other records of the debt in Catasto, 42:443v; 43:841r–844v; 45:704r–705v and 763r–773v.

43 The proviso to grant exemptions is contained in the revised sumptuary statutes dated April 22–23, 1384: Statuti del comune di Firenze, 34, Prammatica sopra il vestire, funerary rubrics at 11v–13v.

44 The following information is derived from Provv. e Massai, Campioni, 1–8. See note 9 above.

45 Klapisch-Zuber, *Women*, 121 n. 17.

46 Provv. e Massai, Campioni, 2, 13r. The permit was bought on March 3, 1385, by Lionardo di Neri di Ser Benedetto for his *nipote* Benedetto. Lionardo's heirs, unspecified by name or relation, in turn bought a sumptuary license for him December 14, 1387. Campioni, 4, 308r.

47 Provv. e Massai, Campioni, 1–8. Of the five permits purchased by men without surnames, two were obtained by men identified by four generations of patronymics: Filippo di Ghino di Piero di Ghino, for his brother Tommaso, and Guccio di Rinieri di Gieri di Berto, for his brother Messer Giovanni: Campioni, 6 (1390), 310r/v.

48 Goldthwaite, "Organizzazione economica."

49 For the illness and subsequent death and burial of Monna Betta, the "buona e onorevole madre" of Bartolomeo and Francesco di Tommaso Sassetti, Cart. Strozz, ser. 5, 1747, 82r, 86v, 88r, 154v, and 155v. Antonio di Lionardo Rustichi buried his niece Mattea, who had fled the plague with the rest of Antonio's *brigata*, in August 1424. Cart. Strozz, ser. 2, 11, 35r.

50 On the customary right of *tornata*, Klapisch-Zuber, *Women*, 122.

51 Manoscritti, 88, Ricordi of Piero di Bernardo Masi, 1452–1513, 160v. Mea's husband Bartolomeo squandered the dowry for which she and her natal family had provided no legal guarantees, leaving her penniless.

52 Manoscritti, 88, 141r, 142v, and 144r. The same household was responsible for burying Bernardo's unmarried brother Tommaso, who had spent most of his life in Rome. Tommaso died in his brother's house in October 1500 and was buried at his own expense in SS. Annunziata, 146v.

53 Herlihy, *Medieval Households*, 83.

54 Libri di Commercio, 102, Ricordanze of Guasparre di Matteo Landini, tessitore, 1516–75, 17v. Judy Brown brought this document to my attention.

55 For the fundamental change in marriage assigns and its implications for late medieval kinship organization see Diane Owen Hughes, "From Brideprice to Dowry in Mediterranean Europe," *Journal of Family History* 3 (1978): 262–96. Hughes further develops the sense of competition between the dotal and lineal faces of the Italian family as seen in artistic representations in "Representing the Family: Portraits and Purposes in Early Modern Italy," *Journal of Interdisciplinary History* 17 (1986): 7–38. Klapisch-Zuber, *Women*, 213–46, views this structural conflict between kin groups through Florentine dowry practices.

56 This phrase is borrowed from Klapisch-Zuber, *Women*, 117–31.

57 Manoscritti, 77, Ricordi of Lapo, Valorino, Barna, and Valorino Ciurianni, 1325–1429, 8v, 20v, 23v, 24v, 37v, and 38r.

58 Provv. e Massai, Campioni, 1–8.

59 Nofri d'Andrea di Neri purchased a license in 1390 for his sister Monna Fora, and the hospital of S.M. Nuova bought one a Monna Filippa the same year. Provv. e Massai, Campioni, 6, 310r.

60 The evidence of Florentine kinship patterns supports Joan W. Scott's argument in "Gender: A Useful Category of Historical Analysis," *American Historical Review* 91 (1986): 1053–75, that gender is a fundamental rather than a marginal category of analysis.

61 Herlihy, *Medieval Households*, 82–83, develops the distinctions between the relative purposes of kin organization.

62 *Cronica del Monaldi*, in *Istorie Pistolese* (Milan, 1845), 443–44. After describing the pomp, Monaldi notes the presence at the requiem of "tutti i consorti e parenti stretti di casa vestiti a sanguigno. Tutte le donne entrate ed uscite di loro casa vestite a sanguigno."

63 Medici's funeral is described by an anonymous diarist in BNF, Panciatichi, 158, 179v–180r. After noting the "molti cittadini e molte donne" who attended the service, the observer described the choir of Santa Maria del Fiore "pieno di torchietti acesi e dal altra parte moltissime donne fra le quali erono le figliuole e lla moglie sua e furono e vestiti a bruno fra uomini e donne sesantotto."

64 Monaldi, 445. Klapisch-Zuber, *Women*, 123 n. 26, discusses the problems and behavior of young widows subjected to the marital strategies of their natal kin.

65 Cart. Strozz, ser. 2, 135, no. 2, Tedaldi Chronicle, 10v.

66 On the cultural significance of clothing in Renaissance Italy, see the important remarks by Diane Owen Hughes, "Sumptuary Law and Social Relations in Renaissance Italy," in *Disputes and Settlements: Law and Human Relations in the West*, ed. John Bossy (Cambridge, 1983), 69–99.

67 On the occasion of his father Parente's death in 1452, for example, Marco Parenti paid 58 florins to clothe his mother, sister, wife, and himself in mourning, or about 73 percent of the total burial expenses; two generations later, in 1519, Piero di Marco Parenti's son paid almost 195 florins to outfit fifteen family mourners for the requiem, a figure that represented 71.1 percent of the total 274 florin burial cost. Cart. Strozz, ser. 2, 17 bis, Ricordi of Marco and Piero Parenti, 1447–1519, 29r, 30r, 128v–129v. All figures in lire have been converted to florins using the rates in appendix 1 in Goldthwaite, *Building*.

68 Cart. Strozz, ser. 2, 17 bis, 86r and 128–129v.

69 Conv. Sopp, 78 (Badia), 313, no. 292, dated February 22, 1449/50.

70 For Checha Masi's requiem, A.S.F. Manoscritti, 89, 18r. Caterina Parenti's burial honors are reported in Cart. Strozz, ser. 2, 17, bis., 1r.

71   Manoscritti, 77, 20v. Valorino spent a total of 25 florins to clothe himself, the manservant Meo, and his father's corpse.

72   Cart. Strozz, ser. 2, 9, Ricordi of Luca di Matteo da Panzano, 1406–61, 23r. A woman's mourning garment customarily required 12 *braccia* of cloth.

73   Manoscritti, 89, 18r. "E vesti di nero charllo e piero li altri si vestirono loro stessi."

74   Manoscritti, 77, 20v. "Per braccia xx di chupo fine levai per mona Pera madre di Barna e per mona Margherita e mona Lena sue sirocchie le quali dichono di paghare la loro parte."

75   Manoscritti, 82, Testament and inventory of Ugolino Michi, 35v. Ugolino, an active officeholder who had been podesta of Pistoia in 1412, was obligated for three dowries: the first to his mother Giemma in the amount of 300 florins; the second, in the sum of 1,500 florins (900 florins of which was tied up in two workshops in Por Santa Maria), was owed to his deceased first wife Checha Panciatichi; and the third sum of 1,050 florins in Monte credits owed to his second wife Lapa. Negotiations over funeral costs began with a question by Giemma to the other executors: "siche si domando loro quello volessino fare delle spese delmortoro e dopo molte parole chonvenne che monna Giemma sobrighi asi alle spese del mortoro in sino in quantita di F. 25. E creditori altre spese echoreano nellonorare mona lapa vestire e veli e tutto cio che lla promesse e cosi fe rimandare uno de due vestiri neri mando la cioppa e ritenne il mantello e rimando il mantello del vaio siche la seppoltura si fe honestamente chome si richiedea."

76   Manoscritti, 89, 19r.

77   Cart. Strozz, ser. 2, 17 bis, 30r, 128v–129v. I am very grateful to Elaine Rosenthal for clarifying Parenti marriage alliances and genealogy.

78   On the legal status of women in late medieval and Renaissance Florence, see the two articles by Thomas Kuehn, " 'Cum Consensu Mundualdi': Legal Guardianship of Women in Quattrocento Florence," *Viator* 13 (1982): 309–33, and "Women, Marriage, and *Patria Potestas* in Late Medieval Florence," *Revue d'Histoire du Droit* 49 (1981): 127–47. Julius Kirshner discusses the legal claims of wives and their natal families in "Wives' Claims against Insolvent Husbands in Late Medieval Italy," in *Women of the Medieval World: Essays in Honor of John H. Mundy*, ed. J. Kirshner and S. Wemple (Oxford, 1985), 256–303.

79   Klapisch-Zuber, *Women*, 178–212, 213–46. Two functional analyses of wedding processions, using evidence from early modern France, are Nicole Belmont, "The Symbolic Function of the Wedding Procession in the Popular Rituals of Marriage," and André Burguière, "The Marriage Ritual in France: Ecclesiastical Practices and Popular Practices (Sixteenth to Eighteenth Centuries)," in *Ritual, Religion, and the Sacred: Selections from the Annales*, ed. R. Forster and O. Ranum (Baltimore, 1982), 1–7, 8–23.

80   Cart. Strozz, ser. 2, 9, Ricordi of Luca di Matteo da Panzano, 1406–61. The burial of Luca's brother Antonio in 1423 appears at 23r, that of his mother

Mattea in 1440 at 104v, his wife Lucrezia in 1445 at 122r, and son Salvatore in 1458 at 193r. Luca's account of his son-in-law's burial is at 125r: "Sabato sera fu messo in santa + e vena da pisa inuna chassa sanza fare altre asequi de lui che cosi mando ubertino suo padre si faciesse."

DONATELLO'S TOMB OF POPE JOHN XXIII

SARAH BLAKE MCHAM

1 See R. W. Lightbown, *Donatello and Michelozzo: An Artistic Partnership and Its Patrons in the Early Renaissance* (London, 1980), 1:26, n. 3, who remarks that its only rivals in terms of size were the Bardi Tombs in the Bardi Chapel, Santa Croce.

2 For a detailed description of the tomb, including precise measurements of its parts and indications of original polychromy, see ibid., 26–31; H. W. Janson, *The Sculpture of Donatello* (Princeton, 1979), 59–65; and Harriet McNeal Caplow, *Michelozzo* (New York and London, 1977), 1:119–40.

3 On the Coscia family arms, see Donald Lindsay Galbreath, *Papal Heraldry*, 2d ed. rev. by Geoffrey Briggs (London, 1972), 82.

4 Lightbown, *Donatello and Michelozzo*, 1:43–44, suggests plausibly that the portrait was made from a death mask, a claim disputed by Janson, *Donatello*, 64.

5 For a biography of Coscia, see C. Hunger, *Zur Geschichte Papst Johanns XXIII* (Bonn, 1876), and E. J. Kitts, *In the Days of the Councils: A Sketch of the Life and Times of Baldassare Cossa* (London, 1908).

6 The best account of the political ramifications of John XXIII's attempts to establish his rule in Central Italy is Peter Partner, *The Papal State under Martin V* (London, 1958), 20–33.

7 In the *Vita di Bartolommeo Valori* [one of the executors of Coscia's will] by Luca di Simone della Robbia, *Archivio storico italiano* 4 (1843): 262, is recorded John XXIII's remark to Valori, "Io confesso che gli è poco senno rimettersi in personaggi ignoti, e che il Concilio non è per me. Ma che debbo fare, se haggio uno fato che mi ci tira?" The contemporary chronicle of Ulrich von Richental records that when John XXIII first saw the Lake of Constance, he exclaimed, "This is how foxes are caught." Quoted in Ludwig Pastor *The History of the Popes from the Close of the Middle Ages*, 6th ed. (London, 1938), 1:195.

8 See H. G. Peter, *Die Informationen Papst Johanns XXIII und dessen Flucht von Konstanz bis Schaffhausen* (Freiburg in B., 1926), and H. Finke, "Flucht und Schicksale Johannes XXIII in badischen Landen," in *Bilder von Konstanzer Konzil* (Heidelberg, 1903), 7–59.

9 One of Giovanni di Bicci's agents, Bartolomeo de' Bardi, arranged Coscia's release and accompanied him on his return to Florence. The ransom was paid through the Venetian branch of the Medici bank; see George Holmes, "How the Medici became the Pope's Bankers," in *Florentine Studies: Politics and Society in Renaissance Florence*, ed. Nicolai Rubinstein (Evanston, 1968),

357–80, esp. 375–76. The *Vita di Bartolommeo Valori* by Luca di Simone della Robbia claims that the ransom was effected through "l'ajuto de' Fiorentini, e le preghiere di Cosimo de' Medici" (263). Coscia's promise to repay Giovanni di Bicci for ransoming him and Bartolomeo de' Bardi's order to the Medici's German correspondents to turn over the payment are published in *Archivio storico italiano* 4 (1843): 432–37. According to Curt S. Gutkind, *Cosimo de' Medici Pater Patriae, 1389–1464* (Oxford, 1938), 177–78, John XXIII's *Liber Quientantiarum (1413–19)* reveals that before leaving for Constance John left monies on deposit with Giovanni di Bicci and Niccolò da Uzzano, which probably formed the nucleus of his ransom. The managing partner of the Rome branch of the Medici bank and some clerical staff had accompanied John XXIII to Constance in order to handle his affairs; see Raymond de Roover, *The Rise and Decline of the Medici Bank, 1397–1494* (New York, 1966), 202–3. According to Holmes, "How the Medici" (p. 373), it is likely that the young Cosimo went along with the Medici contingent since he was issued a safe conduct by the pope along with other members of the Medici group. The *Vite di uomini illustri del secolo XV* by Vespasiano da Bisticci, trans. William George and Emily Waters (London, 1926), 214, asserts that Cosimo went to Constance to gain business experience.

10 See, for example, Leonardo Bruni, *Rerum suo tempore gestarum Commentarius ab anno MCCCLXXVIII usque ad annum MCCCCXL . . .* , in *Rerum Italicarum Scriptores*, ed. Ludovicus Antonius Muratori (Milan, 1731), vol. 19, cols. 914–42, esp. col. 930: "[John XXIII] Erat autem scrupulus quidam apud multos, quoniam depositio, abdicatioque illius violenta fuerat, num jure subsisteret. Quod si illa dubia, Martini quoque electio in ambiguum veniebat; quoniam non vacanti ecclesiae provideri de novo Pastore non potuerit. . . . Ibi quum esset liber, ac sui juris, sive conscientia ductus, sive quod desperabat aliquid proficere posse, sponte sua Florentiam venit, & se se pedibus Martini subjiciens eum ut Pontificem verum & unicum recognovit. In adventu ejus tota civitas obviam profusa multis lachrymis, & incredibili commiseratione respexit hominem de tantae dignitatis fastigio in tantas calamitates prolapsum." We should recall that Bruni was biased but in a characteristically Florentine way. He had become a papal secretary as early as 1405 and was closely linked to John XXIII. Indeed, during the pontificate of John XXIII the papal court became a major center of Florentine humanism; see George Holmes, *The Florentine Enlightenment: 1400–50* (New York, 1969), 60. Lauro Martines, *The Social World of the Florentine Humanists, 1390–1460* (Princeton, 1963), 118, quoted Poggio Bracciolini's oration on the death of Bruni, which noted that through John's favor, Bruni made "a great deal of money."

11 He had made a league with Florence (1408) and for several years effectively countered the attacks of Ladislaus of Naples on Central Italy; see Partner, *The Papal State under Martin V*, 20–22.

12 See H. Finke and J. Hollensteiner, eds., *Acta Concilii Constanciensis* (Münster, 1896–1928), 4:851. Giovanni di Bicci's *Libro Segreto*, the record of his private business accounts, reveals frequent transactions with Coscia between

1404–9. Letters between them were often begun with "amicus meus carissimus"; see Holmes, "How the Medici," 363. Holmes, *Florentine Enlightenment*, 77, also noted the "slanderous, and no doubt inaccurate" stories later written down by Francesco Filelfo that claimed that Giovanni di Bicci had extorted princely sums from John XXIII to pay for Medicean projects like the rebuilding of San Lorenzo and San Marco. Ferdinando Leopoldo Del Migliore, *Firenze città nobilissima illustrata* (Florence, 1684), 95–96, made the same sort of comment in regard to Cosimo and the amount spent on the tomb: "rendendosi falsa una certa voce corrente ancor oggi nel Popolaccio, che Cosimo de' Medici s'arricchisse con la roba di questo Papa, lasciatagli, dicono, quando s'ebbe a trasferire al Concilio di Costanza, di dove ritornato, e richiestala, vogliono, che Cosimo se ne difendesse con dire, esser pronto a restituirgliene, se gli era Papa Giovanni, ma che li sembrava Baldassare Coscia Napoletano."

13 See Holmes, "How the Medici," 362–64, 374; and de Roover, *The Rise and Decline of the Medici Bank*, 198–203. Giovanni di Bicci's political position underwent a volte-face upon the election of John XXIII to the papacy. *Consulte e Pratiche* records reveal that before this he had championed Ladislaus as "the father of [the Florentine] popolo;" afterward he denounced him as the enemy of Florence. See Gene Brucker, *The Civic World of Early Renaissance Florence* (Princeton, 1977), 365. Another proof of their close alliance is that John XXIII made Giovanni di Bicci the Count of Monteverde, an hereditary title; see Gutkind, *Cosimo de' Medici*, 178.

14 On the various political tensions between Martin V and Florence, see Peter Partner, "Florence and the Papacy in the Earlier Fifteenth Century," in *Florentine Studies: Politics and Society in Renaissance Florence*, 381–402, esp. 389; and Brucker, *The Civic World*, 422–23. Bruni, *Commentarius*, cols. 931–32, recounted the anger of Martin V in 1420 when Braccio came to Florence to negotiate with him. Children ran through the streets, praising the condottiere and shouting that his adversary, the pope, was not worth a quattrino. When Bruni tried to calm his wrath by pointing out they were just children, the pope countered that children learned their ideas from their parents. A few months later, Martin V put Florence under interdict; see Brucker, *Civic World*, 423. When the pope finally left Florence for Rome in late 1420, Giovanni Morelli wrote, "et andossene a Roma a dì 9 di Settembre et poco amico della Comunità"; see *Delizie degli eruditi toscani*, ed. Ildefonso di San Luigi (Florence, 1770–89), 19:43. Martin V also terminated the policy of papal sponsorship of Florentine humanists, so marked during the pontificate of John XXIII; see Holmes, *Florentine Enlightenment*, 60–63. Florence's relationship with Martin V marks the nadir of Florentine-papal politics, which had been strained ever since the War of the Eight Saints (1375–78) and the Great Schism; for a summary of Florentine interaction with the papacy since 1375, see Holmes, *Florentine Enlightenment*, 49–53. The tension was particularly acute because the preceding pope, John XXIII, had been so closely allied to the city.

15 On John's last months in Florence, see *Historia Florentina italice conscripta auctore anonymo ab anno Christi MCCCCVI usque ad MCCCCXXXVIII nunc primum luce donata e manuscripto codice Bibliothecae Estensis*, in *Rerum Italicarum Scriptores*, ed. Ludovicus Antonius Muratori, vol. 19, cols. 949–84, esp. cols. 962–64, and *Le Croniche di Giovanni Sercambi Lucchese*, ed. Salvatore Bongi in *Fonti per la storia d'Italia*, 21 vols. (Rome, 1892), 3: 248–49. Gio. Batta Befani, *Memorie storiche dell'antichissima Basilica di San Giovanni Battista di Firenze* (Florence, 1884), 106, recorded the words of John XXIII to Martin V: "Ego solus adunavi Concilium, semper pro S. Romana Ecclesia laboravi. Tu unus es, qui veritatem scis, venio ad Sanctitatem tuam, in quantum possum gaudens de assumptione tua et libertate mea."

16 Del Migliore, *Firenze città nobilissima*, 95: "mortosi, com'ognun disse, di dolore in Firenze."

17 Ibid. and Sercambi, *Le Croniche*, 249.

18 See *Historia Florentina*, col. 963; "Diario fiorentino di Bartolommeo di Michele del Corazzo, anni 1405–38," *Archivio storico italiano*, 5th ser., 14 (1894): 266.

19 See *Historia Florentina*, cols. 963–64; and *Diario fiorentino*, 264–67. Record that the Florentine government paid for the requiem for Coscia held on the thirtieth is found in the unpublished "Ricordanza di Pagolo di Matteo di Piero di Fastello Petriboni, 1419–1459," (Biblioteca Nazionale, Florence, Conventi Soppressi, C.4.895), 100v: "A dì XXX il comune gli fe l'onore nelli detti luoghi, cioè uno grande e bello uficio e spesono insigniori fl. ccc° doro." I would like to thank Prof. Sharon Strocchia for making her transcription of this document available to me. The resolution of the Priori and Consiglio of Florence that the city government would pay up to 300 florins to honor John XXIII with appropriately lavish funeral ceremonies was passed by a vote of 157 to 34 and ratified by 138 to 12. It conveys the city's affection for Coscia: "que talis est videlicet Dilectionem et antiquam beniuolentiam continuis beneficijs demonstratam per reuerendissimum . . . diligens florentinos et eorum statum ut se et suum . . . ut erat toto populo florentino caram." The whole document is printed in Lightbown, *Donatello and Michelozzo*, 2:289–90, appendix A, document 2.

20 The sermon was based on Luke 2:34 which reads "Behold this [man] is set for the fall and rising of many and for a sign." The sermon, "Sermo factus in exequiis domini Balthasaris Cosse Cardinalis florentini et olim pape Johannis XXIII," by an anonymous member of a religious order, is found in Milan, Biblioteca Ambrosiana, MS P 259 sup., fols. 53–56. The manuscript is described in Paul O. Kristeller, *Iter Italicum* (London and Leiden, 1963–), 1:307. I would like to thank Prof. John McManamon, S.J., for providing me with a copy of his notes on the sermon.

21 Petriboni's eyewitness account from his *Ricordanza*, cited above, n. 19, 100v, is also summarized in Del Migliore, *Firenze città nobilissima*, 95.

22 Del Migliore, *Firenze città nobilissima*, 96–97.

23 John XXIII's will was first published by G. Canestrini in *Archivio storico italiano* 4 (1843): 292–96.

24 Ibid., 292–95; "Item sui corporis sepulturam, cum de hac vita migrari contigerit, elegit, et dictum suum corpus sepelliri voluit in illa Ecclesia, et seu apud illam Ecclesiam, de qua videbitur et placebit infrascriptis suis Executoribus, Commissariis, et Fideicommissis. . . . Executores autem suos, et dicti sui Testamenti et ultime voluntatis, fecit, esse voluit, et nominavit, ad predicta omnia et singula exequenda, infrascriptos, videlicet: Bartolomeum Nicolai Taldi Valoris; Nicolaum Iohannis de Uzano; Iohannem Averardi, alias Bicci, de Medicis, et Vierium de Guadagnis, omnes cives notabiles florentinos."

25 "Niccolò di Giovanni da Uzzano, Bartolomeo di Niccolò di Taldo Valori e Vieri di Vieri Guadagni Executori del Testamento di M. Baldassar Coscia Cardinale il corpo del quale era nella Chiesa di S. Giovanni, expongono a Consoli e Consiglio di Calimala che il detto M. Baldassare nel fine della sua vita deliberò e in segreto disse a' detti Executori che ha[v]rebbe ricevuto per favore che il suo corpo fusse stato seppellito nella Chiesa di S. Giovanni, perchè haveva gran devozione a detta Chiesa, come si era potuto vedere per haverli lasciato il Dito di S. Giov. battista, benchè nel suo testamento non havessi parlato di sepoltura per modestia. E che in detto suo testamento apparisce che egli haveva lasciato che si facesse una Cappella che si adornasse e dottase come piacesse a detti Executori, e però domandono a' detti Consoli e Consiglio che voglino dare licenza che l'uno e l'altro si possa fare. Per i quali Consoli e Consiglio disse M. Palla Strozzi che in modo alcuno si conventisse che si facesse in detta Chiesa altra Cappella perchè si guasterebbe, adducendone altre ragioni. E la Sepoltura si consigliò si potessi fare, ma breve e honestissima, sichè non occupi dell'adito della Chiesa, perchè non era poco honore a detto M. Baldassare essere seppellito in tanta Chiesa." January 9, 1421 [1422], filza 2a dal 1425–38; ASF, Carte Strozziane, IIa ser., no. 51, 2, c. 116v and no. 51, 1, c. 116. The document was published in an abbreviated form by C. J. Cavallucci in *Arte e Storia* 7 (1888): 36. The first complete published transcription of the document was provided by Margrit Lisner, "Zur frühen Bildhauer Architektur Donatellos," *Jahrbuch der bildenden Kunst*, ser. 3, 9–10 (1958–59): 117. It should be stressed that this document is the transcription or abbreviation of the original made by Carlo Strozzi in the seventeenth century.

26 Here I depend on the expertise of Prof. Sharon Strocchia; see her *Death and Ritual in Renaissance Florence* (forthcoming).

27 For an analysis of the structure and cultivation of the Medici faction in Florence, see Dale Kent, *The Rise of the Medici; Faction in Florence 1426–1434* (Oxford, 1978). The speculation about the role of the John XXIII tomb in this strategy of Medici aggrandizement is mine and must remain speculation.

28 Cosimo is named *the* commissioner by Vasari: "La quale [Tomb of John XXIII] gli fu fatta fare da Cosimo de' Medici, amicissimo del detta Coscia"; see Giorgio Vasari, *Le vite dei più eccellenti pittori, scultori, et architettori,*

ed. Gaetano Milanesi (Florence, 1787–1818), 2/2:399. Vasari's claim is repeated by many later sources. Platina in his biography of John XXIII even asserted that John XXIII lived in Cosimo's house during his last months in Florence, a claim refuted by Del Migliore, *Firenze città nobilissima*, 95.

29 E. H. Gombrich, "The Early Medici as Patrons of Art," in *Norm and Form: Studies in the Art of the Renaissance* (New York and London, 1966), 36–37, noted that Cosimo, as well as Giovanni di Bicci, were major contributors to the subscription in 1419 among the members of the Cambio guild that funded Ghiberti's *St. Matthew*. This, Gombrich argued, was the first example of Cosimo's patronage. It predates the tomb of John XXIII by several years.

30 The document from the ASF, *Mercatanti di Calimala*, no. 18, *Deliberazioni dal 2 gennaio 1424 a 13 Maggio, 1426*, c. 2r, was published by Lisner, "Zur frühen Bildhauer Architektur," 117.

31 On the arguments concerning the attribution of the parts of the tomb and its dating, see Lightbown, *Donatello and Michelozzo*, 1:24–51; Caplow, *Michelozzo* 1:107–40; and Janson, *The Sculpture of Donatello*, 59–65.

32 Other examples of this type include Tino di Camaino's monument of Cardinal Petroni, Duomo, Siena; the Tarlati monument in the Duomo, Arezzo; Tino's monument of Mary of Valois in S. Chiara, Naples. For a variation on this derivation from the ritual surrounding the dead, see the monument of Cardinal Annibaldi della Molara, S. Giovanni in Laterano, Rome, where a frieze of clerics enact the office for the dead; see G. Swarzenski, "An Early Tuscan Sculpture," *Bulletin of the Boston Museum of Fine Arts* 46 (1948): 2–11.

33 See note 18 above.

34 On the Dome of Heaven, see Karl Lehmann, "The Dome of Heaven," *Art Bulletin* 27 (1945): 1–27.

35 On this common motif see Erwin Panofsky, *Tomb Sculpture: Four Lectures on Its Changing Aspects from Ancient Egypt to Bernini*, ed. H. W. Janson (New York, 1964), 77–78; and Philippe Ariès, *The Hour of our Death*, trans. Helen Weaver (New York, 1982), 250–59. Ingo Herklotz, *"Sepulcra" e "monumenta" del medioevo: Studi sull'arte sepolcrale in Italia* (Rome, 1985), quotes the early thirteenth-century rhetorician, Boncompagno da Segna, who described the images of the deceased kneeling before the Madonna and Child in contemporary tombs as follows: "depingitur etiam quomodo angeli vel sancti mortuorum animas divine maiestati presentant" (191); see 239, appendix 1, for the entire text.

36 The full-length representation of the enthroned Madonna and Child was apparently more common than the half-length image. Extant earlier examples of the latter include the lunette of the painted half-length Madonna and Child on the Baroncelli family monument (Alinari 5874) and the sculpted half-length Madonna and Child on the Gastone della Torre monument by Tino di Camaino, both in Santa Croce, Florence, and dating from the fourteenth century.

37 On this type of iconography, see Helen Ann Ronan, "The Tuscan Wall Tomb, 1250–1400," (Ph.D. diss., Indiana University, 1982), 53.

38 Ariès, *The Hour of Our Death*, 218–22.

39 See Del Migliore's account, *Firenze città nobilissima*, 96.

40 On the papal connotations, see Herklotz, *"Sepulcra" e "monumenta" del medioevo*, 120–23; Francesco Gandolfo, "La Cattedra papale in età federiciana," *Federico II e l'arte del duecento italiano. Atti della III settimana di studi di storia dell'arte medievale dell'Università di Roma, 15–20 Mai 1978*, ed. Angiola Maria Romanini (Rome, 1980), 1:339–66; and Gandolfo, "Reimpiego di sculture antiche nei troni papali del XII secolo," *Atti della Pontificia Accademia Romana di Archeologia*, ser. 3, *Rendiconti* 47 (1974–75): 203–18, esp. 203–7.

41 For an analysis of Coscia's attire, see Lightbown, *Donatello and Michelozzo*, 1:44–46.

42 Ibid., 42–43, makes the connection to the effigies of ruling figures of Northern Europe.

43 On this statue and the rarity of papal statues in precious metals, see Julian Gardner, "Boniface VIII as a Patron of Sculpture," *Roma anno 1300 (Atti della IV settimana di studi di storia dell'arte medievale dell'Università di Roma 'La Sapienza,' 19–24 Mai 1980)*, ed. Angiola Maria Romanini (Rome, 1983), 518.

44 On this tomb slab, see Janson, *The Sculpture of Donatello*, 232–34. It has recently been proved that this sculpture was finished as late as 1445; see Arnold and Doris Esch, "Die Grabplatte Martins V. und andere Importstucke in den römischen Zollregistern der Frührenaissance," *Römisches Jahrbuch für Kunstgeschichte* 17 (1978): 209–17.

45 The oldest tradition regarding the baptistry claims that it was founded as a Christian structure after the destruction of the city by Totila in the sixth century; see *Chronica de origine civitatis* of the early thirteenth century, ed. O. Hartwig, *Quellen und Forschungen . . .* (1875), 59. This Christian foundation is pushed back to the time of the death of Christ by Del Migliore, *Firenze città nobilissima*, 86, who records an earlier tradition. For a comprehensive analysis of the early arguments concerning the date of the baptistry's foundation, see Walter and Elisabeth Paatz, *Die Kirchen von Florenz*, 2 (Frankfurt, 1955): 173. The latest assessment of the dating of the baptistry is Werner Jackson, "Zur Datierung des Florentiner Baptisteriums S. Giovanni," *Zeitschrift für Kunstgeschichte* 43 (1980): 225–43.

46 See ibid. This tradition derives from Giovanni Villani, *Cronica Fiorentina*, 1, cap. 42 and 60, ed. Fr. Ildefonso di San Luigi, *Delizie degli eruditi toscani* (Florence, 1772), 3, as well as from Dante, *Inferno*, 13:143, 146; 19:16. A full account is found in Del Migliore, *Firenze città nobilissima*, 82–83. For citations from fifteenth-century authors like Salutati and Bruni who considered the baptistry a Roman building, see Holmes, *The Florentine Enlightenment*, 175–76.

47 Raffaello Borghini, *Il Riposo* (Florence, 1584).

48 For an analysis of the relationship between Florence and ancient Rome established by late fourteenth- and early fifteenth-century Florentine writers, see Hans Baron, *The Crisis of the Early Italian Renaissance*, rev. ed. (Princeton, 1966), 48–78; and Ronald G. Witt, *Hercules at the Crossroads: The Life, Works, and Thoughts of Coluccio Salutati* (Durham, N.C., 1983), 166, 246–52.

49 Donatello used this dating formula again on the tomb slab of Giovanni Pecci in the Cathedral of Siena; see Janson, *The Sculpture of Donatello*, 75–77.

50 See Enrico Cattaneo, "Il Battistero in Italia dopo il Mille," in *Miscellanea Gilles Gerard Meersseman*, 1 (Padua, 1970), *Italia sacra: Studi e documenti di storia ecclesiastica*, 15:171–95.

51 Del Migliore, *Firenze città nobilissima*, 101.

52 See Cattaneo, "Il Battistero," 188–89. Del Migliore, *Firenze città nobilissima*, 99–100, recounted that Dante was posthumously awarded a laurel wreath in the baptistry and listed the Florentines who were ennobled there. A more general account of the baptistry's role in the civic and religious life of Florence is found in Girolamo Mancini, "Il bel S. Giovanni e le feste patronali di Firenze descritte nel 1475 da Piero Cennini," *Rivista d'arte* 6 (1909): 195–227.

53 See Roberto Davidsohn, *Storia di Firenze* (Florence, 1956), 5:589, 624–25.

54 Romans 6:3–4. For an exegesis on this passage and others by St. Paul concerning the meaning of baptism, see Rudolf Schnackenburg, *Baptism in the Thought of St. Paul: A Study in Pauline Theology*, trans. G. R. Beasley-Murray (New York, 1964). For a brief summary of representative views of medieval theologians concerning baptism, see Richard Krautheimer, "Introduction to an 'Iconography' of Mediaeval Architecture," *Journal of the Warburg and Courtauld Institutes* 5 (1942): 1–33, esp. 26–28.

55 Krautheimer, "Introduction to an Iconography," 28.

56 Ibid., 27.

57 On the mosaic program, see Irene Hueck, *Das Programm der Kuppelmosaiken im Florentiner Baptisterium* (Mondorf, 1962), 58–63.

58 For a catalog of Early Christian sarcophagi and catacomb paintings with images of baptism, see Alfonso M. Fausone, *Die Taufe in der Frühchristlichen Sepulkralkunst (Eine archäologisch-ikonologische Studie zu den Ursprüngen des Bildthemas)*, *Studi di antichità cristiana* 34 (Vatican City, 1982).

59 On the Giovanni Mocenigo tomb, see John Pope-Hennessy, *Italian Renaissance Sculpture*, rev. ed. (London, 1971), 341.

60 See Krautheimer, "Introduction to an Iconography," 20–33.

61 Ibid., 31.

62 Ibid., 23, 29, and J. G. Davies, *The Architectural Setting of Baptism* (London, 1962), 16.

63. Christine Smith, *The Baptistry of Pisa* (New York and London, 1978), 227.

64 Davies, *The Architectural Setting*, 15.

65 See n. 34 above.

66 They were the Councils of Autun (578) and Auxerre (614); see Jules Corblet, *Histoire dogmatique, liturgique et archéologique du sacrement de Baptême* (Paris and Brussels, 1882), 2:29; and Krautheimer, "Introduction to an Iconography," 28–29.

67 Krautheimer, "Introduction to an Iconography," 28, makes the point that the prohibition by the Councils indicates that the practice of burial in baptistries must have been "not uncommon," but cites only the baptistries of Florence, S. Severina, and the Arian baptistry in Ravenna. Corblet, *Histoire dogmatique*, 2:29, adds the baptistries of the cathedrals of Rouen and Autun. These examples consist primarily of burials under the floor, marked only by insciptions.

68 See Krautheimer, "An Introduction to Iconography," 30. The latest argument about the structures under the baptistry is made by Franklin Toker, "A Baptistry below the Baptistry of Florence," *Art Bulletin* 58 (1976): 157–67.

69 Del Migliore, *Firenze città nobilissima*, 105.

70 According to Giovanni Villani, lib. VIII, cap. iii, the decision was made by decree of the city in 1293; see also Del Migliore, *Firenze città nobilissima*, 89–90; F.-A. Gruyer, *Les Oeuvres d'art de la renaissance italienne au Temple de Saint-Jean (Baptistère de Florence)* (Paris, 1875), 25; and Befani, *Memorie storiche*, 103.

71 See Befani, *Memorie storiche*, 103, and Paatz, *Die Kirchen*, 2:205.

72 See Befani, *Memorie storiche*, 104, and Paatz, *Die Kirchen*, 2:206. There is a third Roman sarcophagus positioned to the left of the Velletri sarcophagus, omitted in most commentaries but listed in Paatz as unidentified. Krautheimer, "An Introduction to Iconography," 30 n. 4, identified this as the sarcophagus of Guccio de' Medici [Gonfaloniere of Florence in 1299], transferred indoors at the end of the thirteenth century, but gave no source for his information. Davidsohn, *Storia di Firenze*, 7:720 n. 3, claimed that the sarcophagus was transferred from the baptistry exterior "ai muri dell'edifizio della Compagnia di San Zanobi, vicino al campanile di Sta. Maria del Fiore," then moved to the courtyard of the Palazzo Medici-Riccardi in 1824, and finally to the baptistry interior in 1928.

73 See Hans Dutschke, *Zerstreute antike Bildwerke in Florenz* (1875), 173–74 no. 398.

74 See Wolfgang Wolters, *La Scultura veneziana gotica (1300–1460)* (Venice, 1976), 1:156 cat. no. 17.

75 Ibid., 1:190, cat. no. 80.

76 See Sergio Bettini, *Le Pitture di Giusto de' Menabuoi nel Battistero del Duomo di Padova* (Venice, 1960), and *Giusto de' Menabuoi e l'arte del Trecento* (Padua, 1944), 126–27; Lionello Puppi, "Il Battistero," *Padova: Basiliche e Chiese*, ed. Claudio Bellinati and Lionello Puppi, *Parte prima: Le Chiese dal IV al XVIII secolo* (Vicenza, 1975), 101–11; Bradley Joseph Delanay, Jr., "Giusto de' Menabuoi: Iconography and Style," (Ph.D. diss., Columbia University, 1972), 111–12; and Wolters, *La Scultura*, 1:169.

77 See Konrad Hoffmann, *Taufsymbolik im mittelalterlichen Herrschebild*

(Düsseldorf, 1968), *Bonner Beiträge zur Kunstwissenschaft*, 9; Ernest H. Kantorowicz, *The King's Two Bodies: A Study in Medieval Political Theology* (Princeton, 1981), 12 n. 9, and 319; and J.-P. Bayard, *Le Sacre des Rois* (Paris, 1964), 54, 97, and 198.

78   This example was suggested to me by Prof. Archer St. Clair Harvey. On these plates see John Beckwith, *Early Christian and Byzantine Art* (Harmondsworth, 1970), 43 and fig. 84.

79   On the sacramentary, see Robert Deshman, "Otto III and the Warmund Sacramentary: A Study in Political Theology," *Zeitschrift für Kunstgeschichte* 34 (1971): 1–20. This article was kindly brought to my attention by Prof. Elizabeth Parker McLachlan.

80   Ronan, "The Tuscan Wall Tomb," 63, noted the rarity of Last Judgment iconography on thirteenth- and fourteenth-century Tuscan tombs. From the time of Vasari's second edition of the *Vite* (1568), the scene on the tomb's back wall has been identified as a Last Judgment. Ronan suggests instead that it is one of the first depictions of Particular Judgment, a new theological concept that had been introduced into the teachings of the church at the Council of Lyons in 1274 (p. 60).

81   The position of the portrait of St. Zenobius was also calculated so that it was as near as possible to the Column of St. Zenobius erected just outside the baptistry's northwest wall. The column marks the site where an elm tree broke into leaf when the saint's remains were transferred into S. Reparata; see Arnaldo Cocchi, *Le Chiese di Firenze dal secolo IV al secolo XX*, I, *Quartiere di San Giovanni* (Florence, 1903), 48–53. I would like to thank Prof. Creighton Gilbert for suggesting this correspondence.

82   His sermon about the Gates of the Heavenly City as they are described in the Book of Revelation (21:12–13) tells us: "At the east, that is, through the fate of innocence, the innocents entered; they, who knew how to die before they knew how to speak, were slaughtered for the Lord. Through this gate little children, born again in baptism, enter. . . . From the west, that is, through the gate of penitence, Mary Magdalene entered, who because of her sins had previously been the dwelling place of demons. But later, prompted by the sight of her divine grace, by her weeping and repentance . . . she was made the temple of the Holy Spirit. Also through this gate enter the penitents, who . . . if they renounce completely all the retinue of Satan and the works of darkness, enter into Jerusalem above through the gate of penitence." Saint Bernard of Clairvaux (attrib.), *Sermo de Duodecim Portis Jerusalem* in J. P. Migne, *Patrologiae Cursus Completus: Series Latina* 184 (Paris, 1879): 1118; translated in Eloise M. Angiola, "'Gates of Paradise' and the Florentine Baptistry," *Art Bulletin* 60 (1978): 245.

83   On the statue, see Janson, *The Sculpture of Donatello*, 190–91. Vasari's first edition of the *Vite* (1550) indicated that the Magdalene was placed opposite the tomb of John XXIII; see Corrado Ricci, ed., *Le vite del Vasari nell'edizione del MDL* (Milan, 1927), 48–49.

84 On the Fulgosio monument, see Wolters, *La Scultura veneziana*, 1:240–42, cat. no. 172.

85 The connection between Fulgosio and John XXIII was brought out by Light-bown, *Donatello and Michelozzo*, 1:50.

86 On Michelangelo's tomb, see John Pope-Hennessy, *Italian High Renaissance and Baroque Sculpture*, rev. ed. (New York and London, 1970), 61–62, 366–69. The tent canopy was also adapted frequently by other tombs in and outside of Florence. Although the tomb of John XXIII was not the first tomb monument to use this motif, it certainly popularized it. For a discussion of tombs that adapt the tent canopy and other motifs from the John XXIII Tomb, see Fritz Burger, *Geschichte des florentinischen Grabmals von den ältesten Zeiten bis Michelangelo* (Strasbourg, 1904), 102–12; and Caplow, *Michelozzo*, 1:118 n. 34.

87 On the tomb of Paul II see Renzo U. Montini, "Il Sepolcreto papale delle Grotte Vaticane," *Capitolium* 26 (1951): 269–84; and *Roma 1300–1875: l'Arte degli anni santi*, ed. Marcello Fagiolo and Maria Luisa Madonna (Milan, 1984), 353.

88 Another tomb that suggests an understanding of the way the John XXIII monument worked in conjunction with its site is the tomb of Cardinal Diego de Coca, a collaborative project of Andrea Bregno and Melozzo da Forlì. The tomb, which dates from the 1470s and is located in S. Maria sopra Minerva, Rome, is decorated with a *Last Judgment* lunette painted by Melozzo. This iconography could derive directly from a precedent like the Bettino Bardi Tomb in S. Croce, Florence, but the combination of this unusual imagery with the painted tent canopy suggests instead that both derive from the tomb of John XXIII. On the Cardinal Diego de Coca tomb, see I. P. Grossi, *Basilica di Santa Maria sopra Minerva* (Rome, 1975).

89 For an analysis of how other tombs such as Desiderio's monument to Carlo Marsuppini, S. Croce, Florence, of the 1450s derive from the John XXIII tomb, see Burger, *Geschichte des florentinischen Grabmals*, 102–112.

ON CASTAGNO'S NINE FAMOUS MEN AND WOMEN
CREIGHTON GILBERT

1 The catalog entry on the cycle in Marita Horster, *Andrea del Castagno* (Oxford, 1980), 178–80, provides this and other citations, as well as most basic facts. The 1510 reference (179) is the earliest of any kind.

2 Robert Schroeder, *Der Topos der Nine Worthies in Literatur und bildender Kunst* (Göttingen, 1971).

3 Mario Salmi, *Paolo Uccello, Andrea del Castagno, Domenico Veneziano* (Milan, 1938), 64.

4 Figures from the doors were copied in contemporary drawings, of which two survive (see F. Bellini, *I desegni antichi degli Uffizi: il tempo del Ghiberti* [Florence, 1978], nos. 93, 94); I believe such cases are very rare, though the matter seems not to have been investigated. The figures' influence on a

work of Luca della Robbia is well known. About 1460 Filarete wrote: "If you have apostles to do, don't make them like fencers, as Donatello did in San Lorenzo in Florence." It is commonly and reasonably suggested that he was here echoing Alberti and that Alberti had been thinking of the same figures when he wrote in 1435 about artists whose movements "go too far" so that they make men "seem fencers and mountebanks." (For both texts see Creighton Gilbert, *Italian Art 1400–1500: Sources and Documents* [Englewood Cliffs, 1980], 89, 66.) An influence of the Donatello figures on Castagno's pairs was suggested by Salmi, *Uccello*, 64. Thus the next step would be to suggest that Castagno's gentler figures are taking heed of the Albertian criticism of his model and thus represent an Albertian taste.

5 Horster, *Castagno*, 31, suggests that Cumaea is looking at the Madonna on the other wall. But she does not note the consistent way in which, in these pairs of figures, each one at the right looks at the one to his or her left.

6 A convenient example is Dante, *Purgatorio*, 10:34–35.

7 Leon Battista Alberti, *Della Pittura* (Florence, 1950), 94.

8 Ibid., 92 n. 2.

9 Ibid., 91 ff.; see also 95 (Giotto) and 89 (Meleager).

10 Giovanni Boccaccio, *Concerning Famous Women* (New Brunswick, N.J., 1963), 104–6, 51–52.

11 E. G. Léonard, "Niccolò Acciaiuoli," in *Dizionario biografico degli Italiani*, 1 (Rome, 1960): 87–90.

12 *Mélanges . . . Hauvette* (Paris, 1934), 139–48.

13 Giovanni Boccaccio, *Il Comento . . . sopra la Commedia* (Florence, 1863), 223.

14 This report occurs in one manuscript, the "Libro di Antonio Billi," in a list of Castagno's works which cites the title and location of each. A unique exception is a work at the church of San Giuliano for which no title is given; from other sources we know this lost painting was a Crucifixion with other figures. This item in Billi's list is followed by our villa, where he lists this Crucifixion, while omitting the nine famous men and women cited in every other similar source. It becomes apparent that the scribe shifted the Crucifixion down by one line, and then compensated by omitting the title belonging to this lower line. It seems extremely doubtful that this writer could be aware of an otherwise unknown work there yet unaware of its famous image; this makes the scribal error the only acceptable hypothesis. All this was duly pointed out by Cornelius von Fabriczy, "Il libro di Antonio Billi," in *Archivio storico italiano*, ser. 5, 7 (1891): 349, but in a quite succinct way. The apparent effect was that some later writers, reading the Billi text without his annotations, have treated the Crucifixion in the villa as a possibly real work, as Horster does by citing it without comment. Hence, it may be useful to repeat the basis of its invalidity.

15 Cennino Cennini, *Il Libro dell'arte* (Florence, 1943), 19–21.

16 As a recent art historian has neatly summarized it, Vincent of Beauvais's "*The Mirror of Instruction* begins with the Fall of Man, the immediate

consequence of which is the necessity for toil, and the ultimate consequence of which is the need for redemption. The Mechanical Arts are invented to fulfill our physical needs whereas the Liberal Arts develop our intellectual capacity." Anita Fiderer Moskowitz, *The Sculpture of Andrea and Nino Pisano* (Cambridge, 1986), 33.

17   Although it is often said that the earliest images of St. Luke actually painting only appear in the fifteenth century, one of the early fourteenth century in Venice is reproduced by George Kaftal, *Iconography of the Saints in the Painting of North East Italy* (Florence, 1978), fig. 799.

18   Phyllis Pray Bober and Ruth Rubinstein, *Renaissance Artists and Antique Sculpture* (London, 1986), 67.

19   Cennini, *Libso*, 19.

20   Moskowitz, *Pisano*, 37, developing comments of previous writers, finds it necessary to explain why the campanile reliefs omit the image of the Fall of Man, proceeding directly to the "work." Her explanation that the planners "suppressed the traditional view of world history" in which work was required by sin, and instead presented "manual labor as an achievement," is not supported by evidence and seems doubtful. It is notable that, if the added images hypothesized above did not actually exist, the Brancacci Chapel conversely showed the sin but not the toil of Adam and Eve and so did the Fonte Gaia. Cennino's text attributes the need to work to the whole history of Adam and Eve involving both sin and their work. Thus it may be that either image could present this idea adequately.

21   Horster, *Castagno*, 179, transcribes all the inscriptions.

22   Boccaccio, *Famous Women*, 104–5.

23   Léonard, as in note 11.

24   Maria Elizabeth van Lohuizen-Mulder, *Rafaels Encomium van Scipio Africanus Major* (Utrecht, 1973), 5–11, surveys the principal hypotheses.

25   J. P. Trapp, "The Owl's Ivy and the Poet's Bays," *Journal of the Warburg and Courtauld Institutes* 21 (1958): 246.

26   Baldesar Castiglione, *Il Cortegiano*, 1:42–46.

27   Dora and Erwin Panofsky, *Pandora's Box* (New York, 1962), 40.

28   Barbara C. Bowen, "Renaissance Collections of Facetiae," *Renaissance Quarterly* 39 (1986): 8.

29   William Harrison Woodward, *Vittorino da Feltre and Other Humanist Educators* (New York, 1963), 103–4, paraphrased.

30   Ibid., 136 ff.

31   Matteo Palmieri, *Della Vita Civile* (Florence, 1982), 38–39.

32   Ibid., 8–9, 115.

33   Ibid., 120.

34   Ibid., 6.

35   Léonard, as in note 11, presents the bibliography. The only printed edition of Palmieri's life in the original Latin is in *Rerum Italicarum Scriptores*, 8:2. The content does not suggest any association with our cycle.

36   Rinaldo degli Albizzi, *Commissioni* (Florence, 1873), 2:595.

37 Cornelius a Lapide, *Commentarius in . . . Esther* (Venice, 1701), 110. Lapide's biblical commentaries are helpful in such enquiries because he devoted most of his space to repeating the most usual formulae from earlier commentaries.

38 Martin Davies, *National Gallery Catalogues: the Earlier Italian Schools* (London, 1951), 94–98.

39 Mario Salmi, "Gli affreschi di Andrea del Castagno ritrovati," *Bollettino d'Arte* 35 (1950): 295–306. It has been noted that the fresco shows losses around the door frame, but not that this could be a sign either of a new door (the inference generally drawn) or of repairs on an old one.

40 Palmieri, *Vita Civile*, 208.

41 Woodward, *Vittorino da Feltre*, 197.

42 Ronald Lightbown, *Sandro Botticelli* (Berkeley, 1978), 1: 94ff.

43 Eric Zafran, *Fifty Old Master Paintings from the Walters Art Gallery* (Baltimore, 1988), 44, offers a judicious summary of the present state of knowledge, citing the significant previous studies, i.e., recent writing by Mode, Zeri, Tatrai, and Angelini. These are cited below herein as to certain details, with the exception of Angelini. His study provided new attribution for one of the panels, to Orioli instead of Pachiarotto.

44 Robert L. Mode, "Ancient Paragons in a Piccolomini Scheme," *Hortus Imaginum: Essays in Western Art* (Lawrence, Kans., 1974), 75, remarks that this set of eight, as he considers it, is "a departure from the traditional" number of nine.

45 Mode, "Ancient Paragons," 75.

46 Mode (ibid.) notes as a possibility that the set is incomplete, but provides a reconstruction of the layout based on its being complete with eight. His arrangement separates the sexes, but beyond that seems to depend entirely on suggestions about balancing the composition through gestures, background buildings, and the like.

47 V. Tatrai, "Il maestro della storia di Griselda," *Acta Historiae Artium* 25 (1979): 44.

48 The Roman story is that of the continence of Scipio, perhaps the most familiar of all anecdotes of classical virtue. In this as in the other two known pairs, it seems that some effort was made to find a sufficiently similar Greek story; Eunostos is a very obscure figure, and Artemisia, as noted, matches her Roman analog only fairly well. As to the analog of Scipio, the inscription on the Alexander panel simply places him for restraint in general. The instance, which shows that he like Scipio was restrained toward women, emerges when we look at the small background figures, the family of Darius which he treated with clemency. Federigo Zeri (*Italian Paintings in the Walters Art Gallery* [Baltimore, 1976], no. 91), following others, reported that most of the stories are taken from the classical text of Valerius Maximus. However, the passage he cites for Alexander does not refer to the Darius incident. Eunostos is also absent from Valerius. This apparent pattern of a wide-ranging hunt for the Greek stories may support a view that

they, all painted by the Griselda master and hence suggesting a different chronological phase of the project, were done later, following an earlier phase in which the project was more ambitiously initiated by five major artists.

49 Mode, "Ancient Paragons," 82, n. 21.

Index

▼

Library of Congress Cataloging-in-Publication Data
Life & death in fifteenth-century Florence / editors, Rona Goffen,
Marcel Tetel, Ronald G. Witt.
p.   cm.—(Duke monographs in medieval and Renaissance
studies : no. 10)
Based on papers presented at a colloquium held at Duke University,
Oct. 1986.
Bibliography: p.
Includes index.
ISBN 0-8223-0872-X
1. Florence (Italy)—Social life and customs—Congresses.
2. Death—Congresses. 3. Life—Congresses. I. Goffen, Rona,
1944–   . II. Tetel, Marcel. III. Witt, Ronald G. IV. Title: Life
and death in fifteenth-century Florence. V. Series.
DG735.6.154 1989
945'.51— dc 19 88-7924 CIP